ISBN 978-0-282-95779-7
PIBN 10140668

This book is a reproduction of an important historical work. Forgotten Books uses state-of-the-art technology to digitally reconstruct the work, preserving the original format whilst repairing imperfections present in the aged copy. In rare cases, an imperfection in the original, such as a blemish or missing page, may be replicated in our edition. We do, however, repair the vast majority of imperfections successfully; any imperfections that remain are intentionally left to preserve the state of such historical works.

1 MONTH OF
FREE
READING

at
www.ForgottenBooks.com

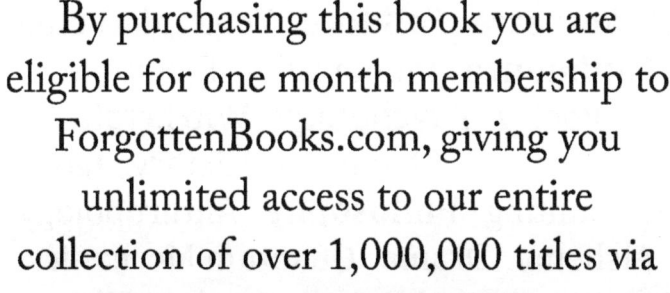

By purchasing this book you are eligible for one month membership to ForgottenBooks.com, giving you unlimited access to our entire collection of over 1,000,000 titles via our web site and mobile apps.

To claim your free month visit: www.forgottenbooks.com/free140668

English
Français
Deutsche
Italiano
Español
Português

www.forgottenbooks.com

Mythology Photography **Fiction**
Fishing Christianity **Art** Cooking
Essays Buddhism Freemasonry
Medicine **Biology** Music **Ancient
Egypt** Evolution Carpentry Physics
Dance Geology **Mathematics** Fitness
Shakespeare **Folklore** Yoga Marketing
Confidence Immortality Biographies
Poetry **Psychology** Witchcraft
Electronics Chemistry History **Law**
Accounting **Philosophy** Anthropology
Alchemy Drama Quantum Mechanics
Atheism Sexual Health **Ancient History**
Entrepreneurship Languages Sport
Paleontology Needlework Islam
Metaphysics Investment Archaeology
Parenting Statistics Criminology
Motivational

ADDRESSES

AND

REVIEWS

BY

T. A. D.

(Theodore Ayrault Dodge)

———:———

PRIVATELY PRINTED
HENRY S. DUNN,

TO MY WIFE,

•

AT WHOSE SUGGESTION

AND FOR WHOSE ENTERTAINMENT

THESE PAGES WERE GATHERED

TO MY WIFE,

·

AT WHOSE SUGGESTION

AND FOR WHOSE ENTERTAINMENT

THESE PAGES WERE GATHERED.

CONTENTS.

THE FIGHT FOR UNION.

THE FIGHT FOR UNION.*

COMRADES:—Twenty years ago there came to a close one of the most gigantic struggles of modern days. During four long years nearly five millions of brothers had fought over the larger part of the area of this great country—brothers in race, language, religion, but foes in political ideas. One of the adversaries lived under the glowing rays of a Southern sun; the other in the rugged cold of more Northern—but none less beautiful skies.

From their ancestry both inherited that courage which springs from strong convictions. From his fervid climate the Southerner had drawn a more potent fire, which burned fiercely within him to accomplish as quickly that for which his soul might long, as his tropical vegetation waxes into gigantic masses in the course of a few short days.

* Delivered at Pittsfield, Memorial Day, May 30, 1885.

From his colder clime the Northerner had slowly garnered that sturdy patience which never yields in the pursuit of its cherished end, long though the road may be. Swift as the greyhound, the Southerner could rush upon his quarry full in sight; true as the sleuth-hound to a certain scent, the Northerner could follow up his purpose through weary disappointment.

The Southern education and servile institutions made its people homogeneous to the core; the Northern struggle for individual success had bred each man to act his own strong part. No need to day, comrades, to question who was right or who was wrong. Both we and they now recognize which cause was just, which object wise, which purpose was smiled upon by the Great God of Hosts. Selfish men there were on both sides. Ambitious men there were, to whom individual advancement or profit stood in lieu of patriotic zeal. Nor in the North was there a lack of men who were traitors in heart, but cowards too, who dared not act their perfidy. In the South there were, among the leaders, wicked men, untruthful men, men steeped to their souls in treachery and mean, low cunning. But the brawn and heart of the South was true—according to its light. The men who bared their breasts, comrades, to your cold steel, fought for the right as they then understood it; fought for their firesides, their mothers, wives and sweethearts, their tender offspring and all that you and I could hold most dear.   Did we not know all this, the proof of their truth lay in their strong right arms.   For no people ever did or ever could fight as did they, for a faith but half embraced.   As truly as I esteem that the Northern cause was just, as truly as I thank God that the victory of our arms gave freedom to millions of our dark skinned brothers, so truly am I satisfied that our Southern foemen believed that they were right. And glory to our American manhood that they did so believe!

I have searched the annals of the history of the wars of the world.   I have felt the inspiring thrill of Freedom won by the blood of heroic nations of ancient days. I have gloried in the triumphs purchased by the heroism of the martyrs in the cause of religion and of political independence.   But nothing, comrades, has ever warmed my heart, nothing has ever made me exult in the pride with which I can claim to be an American citizen, as does the knowledge that the men whom we fought four long years to conquer, are by birthright of the same blood that courses in our veins; that the men whom we outnumbered many times, who were hungry when we were fed, who marched barefoot when we were shod, who opposed worthless weapons to our perfected arms, who saw their homes laid waste and their dear ones cowering with terror within their enemy's lines; who believed that the war was one solely of conquest and of cruelty, and who yet fought on until they as truly died in the last ditch as they pledged themselves to do—that these men are our brothers, and that we may point with exultation to their courage, unfailing purpose and manly resistance to what they deemed an invasion of their rights. The manhood of America, at Lexington or Valley Forge, had no truer champions than were the Southerners when they charged upon our ranks at Gettysburg, or laid down their arms with bowed heads and saddened hearts to our hosts at Appomattox. And I glory in this manhood! And comrades, so do you!

Though, indeed, we may dissent from their opinions, how can we but admire their spirit? We have every cause for gratitude to an over-ruling Providence which preserved us here at home from being driven to put forth such efforts, to go to such lengths of individual and national self-sacrifice, as did our Southern brothers.

Have you ever considered, comrades, what those sacrifices were? Do you know that, in very truth, the ranks of the Southern armies were kept full by robbing the cradle and the grave? That the people of the South were reduced to a generation's poverty, wretched beyond our conception who live in the midst of plenty? And that, as in Egypt of old, over the length and breadth of that fair land, there was not a house in which there was not one dead? Is it to be wondered at, that it was easier for us to forgive the South its act of rebellion than for the South to forgive us our enforcement of its disputed obligations to the Union?

A couple of years after the war, duty called me down into the heart of Virginia. I had to spend several days distant from any town where I could find a sheltering hostelry. Not far from the scene of my labor was a large brick house, evidently once a beautiful homestead. Its approach had been through a noble avenue of ancestral oaks, whose mutilated stumps alone now testified to their age and shadowy grandeur. The landscape was naked of fencing or crops, except that near the house was one small patch of corn. Not an animal was to be seen, save a stray dog, which howled its protest at the infrequent visitor. The dwelling was one of those large mansions, with ample porch and pillars, seen often in the South. The heavy doors were off their hinges or altogether gone. The windows were shattered. The garden showed only by its wild growing flowers its normal taste and splendor. I was met at the portal by an aged negress, whom I asked for shelter for the night. With that old-fashioned servile grace possessed only by the domestics of the Southern upper classes, the old servant ushered me into what had been a spacious drawing room, now dismantled of its glories, but showing what it once had been by the relics of the frescoed ceiling, a few massive pieces of antique furniture, sadly mutilated, and the heavy frame of an enormous pier-glass, whose mirrored surface had been shattered by musket balls. I was shortly received by the lady of the house, who with her two daughters were the only members of the family, and was invited to consider myself at home. They had as servants only the old negress and her husband, who though free, refused to leave the home where they, and their fathers before them, had eaten the bread of kindly slavery. The man tilled the field; the woman worked within. I tarried under this roof for nearly a week. My bed was clean, everything about the house was scrupulously neat, but biting want showed her scanty face at every turn. My hostesses were women of reading, culture, travel; gentle but distant. Three times a day corn meal and a few wild fruits furnished forth the entire repast, supplemented at noon by bacon. They were too poor to own a cow or chickens. Yet never did princely courtesy grace an abundant banquet better than the urbane civility of those three women and the absence of explanation or apology. Our conversation dwelt necessarily upon things of long before the war. Only on the day I left, did the lady of the house refer to the ruin of her home. As her old negress had tearfully told me, her husband and three sons had been victims of the war. Do you wonder, quoth she, that we women cannot forget or forgive?

And this, comrades, was no isolated case. Its parallel was to be found everywhere throughout the South. Such uniformly were the sacrifices of the men of the Confederacy. They had mutually pledged to each other their lives, their fortunes, and their sacred honor, mistaken though they were. And bravely they paid the pledge!

Comrades, such were the men you fought! Such were the men from whose gallant hearts and strong

And what were the heroic souls who, after this mighty struggle, waged for the Union and for the freedom of another race, overcame so wonderful a people? There have been indeed few wars waged during the world's history as great as that which you, my fellow soldiers, fought in. Fewer still have there been of such gigantic struggles for liberty. None in which the conquerors fought for the liberty of others and won it for them, paying themselves the price.

Let me recall to your minds who these heroes were. They were your comrades and mine. We all remember them well. Let us go back in memory some twenty years.

Think of that small, puny, weak-looking lad of eighteen summers, scarcely fitted, we used to say, to carry that heavy musket, that plethoric knapsack, five days' rations and forty rounds of ammunition under the burning rays of a July sun. Of gentle nurture, as shown by his hands unused to toil, and a visible shrinking from the many coarse sights and words too common, alas! in camp; of open bearing, and with a face which shows the truth and honor his mother's loving precepts and daily prayers have planted in his heart; of a sensitive frame, shocked to the marrow, physically, mental-

ly, morally, by what the most of us pass by unheeded
as an every day affair which it isn't worth our while to
try to mend; of a mould which seems too fine in grain
ever to toughen to the hard fabric of a soldier; yet this
lad has trudged beside you and me, comrades, throughout the many weary miles we have had to cover twixt
early dawn and sunset, and though his face may have
shown keen physical distress for hours, that strong purpose which has come to him with the blood of his Puritan forbears, (though indeed, too, it be coupled with
the germ of that fell disease with which the bare shores
of Massachusetts greeted the half-clad, half-fed pil-
grims), that purpose has been gleaming in his eye, and
his pleasant smile and high-bred word of cheer have
been grateful to our eye and heart. And this same lad,
comrades, on the morrow, though he has never been beyond the precinct of his peaceful home, though danger
be to him a mystery yet unsolved, this same lad will
set his blenching lips and steel his dreading heart, and
stand steadfast in the ranks, where the fearful enginery
of war is working its noisy horrors, and grisly Death is
playing his ghastly pranks, and hundreds of well known
friends, playmates of olden days, are stricken down
around him. And he, too, will fall in his tracks, nor

utter complaint nor groan, and yield up his young
life,— because to do his duty is dearer than to live.

That boy, comrades, is your hero! It is his grave
we deck to-day with flowers!

Do you remember that handsome, well grown, hearty
fellow, in the prime of early manhood? With warm
and honest blood threading its vigorous course through
artery and vein, the very type of a sound heart in a
sound body, you may see that his hold on life is strong
and full of hope. Behind him at home he has left his
sweetheart wife, married and kissed good-bye the self-
same hour, and only married so that should he be sick
or wounded, his beloved may come by right and nurse
him. His breast pocket, you remember, is always full,
and growing fuller of letters. We know indeed who
wrote them, and what their contents are. We may recall the look of proud delight which greets each coming
mail; for in it there is always that neatly addressed,
sweet smelling missive from her who sits in the father's
old farm house, dreaming of her lover husband, and
praying God to shield his head in the day of battle, and
keep him safe amid the unknown but dreaded terrors of
the tented field. To this man, comrades, mere labor is
always easy. Long marches, sleepless picket duty

worry not him. The dangers of the fight he faces as he has been used, since a boy, to climb the tallest tree or subdue the restive colt. But think you that this man has not battles of his own to fight? Think you that a three years' separation from the one loved object has not required, does not hourly require, the highest courage, the bitterest self-denial, as he gulps down the rising regret and grinds the restless longings of his yearning heart under the heel of his patriotic will?

Him, too, we shall see mowed down, and clinging convulsively to life, fed only by the ardent desire once more to gaze on the one loved face, (and this, thank God, he does) and then we shall hear that he has bid a brave farewell to a life which promised a store of happiness far beyond what most of us can reach. And this is his sacrifice to duty.

Is not he indeed our hero? Do not our hearts yield him glowing tribute to-day?

Mark that sturdy father of a family. From the rugged beauty of the Berkshire hills he has sucked strength and honest purpose. His boys are too young to stand the hardships of a soldier's life. But shall no one bear the honor of his name to the dangers of the front? His pride and patriotism give the answer crisp and clear. He has left the lads to till the soil, and herd the kine, and keep the home unbroken, while he, the one grown man of his fireside, shall do his three years' duty to his father's and his children's country. He knows full well what he has left behind. The sweet joys of home, the wife's bright smile, the child's caress, and happiness, comfort, and cheer and prosperous gain. He knows full well what he has come to face and why he has come to face it. He forgets not how he is needed by his dear ones; how the nurture and education of his pretty girls and the training of his brave souled boys depends upon the preservation of his life. And yet he has laid, he daily lays all this a willing sacrifice upon the altar of his fatherland. As he marches beside us, comrades, do we not know that under that blue blouse there beats the true heart of an American? And when the poisonous exhalations of the swamp, where he has tramped to and fro his many soldier's vigils, have sown the seeds of grim disease from which he will never rise again, as he lies prone upon the hospital cot, do we not recognize in the wasted form and hectic cheek the garb which clothes the true soul of a hero? And do we not to-day strive to learn our lesson from his fortitude and love of conntry, as we lovingly lay a

At the head of Company A trudges the gray bearded Orderly-Sergeant. Two of his sons are the pattern soldiers of the company. The third, his baby, is the tiny drummer who has won his way into all our hearts. How his father's rugged face softens when he looks at this little son of Mars! At home the mother and the girls are working bravely and choking down their tears to keep the household gods intact against father's and brothers' return. In the Sergeant's knapsack is his well-thumbed Bible. Rather lose rations than this soul's food. In the hearts of his boys are garnered the truths which he has harvested from the Book and fed to them since ever they could listen to its stories. Unwilling to deny his sons to the war, unwilling that they should lose the watchful care of the father's eye, he goes with them to the field, unmindful of his years, unmindful of the comforts left behind. And, comrades, such a father and three such sons I saw shot down around the colors at Chancellorsville, each one seizing them as they fell from the death grasp of the other, while the boy perished clasping the dead father he would not leave.

Was not that gray headed Sergeant the hero of them all? Shall we not stand with uncovered heads and meekly reverent hearts beside his simple tomb to-day?

And, comrades, there is another hero. He was the only son of his mother and she was a widow. His soul consumed itself with ardor to join his fellows at the front. The very love of his heart of hearts dwelt in this one idea. True, brave, strong, a worthy citizen, a broad man, his was the stuff from which to make your soldier. His two brothers had preceded him. One had gone down before the ordeals of a prison, one had fallen at Fair Oaks. His mother, crushed by her sorrows, yet never bade him stay. But she could not utter "Go, my son!" though she would not have said him nay, had he pleaded for leave to serve his country. By night his pillow was drenched with tears, wept in the bitterness of his disappointment. By day his cheek burned with needless shame, and his ears tingled with imagined taunts. He could not look at the gay ranks of his fellows marching cheerily to the war. Yet he silently gave up his life's ambition as a duty to her who bore him and his martyred brothers.

Comrades, may *he* not have been the truest hero yet?

And there was the whole-souled captain of the company. Patient, hard working, just, liberal, with always a fellow feeling for the over-taxed soldier as he had no pity for the man who shirked, doing twice the duty of any of his men, did he not wear his shoulder straps with honor? And, comrades, as we lay under our shelter tents, the day's march over and the simple supper eaten, enjoying our well earned rest, have we not heard the footsteps of this large souled man, whose self imposed duties would not be over for yet many a weary hour?

And do you remember the trig young Major, who sometimes, we could not help feeling, had quite too easy a time, detailed on the division staff? But, comrades, let me remind you of the day when he was ordered to guide our regiment to that memorable slashing when we had the hardest fight the regiment was ever in; and when, having pointed out our proper place in the line, instead of riding back—his duty well performed—he stayed behind to see his old brothers-in-arms through the struggle which we all knew would be a fierce one. As he rode into action beside us, animating us all by his cheerful, almost careless, gallantry, did not our hearts warm toward him, each and every one? And when we saw his proud black charger rear and fall crashing together, and found that both horse and rider had gone down never to rise again, do you not remember the exclamation of sympathy wrung from the whole line? And did we not all feel that he had well earned the

And perchance we used often to think that the generals as well as their staffs had an easier time than we. But as we lay on our arms after the battle or in anticipation of the fray to come with daylight, have we not seen these same generals and their aides working the livelong night, anxiously preparing for the morrow, or repairing the disasters of the day? Did we not then recognize that, when he has done his duty, the soldier has had to perform more labor and bear more strain, mental and physical, the higher he has climbed in his profession? And when we have lain behind the sheltering breast-work, has not our commanding officer ridden to and fro in the saddle, forgetful that he is in the line of fire of a thousand rifles, encouraging us to do our simple duty, for the performance of which he alone was held to account? And have we not seen him fall while thus engaged, when he might have been safe in the ranks beside us? Let us then honor to-day our heroic dead, from him who bore the marshall's baton to him who shouldered the private's musket, each one equal to the other; each one to-day mingled in equal humbleness with his native sod, but each one enshrined with an equal halo, in the temple of our inmost hearts.

And there is that grand old hero by whose bedside

we have all been watching, whose calm courage and steady will have brought him back from the very confines of the Valley of the Shadow of Death. The same self-confidence, for the country's sake, regardless of himself, now twenty years ago, was what united all men to trust in him and to continue his leadership of our armies, despite reverses and disaster and holocausts of slaughter. And though he may not have been the greatest of our soldiers, nor the wisest of our statesmen, nor the most astute in the busy marts of commerce, will he not always be borne upon the roster of History as one of the greatest of Americans?

And again there is our martyred Lincoln, the type of all worthy the imitation of man. The son of a poor Southern white, building his own career on the foundation of guileless poverty, gathering the rudiments of knowledge at the expense of bread, studying the law by the light of burning shavings, he made his impress on his adopted Northern state simply as honest Abe Lincoln. Embracing emancipation as his earliest political creed, he grew apace in the Nation's life until his hand, under the guidance of Providence, sealed Freedom to four millions of his fellow-men. It has been one of my great privileges to have served, during the last year of his life, in the War Department, in a capacity which enabled me to see and know Mr. Lincoln. And among the great of the earth, in the presence of many of whom I have stood, never was one who could impress you with a sense of the dignity of that noblest work of God, as did this honest man, the Preserver of the Union. His life, his death, his fame, need not a word from me. They are secure within your hearts, my country-men!

Nor must we forget that second martyr, Garfield. A worthy citizen, a sturdy soldier, an incorruptible statesman, an honored President! He fell at the last insane flicker of the torch of sectional hatred, as Lincoln fell when its flame was full of heat. And he was its last sacrifice!

Whether he wore the stars of a Major General, or whether his coat-sleeves boasted not even a chevron, every man who did his duty was a hero whom his country delighteth to honor. And though republics be called ungrateful, can this be said of our American Union? For has not the treasury of the land poured out in shining millions what the hearts of our citizens have poured out in affectionate gratitude? And, brother, many will be the generation before the musket you bore will cease to be the pride of the lisping child who will point to it as to his badge of nobility.

But, comrades, we are not here as to a feast of the living. We are here to honor the memory of our dead.

Their bones are dust,
Their good swords rust,
Their souls are with the saints, we trust.

To us, the living, the country has requited what we have tried to do, and a life saved to future usefulness must be our meed. It is the lesson we may learn from what our dead hero has done which stands for text. Through every form of human self-sacrifice he has spoken to us. He has taught us by his courage, as he fell in the glorious enthusiasm of the charge upon the serried ranks of a foe whose guns belched death from a thousand mouths. He has taught us by his staunchness as his death-knell rang when he planted his standard upon the captured rampart, and stained the stars and stripes with his own hot, gushing blood. He has taught us by his fortitude, on the disheartening retreat from a field where all was lost save honor, where he fell at the head of the rear-guard, to save his fellows from the sword. He has taught us by his silent agony as he died far from kindly succor, wounded on the field deserted by friend and foe. His charred bones, where the underbrush fire has consumed the dead and wounded alike, teach us the lesson taught by the martyred saints of old. The simple slab, with its sad inscription, "Unknown," teaches us that self-denial and simplicity which storied urn and animated bust can never teach. He teaches us patience to-day, as he bravely conceals the running wound or crippled limb while doing his work like the man he is, as he taught us patience long ago when he lay racked by disease and wounds in the hospital-ward or under the dews of heaven. No hour of the life of the American soldier but what can teach us its lesson, if we read the life aright.

And, brother-soldiers, we have had in our own midst examples which we should gratefully remember. Can we forget that tall, fair-faced man, whose gentle dignity was equalled only by the strength of his manly character? Whether drilling his officers and men as he stood upon his one remaining leg, or whether riding at the head of his departing regiment with his crutch strapped to his saddle, or whether facing danger with a coolness which drew forth the chivalric respect of even his bitterest foes, or whether speaking the first word of welcome to our Southern brothers, or whether, the uniform laid aside, pursuing his daily avocation as an honored citizen, was he not, in the manly beauty of his person and his heart, the typical American Anglo-Saxon, as he was so truly the *chevalier sans peur et sans reproche?* And does not his life teach us each and every of the virtues cardinal?

With one of the soldiers, a most honored officer and member of this Post, now passed from among us, have I played through the happy hours of many a long holiday a generation ago. Many an afternoon have I spent with him, each seated in his chosen willow tree on the banks of the Housatonic, fishing for finny dwarfs in its pretty pools, little conscious that in the future both of us would grasp arms in the defense of the Union. Though, comrades, I was but a lad when I left these beautiful Berkshire hills, to return only at rare intervals, I am fain to ask for, nay, to claim my place among you. Here is the home of my kindred; upon the registry of yonder church you may see the record of my birth; here is the school and play-ground of my youth. Though I may not personally have known many of the brave, the generous, the heroic dead whom particularly we remember to-day, yet their names are no less household words to me than they are to you.

Of him for whom this Post has been named, I know but by hearsay. But to him whom his fellow soldier delighteth to honor, every one who has borne arms most willingly does homage. I have heard of Major Rockwell's generous qualities as a man and gallantry as a soldier; of the friends he made in life and the still warmer friends he made in death. But I can bear witness of him only as the soldier whom you, my comrades, have chosen as your type, and lay to-day upon the sod which covers his honored dust my "rosemary, that's for remembrance."

It was by the virtue of such men, comrades, and by their struggles on many fields, that the death-knell of slavery was tolled and that the American people proved its right to be one and indivisible. No man who carried arms in our civil war but may tell the tale with glowing pride. No scar there won but yields its meed of honor. Surely then each life laid down in this struggle for our country and for our own and our fellow-men's liberties, will inscribe his name who bravely gave it up on the roll of imperishable renown.

Rest to his ashes! Peace to that nobler part which dieth not!

THE GETTYSBURG CAMPAIGN.

THE GETTYSBURG CAMPAIGN.*

GETTYSBURG is not only one of the greatest battles of modern days, but it is the culminating point of our civil war. Up to the time of their defeat on this ever-memorable field, the Confederates had been on the whole more successful than unsuccessful. After midsummer of 1863, the course of the Confederacy was downward, steadily downward to the end.

Hundreds of volumes have been written about this most magnificent of the scenes in our great fratricidal drama. Hundreds more will be written. Nor will they exhaust the fruitful theme. Like Waterloo, every generation will listen to its story with fresh interest.

The Southern leaders started out with great anticipations. At the outbreak of the war, they seriously

* Published in The United Service Magazine, July, 1885.

expected to make their initial line of defense along the Ohio River and the northern boundary of Maryland. The North was to be made the attacking party. The South was to wage a defensive warfare. As their political chief, Jefferson Davis, expressed it, all they asked was to be let alone. There was no doubt in their minds that Maryland, Virginia in its then entirety, Kentucky, and at least all of Missouri south of the Missouri River, would be one body indivisible. The map shows how large a territory they thus expected to control. No wonder the scheme of secession looked feasible abroad.

But early events disappointed the expectations of the Confederate leaders. Cairo and Paducah, keys to the Ohio and Mississippi Rivers, were seized; Missouri was rescued from secession government; Kentucky's lukewarmness enabled us to get a foothold, political and military, on her soil; West Virginia affiliated with Ohio, whence had come the bulk of her population up the western slope of the Appalachian water-shed; and Maryland was seized *flagrante delictu* and held in half-willing subjection. Thus instead of the easily defensible line of the Ohio, Mississippi, and Missouri Rivers, flanked by the Blue Ridge, and leaning upon the sympathetic States of Maryland and Virginia, the Confederates were at once, and with scarce a drop of bloodshed, forced back to a line across the open country from the great river to the coast.

The trans-Mississippi conflicts were early eliminated from our military problem, and this was confined to two great strategic fields, one on each side of the Alleghanies, and extending respectively to the Father of Waters and to the Atlantic; the navy meanwhile, backed by sundry military expeditions, doing its share along the Southern coasts.

In the Eastern field stood the two. rival capital cities, each waiting to be crowned as queen when her champion should unhorse his opponent. Here, too, were the flower of the secession troops, led by the most skillful of the soldiers of the Confederacy. And here, too, the armies wrestled, without the final mastery of either, over the same ground for four long years.

The Western strategic field was more open. No one point was here so necessary to the existence of the new state as was Richmond in the East. Kentucky was but half a Southern State. Eastern Tennessee was full of Union men. This territory was not, therefore, clung to with the deperate tenacity exhibited in Virginia. And it was here that our soldiers tasted the success of victory, while in Virginia barren results alone followed a battle won.

The year 1861, however, was but a period of drill and preparation, varied only by minor conflicts which savored of schooling in the new and difficult art of war. In the West swords were barely crossed. In the East political impatience had brought about the battle of Bull Run, where simple accident turned our victory into a defeat. This was followed by many months when all was quiet along the Potomac.

Early in 1862, Grant moved up the Tennessee River and captured Forts Henry and Donelson, while Pope moved down the Mississippi and gained a footing at New Madrid and Island Number 10. Meanwhile the blockade had become a *fait accompli* along the coasts, and Farragut had captured New Orleans.

Spring was now well upon us. The first year of the war was over. The troops on both sides were fairly seasoned and ready for work. Grant had moved still farther up the Tennessee River after rupturing the Confederate line at Donelson. Buell had marched cross-country to meet him, and both had fought the sanguinary battle of Shiloh, which necessitated the enemy's retreat to Corinth. McClellan had moved to the

Peninsula, where, after three months of useless struggle, he was forced to retreat, having fought a dozen bloody battles, to a new base on the James.

The scattered forces in Virginia were brought together under Pope; the Army of the Potomac was dismembered and sent to join the new Army of Virginia, and our forces again suffered a galling defeat on the old Bull Run field.

From here Lee marched into Maryland full of high hopes. McClellan was reinstated, followed him up, defeated him at the Antietam, and pursued him back to mid-Virginia.

While these Eastern successes by the Confederates were going on, Bragg had seized Chattanooga, the strategic key of the Tennessee Valley region, had outflanked Buell and had driven him back to the Ohio, all but securing Louisville and Cincinnati as the reward of his daring. But defeated by his own tardiness, he again retired to Chattanooga.

Thus both the Eastern and Western schemes of invasion of the Northern States by the enemy had failed, in the early fall of 1862, while Grant had completed his hold on the Memphis and Charleston Railroad, after the capture of Corinth and Memphis. We had

There were thus three main armies of operation against the Confederacy. The Army of the Potomac in Virginia; the Army of the Cumberland (Army of the Ohio) on the Nashville-Chattanooga line; and Grant's and Sherman's troops along the Mississippi. Innumerable smaller forces operated on their flanks, along the coast and at available outlying points.

While advance and retreat were thus occupying the Army of the Potomac and the Army of the Cumberland, Grant and Sherman had planned a joint land and water attack upon Vicksburg. Grant's march overland was summarily cut short by severed communications; and Sherman, who had moved down the Mississippi, was unable to cope single-handed with the Vicksburg defenses. A new advance in one body down the river had to be planned against this Confederate stronghold. Its details occupied Grant and Sherman until spring.

In the same last week of 1862 which saw Sherman recoil from the bluffs of Vicksburg, Rosecrans, who had superseded Buell, advanced from Nashville at the head of the Army of the Cumberland, and after the drawn battle of Stone River compelled Bragg to retire from Murfreesboro'; while but a couple of weeks before, the Army of the Potomac under Burnside, the successor of McClellan, had lost all save honor in front of the horrible slopes of Fredericksburg. It had become evident that the struggle had but begun.

The spring and early summer of 1863, in the West, saw Banks move from New Orleans up the Mississippi towards Port Hudson, and Grant undertake his finally successful though erratic manoeuvre against Vicksburg; Rosecrans the while resting on his oars at Murfreesboro'.

In the East, Hooker had superseded Burnside, and in May had afforded the enemy his wonderful triumph at Chancellorsville.

Here apparently was an excellent chance for Lee. His career had been one of almost uninterrupted victory. He had driven McClellan from Richmond. He had outgeneraled Pope. He had invaded the North, and, though forced back, had defeated Burnside with fearful slaughter at Marye's Heights. He had just won by sheer skill (or lack of it) a campaign against Hooker in which he numbered less than half the force of the Army of the Potomac. No wonder his rugged, ragged veterans felt invincible.

But was an invasion of the North a wise step? It

might be of value to conduct a raid into the Northern States, on which the Northern peace-politicians could found more clamor against the Lincoln government, and the European powers could be persuaded into giving their long-delayed assistance. But to all but stake the existence of the Army of Northern Virginia on the result of an important campaign beyond his own borders, where every mile of advance would weaken him and strengthen his adversaries, argued very questionable foresight. Still, Vicksburg was notoriously about to fall, and this disaster must be compensated for by some brilliant feat of arms. The Confederate agents abroad sent home assurances that England and France would recognize the Confederacy if Lee could but establish a foothold in the Northern States, while the Copperheads could be counted on to afford him open assistance there. The Army of Northern Virginia was sadly in lack of rations, shoes, clothing and horses. The Richmond commissary had replied to a requisision for rations that the general commanding might go to Pennsylvania and get his rations himself. The Davis *régime* insisted,—and Lee decided upon invasion.

To attack, in either military or civil warfare, is doubtless often the surest defense; but like a lunge with the foils, an assault must not be beyond the point of instant recovery. Invasion meant weakness in parrying skilful return-thrusts.

In Lee's last campaign he had lost his right-hand man,—that wonderful soldier, Stonewall Jackson. But he was still fortunate in his lieutenants. Longstreet, Ewell, A. P. Hill, Stuart, were all of the right stamp. No captain has ever leaned on bolder, truer men. Few changes needed to be made by Lee. His three infantry corps and his cavalry were all that any leader could ask. For what his men lacked in equipment they more than made up in courage, discipline, belief in their own invincibility, and more than all, untiring legs and uncomplaining stomachs.

Lee had two plans from which to choose. He could either cross the Rappahannock and turn Hooker's flank as he had done Pope's a short year ago, or he could steal a march on him through the Shenandoah Valley across the Potomac into Pennsylvania. He imagined Hooker to be too keenly on the lookout for the first plan to succeed, and choose the latter as affording him, moreover, the better protected line of march. For, after once disengaging himself from Hooker's grasp, he had the Blue Ridge between himself and the Army of the Potomac, with only a few gaps to hold to insure him security on his marching flank.

Early in June he accordingly advanced his left wing under Longstreet, followed by Ewell, to Culpeper, and thence threw Ewell into the Shenandoah Valley.

Hooker had sent Sedgwick across the Rappahannock at Franklin Crossing on the 6th to ascertain what Lee was doing. But Hill met his demonstration with so much vigor that he reported the Confederate lines to be held in force.

Hooker's army had been much depleted by expiration of service, but he still outnumbered his adversary. Indications were too numerous to doubt some projected movement by Lee. A forced cavalry reconnoissance was therefore made on June 9 across the Upper Rappahannock. Pleasonton and Stuart had a smart combat at Brandy Station, and this gave Hooker an inkling of Lee's plan. He at once notified Halleck of his suspicions (as he had in fact previously done), but received as usual no satisfactory instructions. The Union forces were parceled out in wretched driblets all over Virginia, under command of independent generals.

Lee continued his movement. On June 13, Ewell was well down the Valley. Hill was still in the defenses at Fredericksburg. This line, one hundred miles long, was fraught with grave danger for Lee, and argued an almost contempt of his adversary. Yet Lee was afraid to let go of Fredericksburg until he had enticed Hooker away from Falmouth opposite.

Hooker was held in the leash by Halleck. He pleaded for leave to cross the Rappahannock and attack Hill. The problem was simple. He could overwhelm this one corps before Lee could possibly get back to it, and could then march straight on Richmond. Washington had thirty-five thousand men in garrison, and this number could speedily be increased to fifty thousand. The Army of the Potomac could do vastly greater damage to the Confederacy than the Army of Northern Virginia to our cause in the next two weeks. Lee knew this, and Hooker knew that he knew it. Hooker had every chance to capture Richmond by a *coup de main*, and at the same time to call Lee back from his quarry. If there is any well-settled problem in war, it is to attack a divided army whenever you can catch it so. But Halleck, unmindful that to beat the enemy was the true way to protect the capital, forbade any movement which would "uncover Washington;" good Mr. Lincoln feared that the Army of the Potomac would get caught astride of the river "like an ox jumped half over a fence, and liable to be torn by dogs front and rear without a fair chance to gore one way or to kick the other;" and, instead of having the initiative, Hooker was obliged to move towards the Potomac to hold head against the Army of Northern Virginia, according to the weak methods of the general-in-chief.

The only force to oppose Ewell's free march down the Valley was Milroy at Winchester. Milroy had no definite instructions from Halleck, though the latter had had abundant notice of Lee's probable direction a week since from Hooker. Ewell had occupied all the gaps in the Blue Ridge by June 18, and found no difficulty in trapping astonished Milroy and in capturing four thousand prisoners. From here his vanguard boldly advanced into Maryland and Pennsylvania, reaching Chambersburg on the 17th.

Hooker's parallel march was conducted with logistic skill. His cavalry covered his left flank, and at Aldie and Ashby's Gap from the 17th to the 20th crossed swords repeatedly with Stuart, who sought to screen Ewell's movements with his own tireless horsemen.

Hill and Longstreet now followed up Ewell with

alacrity, and crossed the Potomac at Williamsport and Shepherdtown on the 24th and 25th of June. On the succeeding days they were followed by the Army of the Potomac at Edwards Ferry, lower down.

It must be said in honor of the Confederate troops, and especially of their leaders, while on Union soil, that discipline was well maintained, and that, beyond contributions levied in accordance with strict legal warfare, no more than accidental harm was done to the districts through which they passed. However unjustifiable, so much that is beyond description horrible might have been wrought by the men who had seen their own smiling fields made a howling waste by the misfortunes of war, that we should remember their forbearance in the midst of our own happy homes.

Ewell reached the vicinity of Harrisburg June 27. Lee was following hard after him west of the South Mountain Range, Longstreet and Hill being at Chambersburg the same day. Hooker concentrated around Frederick and closely watched his foe. A glance at the map will make it apparent that Lee, the farther he advanced, was more openly presenting his rear to the assault of the Army of the Potomac, while Hooker was planted where he could readily place himself astride all the roads leading to Baltimore and Washington. The Army of Northern Virginia was strategically compromised.

So soon as the Army of the Potomac was fairly over the river, Hooker sent the Twelfth Corps to Harper's Ferry, occupied Turner's and Crampton's Gaps in the South Mountain, and planned to make a diversion against Lee's communications. Reynolds with the First, Third and Eleventh Corps lay in the gaps and at Middletown. Their presence was both a threat to Lee's rear and a corresponding protection to Baltimore and Washington. For if Hooker advanced into the Cumberland Valley, where last year the Antietam battle was fought, he could not only compel Lee to a hasty retreat, but could choose his own ground for a battle. He now asked of Halleck that French at Harper's Ferry be ordered to him for duty with the Army of the Potomac. But useless as Harper's Ferry now was, Halleck loved it as the apple of his eye. He refused. Unwilling to fight the enemy with his hands tied, Hooker at once resigned. Meade was appointed to his place, and to the new commander was granted all the old one was denied. Harper's Ferry was evacuated and the *matériel* sent to Washington, while French re-

Lee now had a taste of the same difficulties we had always experienced in Virginia from lack of information. He was in the enemy's country, where every farmer was a Federal spy, and tongue-tied to the Confederates. Worse still, his "feelers" (for cavalry are the antennæ of an army) under Stuart were off on an erratic mission. Stuart's perceptions and military instinct were, as a rule, singularly keen. But his boldness had this time misled him. By a misunderstanding of the scope of Lee's permission to harass our army in crossing the Potomac, he had got intercepted by Hooker's advance and was compelled to make a hazardous and useless circuit of the entire Union forces, by way of Seneca Ford, Rockville, Westminster and Carlisle. For many days (June 24 to July 2) he was useless to his chief while doing us but little mischief. Thus Lee was deprived of his eyes.

Moreover, at this moment an advance by some Union troops up the Peninsula, in the hope of capturing Richmond, was being made, and, however weakly the plan was executed, it was by no means calculated to allay Lee's fears. There was enough Federal force in the vicinity of the enemy's capital to compass a good measure of success, but the attempts made were la-

Meade, on acceding to the command, preferred not to carry out Hooker's manœuvre against Lee's communications, and decided to follow him up instead on a line east of the South Mountain Range, so as to call him off from the Susquehanna region, and to intervene between his army and Baltimore. He believed, as was the fact, that his presence had relieved Harrisburg and Philadelphia from immediate danger.

But the scheme of Hooker had its advantages, and had at once caused no inconsiderable apprehension to Lee. And Ewell, who was at Carlisle and York on June 28, was no sooner ready to cross the Susquehanna, and to knock at the doors of the capital of Pennsylvania, than he was recalled by Lee. Beyond the burning of the bridge at Columbia, no great harm had so far been done.

The Confederate chief had only heard of the proximity of the Army of the Potomac on the 28th. Both armies had been playing at "hide and seek." He at once divined that this proximity meant retreat, and probably battle. For if cut off from his base, while he might be able to ration his men on the country, he could supply them with no more ammunition, and cold steel can only on rare occasions take the place of pow-

He, therefore, began to retrace his steps, concentrating his forces somewhat slowly. He decided to move east of South Mountain, both to threaten Baltimore and to call Meade's attention away from his line of retreat, about which he was now extremely solicitous. Meade meanwhile selected the general line of Pipe Creek for defense, but threw forward his left under Reynolds towards Gettysburg to develop the enemy.

Meade perhaps lacked strength in planning a defensive battle; for he gave Lee, thereby, the opportunity to hold him in his lines with two of his corps, while with the third he was inflicting incalculable injury to Pennsylvania. Hooker's plan seems on the whole preferable.

On the 30th of June, then, the Army of the Potomac extended substantially from Emmetsburg to Westminster, and the Army of Northern Virginia from Cashtown to Heidlersburg. Lee had, as already stated, his three corps,—Longstreet's First, Ewell's (old Jackson's) Second and Hill's Third, with Stuart commanding the cavalry. The Army of the Potomac had seven corps, each numerically smaller, the First under Reynolds, and later Newton; the Second under Hancock, later Gibbon; the Third under Sickles, later Birney; the

Fifth under Sykes; the Sixth under Sedgwick; the Eleventh under Howard; the Twelfth under Slocum, later Williams; and the cavalry under Pleasonton. As casualties occurred, or necessity dictated, the specific duties of these commanders were shifted. But we have only to do with bodies of men, not individuals. Names will only be used for ease of reference.

In the process of concentration, Lee was not unmindful of supplies. Hearing that there was a goodly stock of shoes in the stores of Gettysburg, he ordered Hill upon this town; and as Gettysburg is a centre of converging roads, Ewell was likewise heading thither. Neither Lee nor Meade had any knowledge of the local topography. Reynolds was, as before stated, at the same time moving with the First and Eleventh Corps, the Third in reserve, upon the same point; Buford's cavalry having preceded him, and having actually occupied the town on the 30th.

Gettysburg is surrounded by hills. On the west, running north and south, is Seminary Ridge, with Willoughby Run a half-mile farther on. Rock Creek makes north and south on the eastern side. South of the town is the fishhook-shaped hill where victory was to perch upon our banners. The Chambersburg turnpike

enters from the northwest, the Harrisburg road from
the northeast, the Carlisle road from the north, the
York road from the east, while the Emmetsburg,
Taneytown, and Baltimore pikes run respectively in a
southwesterly, southerly, and southeasterly direction.

Buford's cavalry had gallantly held the Chambersburg pike beyond Willoughby Run against the van of
Hill from an early hour on July 1. Reynolds hurried
up with the advance of the First Corps about 10 A. M.,
pushing, as was his wont, towards the sound of the
guns. Mounting the belfry of the Seminary buildings,
he carefully scanned the landscape. What he determined he did not live to tell. But he quickly threw
his arriving troops into action on both sides of the
Chambersburg pike. The enemy, who was in greater
force and had reconnoitred the ground, soon overpow-
ered some regiments on the right of the road, causing
them to fall back on Seminary Ridge. A dangerous
break was threatened, but an opportune attack upon
the flank of the pursuing Confederates by the Iron
Brigade, which lay on the left of the road, where it
had captured a *point d'appui* in a little stretch of woods,
enabled us to turn the tide, to strike the right of the
successful line, and to capture several regiments of the

enemy. It was here, directing the dispositions of the fight in person, that gallant Reynolds fell. So vigorous had been the onset of the First Corps men that the enemy had overrated our numbers and become more circumspect in his advance.

Rashness has been charged on Reynolds for thus precipitating the action of July 1. His motive is not known. But he may have gauged the value of the hills in his rear as a battle-ground, and have determined to hold them; and it is asserted that he sent a dispatch ordering Howard up to take position on them in reserve, of which, however, Howard denies the receipt. Hurried field dispatches are not always clear.

The line astride the Chambersburg road was thus re-established, and new brigades coming up were thrown in on the left and right of the wood held by the Iron Brigade. But now appeared from the direction of Carlisle the advance of Ewell's corps, and to meet this accession to the enemy, the fresh arrivals were utilized to prolong our line towards the Mummasburg road.

Howard now put in an appearance and as senior assumed command, and sustained the right with two divisions of the Eleventh Corps, leaving one on Cemetery Hill as a reserve. But this line, which extended from beyond the Chambersburg road over to Rock Creek, was much too extended and thin. Ewell had secured for his batteries a footing on Oak Hill (an eminence one and a quarter miles northwest of Gettysburg), which was the key-point of the field over which the opposing forces were manœuvring, and without great pressure broke through the line where the First and Eleventh Corps joined hands, while some fresh brigades appearing from Hunterstown, sharply assaulted the right of the latter body.

The Eleventh Corps was driven back in disorder and huddled along the roads, converging into the town in tangled masses. The impression of its experience at Chancellorsville had not yet been effaced, and it did not long resist the enemy's assault. The First Corps, on the other hand, had fought with its accustomed nerve. Doubleday, on his right flank being thus turned, applied to Howard for reinforcements or for orders to retire. But neither came. The enemy was closing in on him from three sides, and it was with difficulty that the remnants of the corps made a steady retreat. A short defense at the entrance of the town was resorted to. But it was lucky for the event that the Confederate success was not pressed home.

In order to hold the Gettysburg ridge, it had been necessary to check the enemy in his concentration. This was most readily to be effected by a demonstration beyond the town of sufficient vigor to impose upon the enemy an exaggerated idea of our force at this spot, and oblige him to use up his first efforts on the outlying ground. The scheme failed, to a certain extent, by the Eleventh Corps not holding head against the Confederate onset. But the result of July 1 was to leave Cemetery Ridge in our possession. This fact justifies even the enormous loss we sustained. There had been some sixteen thousand five hundred Union troops engaged against about twenty-two thousand Confederates; but when the routed Federals were assembled in the rear, a bare five thousand men responded to the roll-call.

Hancock now arrived in advance of his corps,—sent by Meade, on hearing of the death of Reynolds, to take command and send back word how the Gettysburg terrain would suit an advance to sustain the action already engaged. His arrival was opportune, for his magnetic cheerfulness aided wonderfully in restoring order. The reserve division of the Eleventh Corps still occupied Cemetery Hill, and here Hancock and Howard disposed the remnants of the First and Eleventh.

Towards evening the Twelfth Corps began to arrive, Howard having by several dispatches urged it forward to his aid, and Slocum as ranking general assumed command. Hancock carried back word to Meade that the ground was greatly in our favor, and urged him with the utmost warmth to come forward with the rest of the army.

The hills on which the Army of the Potomac was then to form—the honor of selecting which belongs to Reynolds, Howard, and Hancock alike—describe a curve not unlike a fishhook. At the barb rises Culp's Hill; along the back, what is known as Cemetery Hill; and the shank ends its north and south line in a rocky, wooded peak called Round Top, having as a spur Little Round Top at its foot. Culp's and Little Round Top are not far from one hundred feet above the town. Round Top is over two hundred feet. Just north of Little Round Top the ground falls away so that the ridge is barely traceable. The general line of these hills is some four miles long, and the position covers the approaches of Baltimore. The ground is mostly open fields alternating with small patches of woods. Distant about a mile west is the parallel Seminary Ridge, and the ground between the two hills has still another slight elevation, along which runs the Emmetsburg road. At the rear of the concave line we were occupying, the ground slopes away and affords excellent cover for reserves and trains.

Hancock's urgent advice determined Meade to fight at Gettysburg. The Third Corps was already on its way, likewise summoned by Howard. Its van reached the scene about sunset. The Second Corps was hurried on and placed in reserve. The Fifth and Sixth were respectively at Union, twenty-three miles, and at Hanover, thirty-six miles away, but could be probably got upon the ground as soon as the enemy would himself have concentrated for action.

Lee's slowness was attributable to his lack of knowledge of our movements, due primarily to his being in hostile territory, but in almost equal measure to the absence of Stuart. The distance over which the Army of Northern Virginia had to move in its concentration averaged short of twenty miles. But until Lee and Meade were by the already related accidental occurrences precipitated into action, the Confederate chief had not hurried forward his troops with his usual vim.

Now that the Federals had been driven back through

the town, Ewell was ordered to carry Cemetery Hill if practicable, but not to bring on a general engagement till the bulk of the army was up. Had Jackson been still alive, the attack would have certainly taken place. But as good luck would have it, Ewell declined the attempt, and during the night our position was fully occupied and intrenched.

At nightfall of the 1st, then, Meade had to contemplate a loss of nearly ten thousand men, and the fact that the Army of Northern Virginia, redolent of victory, was perhaps all in his front, ready to attack at daylight, the Army of the Potomac meanwhile being much scattered. But to offset this, his ground was as good as possible. He naturally overrated Lee's force, and heartily wished he were reinforced by a part of the nearly one hundred thousand men who at Washington, Suffolk, Yorktown and other places, were being held to defend what a bare third of their force could well have cared for.

Neither could Lee feel quite satisfied with his situation. He had promised his corps commanders that he would not assume in this campaign a tactical offensive, but would fight only if he could do so at a great advantage. Longstreet, who was established on the

Emmetsburg road, could, by moving on Frederick, seriously compromise Washington, the nervous timidity of whose leaders was only too well known. And Longstreet desired to do this very thing, though confessedly hazardous. But there lurked in the healthy body of the Army of Northern Virginia a poisonous contempt of its adversary. This was the natural outcome of Manassas, Fredericksburg and Chancellorsville. Lee was morally unable to decline battle. He could not imperil the high-strung confidence of his men.

As the second day dawned he must, however, have watched with throbbing anxiety the Federal line rapidly throwing up defenses on just such a formidable crest as himself had held at Marye's Heights. For Lee gauged better than his men the fighting qualities of his foe.

On the morning of the 2d of July, then, the Army of the Potomac, save only the Sixth Corps, which was rapidly advancing, lay upon the hills of Gettysburg. Slocum had general command on the right; Hancock on the left centre. The men were exhausted by their long marches, but they were in place and resting on their arms. The divisions of the several corps had been placed on the crest and slopes, after considerable shifting to and fro, in substantially the following order from the right. The First Corps was partly at Culp's, and, at a later hour, the Twelfth, with the Fifth in reserve, took place upon its right. The Eleventh Corps held Cemetery Ridge, with the balance of the First Corps on its left. Next came the Second Corps, while the Third prolonged the line along the lower-lying ground as far as the slopes of Little Round Top. Here had lain the Twelfth Corps, and Sickles was ordered to occupy the same ground. The usual field-works were constructed.

The least commanding position of the entire line was thus held by the Third Corps. Sickles' orders appear to have been somewhat indefinite as to his actual line, Meade's attention being attracted more to the right, where he expected the attack. He could not tell exactly where the Twelth Corps had been, and had not particularly noticed the advantage of leaning upon Little Round Top, his line being barely long enough to reach its lower slopes. But the rising ground in his front, at Peach Orchard, tempted him to throw forward substantially his whole line to that point, from which Humphreys prolonged his right flank along the Em-

metsburg road, and Birney threw a part of his division
back crotchet-wise in the direction of Little Round
Top. This made our left flank vastly weaker than if
it had been leaned upon Little Round Top, as Peach
Orchard was commanded by higher ground held by the
enemy on its north.

By mistake of orders, our cavalry was not on hand
to patrol and protect the left. Sickles' position was
weak enough as it was, and he had no idea that Longstreet was massing to crush his left flank, thus almost
in the air. But he was keen enough to doubt the sol-
idity of his lines, and repeatedly applied to Meade to
inspect his dispositions. Busy with other parts of the
field, however, Meade was unable to do so at once, and
before he arrived upon the spot, Longstreet had attacked.

Lee had had his choice of several plans. *First,* he
could retire to the South Mountain passes, thus protect
his line of retreat and lure on the Army of the Potomac
to attack him. This was perhaps his wisest course, for
in it he had the double advantage of pressing his strategic offensive and tactical defensive. He was on the
enemy's territory, and yet might compel the enemy by
active diversions to attack him on his own chosen bat-

tle-field. *Second,* he could attempt to manœuvre Meade out of *his* chosen position. This was Longstreet's idea. It was hazardous, because during the operation he was exposing his flank; but it was feasible. *Third,* he could await attack on Seminary Ridge. This was a doubtful scheme, for Meade was in position to tire him out at his own game. *Fourth,* he could boldly attack. This last course he selected, probably impelled thereto by the temper of his army, which he could not endanger by a retreat, the reason for which they would be unable to understand.

The difficulties we always labored under in Virginia are well illustrated by Lee's slowness of attack in Pennsylvania. On the 1st he delayed in attacking Cemetery Hill when it could have been taken. On the 2d, instead of attacking at daylight, as was his wont, his orders to Longstreet were not imperative enough to bring on the actual clash till late in the afternoon. His ancient habit of barely suggesting to Jackson, who needed no more to start his troops into instant vigorous action, was lost upon his present lieutenants, however excellent as soldiers. Moreover, when Lee determined to strike our left flank, it was wisdom to subordinate everything else to the execution of this one manœuvre.

To leave Ewell in force on our right with a similar purpose was scarcely defensible in a military sense. It is especially necessary, when the weaker army attacks the stronger, that its blow should be concentrated to the last degree. A notable instance of this is Frederick's assault with but thirty thousand men on eighty thousand Austrians at Leuthen. Frederick's front covered barely the Austrian's left wing; but the vigor of his onset in a short winter's afternoon rolled up his enemy's entire force as it had been a scroll.

Lee would perhaps have been wiser to concentrate all his forces along the line of Seminary Ridge. But Ewell was so strong in his belief that he could capture Culp's Hill if Longstreet would make a strong demonstration upon the left, that Lee was loth to withdraw him.

The Union army thus lay in convex line of battle about four miles in length, with a chord of less than a mile and a half over which to move troops from one to another point in the line. The Confederates on the other hand were in concave order, on a line all but six miles long, and in no place of such strength as to be able to mass for a single overwhelming blow. However admirable Lee's tactics generally were, however easily he stands chief among the soldiers of our Civil War, he was here open to criticism. He was doing just what Hooker had done two months before at Chancellorsville, and just what, despite superior forces, Hooker himself had paid a heavy penalty for doing. And this was an open country, where his movements could not be concealed as they might be in the woods of his native State.

In possession of charts, the materials for which the investigations of a thousand minds for twenty years have combined to give us; having the benefit of the research and acumen of the best military judges; viewing the field as we do a problem on a chess-board; with absolute knowledge of the numbers engaged and the terrain upon which they are to move, it is easy to pass criticism upon even Lee, whom history will enroll upon the short first page of Captains of the World. But to stand where Lee stood, with threescore and ten thousand human lives in his keeping; with the fate of the cause he loved and led hanging upon his word; with unknown ground, unknown forces, unknown obstacles in his front, was indeed another task. Unless our criticism is made as earnest students in peace of the great deeds these giants did in war, it is pitiable indeed.

That which has been here indulged in is meant to be temperate as well as honest. It is made with a full appreciation of the unusual difficulties which beset our generals, North and South, with a sincere admiration of their qualities and services, and in that spirit of diffidence which should become a soldier who bore but a modest part in the great struggle which they conducted to what is now accepted by all as its happy outcome.

Ewell, then, was waiting for the signal of Longstreet's attack. But hours passed and Longstreet was not ready. Some of his brigades were not yet up. He was still perfecting his dispositions. His activity was not unperceived by our Signal Corps on Little Round Top. Meade imagined that he might be intending a manœuvre to turn our left, and like a wise commander he prepared his plans to meet this phase of the conflict if it should happen to be suddenly thrust upon him. For such a movement by the Army of Northern Virginia in force might necessitate an immediate withdrawal towards Pipe Creek. Out of this simple precaution seems to have arisen the allegation that Meade deliberately planned a retreat from Gettysburg. The weight of evidence is certainly in favor of his readiness to fight there; and the fact remains that he did fight—and win there.

The Sixth Corps had arrived on the field about 2 P. M., after a march of thirty-five miles in twenty hours, and had been posted in reserve a little back of Round Top.

About 4 P. M. Longstreet opened his attack on Sickles. The Confederate line had not advanced far, before Hood, who was on the right, caught sight of Little Round Top, guessed that it was the key of the battle-field, and instantly made a bold move to capture it. At the moment, it was only occupied by our Signal Corps. Its loss would have taken our left in reverse. Warren, then on the general staff of the Army of the Potomac, had just arrived on the spot to watch the enemy's movements. At once foreseeing the danger, he hurried down the hill for troops to occupy the threatened cliff. The van of the Fifth Corps was just coming up, ordered by Meade from the right to the now seriously threatened left. Seizing on Vincent's brigade, Warren hurried it *pas de course* up the rugged southern slopes, and after a desperate struggle rescued our menaced flank from this crucial peril.

Hood's general attack on Birney was, however, vig-

orous enough to require Sickles' line to be reïnforced
by part of the now arriving Fifth Corps and a brigade
of Humphreys'; despite which the salient at Peach
Orchard was speedily broken through, and Birney and
Humphreys both taken in reverse by McLaws, while
Anderson pushed in on his other flank at Zeigler's
Grove.   In fact, the onset at the latter point had actually pierced our line, and, if followed up, could have
been made a turning-point in favor of the Confederates.

Sickles' difficulty lay in conducting an orderly retreat so as to reoccupy the proper line from Cemetery
Ridge to Little Round Top, and to hold it.   The en-
filading fire made the retiring lines very unsteady.
Gradually, however, under the protection of reïnforcements from Hancock and the Fifth Corps, and of
Ayres' regular division, which left one-half of its number on the field in killed and wounded, the withdrawal
was accomplished, and the line patched up.   A small
force now took position on Round Top.

Repeated attempts by our reïnforced line were made
to recover the lost ground, but uselessly.   We occupied
the wheat-field, but left the enemy the Devil's Den.

The Twelfth Corps had likewise been ordered over
to the point of danger.   But it lost its way and did

not get into action. This seriously depleted the right of the line, without adding to the left.

Ewell's attack on our right had been as greatly delayed as Longstreet's. He had not heard the latter's fire. It was sunset before he assaulted. Early moved on Cemetery Hill, Johnson on Culp's. The former met with no success, though he struggled hard till late at night and once drove our troops out of their intrenchments. His columns had not been simultaneously moved to the attack. But at Culp's, owing to the absence of the Fifth, and the bulk of the Twelfth Corps marching over to the left, Johnson managed to make a lodgment with small effort in the lines abandoned by the Twelfth Corps, and held it during the night. Only a small force of cavalry was between him and both the headquarters of the army and the reserve artillery.

The night was spent in preparation for the eventful morrow. The troops were reformed; weak portions of the line were reïnforced; ammunition was distributed; the field-works were strengthened; the situation was inspected in its every detail; and plans for every probable contingency discussed. The men lay on their arms in line of battle.

Meade, who had been but a few days in command, felt that he must rely greatly for his action upon the opinion of his late companions-in-arms, now his subordinates. He called together his corps commanders during the night and put to them two questions. First. Shall we fight the battle out here? Second. If so, shall we attack or await attack? The situation was grave, but not unpromising. Longstreet had lost heavily, and had gained only an apparent, not a real advantage. The left was safe, and in the position originally designed for it. On the right, however, the enemy had a foothold very near the Baltimore pike on Culp's Hill. This was a serious matter, but it might be mended. The troops were in fine spirits, and despite their extensive losses—some twenty thousand men—were ready for yet another day. It was decided to fight a defensive battle on the morrow, without change of position.

Lee must of course have scanned the situation most critically, too. He was inclined to believe that Longstreet had made an actual lodgment in our left centre; while Ewell reported that he could certainly hold his position at Culp's. The Army of Northern Virginia felt confident of victory. There was no question of what Lee must do.

At one time Lee contemplated a renewed attempt to turn the Union left, so nearly broken through already; but on second thought he abandoned this idea, and determined to assault where Anderson seemed to have have made a feasible breach at Zeigler's Grove. Lee had always been much in the habit of relying upon his subordinates. Jackson's splendid individuality of action had to a certain extent weakened his own. And his desire not to interfere with what Ewell felt sure that he could do, led him to leave his line in its then long and weak condition. Lee's powers in Pennsylvania seemed to be less active than on his native soil.

Meade, to prepare for the morrow, ordered the Twelfth Corps, reïnforced by some troops from the Sixth Corps, back to Culp's. Here, on its arrival, it found the height which itself had occupied, in the possession of the enemy. It went into position, however, determined to drive him out at daylight.

The Fifth Corps had been placed on the left, leaning on Little Round Top, with the Third, whose losses had been the most severe of any in the army, in reserve. The First Corps had been placed in the most necessary gaps on the right and left of Cemetery Hill.

During the night batteries were established on all

the heights which could be made to command the ground held by Johnson, and at early dawn on July 3 the Twelfth Corps engaged the veterans of Jackson along the rugged slopes of Culp's Hill. The Federals fought with the knowledge that this flank must be preserved intact at any sacrifice, while the vicinity of the Baltimore road invigorated the enemy, who well understood how grievous a blow could be inflicted upon the Army of the Potomac by gaining possession of its trains, reserve ammunition, and main line of retreat. And Jackson's men were rarely to be denied the victory they fought for. But Johnson was unsupported by artillery, which could not be utilized on the steep and rocky hill-side, and the efforts proved vain. Until an hour from noon they persevered in their attempts to dislodge Slocum. Finally exhausted, Johnson was fain to beat a recall. Ewell's anticipations had come to naught.

Longstreet was still in favor of a strong manœuvre upon our left, and looked with no kindly eye on the proposed assault at Zeigler's. This, meanwhile, was being unaccountably delayed. In fact, Longstreet had planned a diversion against the Round Top with a small column, but Kilpatrick's cavalry turned up opportunely on his right, and not only checked the attempt but required some effort to drive him back.

A lull of several hours of precious time had occurred in the preparations for the assault on our centre. Finally, about 1 P. M., the Confederate batteries which had been massed along Seminary Ridge—one hundred and thirty-eight pieces in all—opened fire upon that part of our line which Lee had selected for the assault. The Union batteries, of some eighty guns,—more could not be crowded into the available space,—began to reply so soon as they could determine the location of the enemy's guns.

The Confederate fire was too much spread. There was an appearance of that lack of unity among the Southern chieftains which did in fact exist. But the column destined for the supreme effort was slowly forming, and would move whenever a sufficient impression had been made on the Union lines by the artillery fire.

Pickett's division, consisting almost exclusively of Virginia regiments, which had just reached the field, was assigned as the forlorn hope. The duty could not be in better hands. The Ney of the Rebel army, backed by his gallant Virginians, could pierce the Union centre

Under the cover of the guns, Pickett formed his five thousand men in double line of battle. On his right Wilcox was to march in support, and on his left Pettigrew, each in column by battalions. The whole body was fourteen thousand strong. To save up ammunition for closer range, our guns had temporarily ceased their work. The enemy believed that he had silenced them by his own heavier fire. Now was the moment for the blow. In superb alignment, as on parade, Pickett's heavy column moved out from the cloud of smoke. A clump of trees within Hancock's line was the goal marked out by Lee. Our guns again opened fire, using canister as soon as the range allowed. The men lay behind their breastworks and in the shelter of the stone walls somewhat below, which they had strengthened as defenses, calmly watching the advance. In the breast of every man who fought on December 13, must have lurked the feeling that this was the day which should avenge us for the bloody work at Marye's Heights.

The point aimed at by Pickett was on Hancock's front, covering a space defended by perhaps some five or six thousand men. Our supply of canister had been mostly exhausted, and the gaps which had been torn in the enemy's ranks had been filled up as, with only such pauses as would enable the men to throw down the walls and fences in their path, the devoted column swept on. The Federal infantry reserved its fire with exceptional steadiness. The artillery was using grape.

On the right of the advancing column a small wood extended in front of our line. Here Stannard's brigade had been posted. As Pickett's column approached, these men opened an oblique fire which caused the enemy, in edging away from it, to move somewhat to their left; and as their lines arrived opposite the wood (Wilcox's delay on their right having entirely uncovered their flank) Stannard changed front and poured some destructive volleys at close quarters into their midst. But these Virginians were not to be thus stopped, though their right and left were naked of support. The column pushed on, struck Webb's brigade at the stone wall, and planting their battle-flags upon it, the men rushed over the obstacle, blue and gray struggling in one mass, and sought to hew their way to the line of breastworks above.

But the effort had exhausted itself. Webb's resistance was superb. Fresh Union troops poured in from every side, filling up the vacant spaces, until the men stood four deep and upwards. Not a sign of demoralization was apparent. Our broken line was speedily rehabilitated. Too few of the enemy were left to continue the struggle, and the gallant body, surrounded on every side, and with but a tithe of its force unhurt, laid down its arms. A few had escaped to the rear. Barely one in four returned to the cover of the Confederate guns. Two thousand stayed within our lines.

The column of Pettigrew never reached our line. It broke before it could accomplish anything of moment. Hays' sharp fire had quickly checked its onset, and we captured two thousand five hundred prisoners.

Wilcox's column for some unknown reason had obliqued too much to the right, as Pickett's had to the left, and as it later passed by Stannard's wooded salient, was, by another change of front, in similar fashion taken in flank upon the opposite side. Deploying his command, Wilcox opened fire, but was speedily driven back, with heavy loss in prisoners and battle-flags.

Thus ended the attack on our centre, like its predecessors on our right and left. The Army of Northern Virginia had suffered a disastrous defeat.

The instinct of a great commander might have

seized this moment for an advance in force upon the broken enemy. But Meade cautiously held what he had already won rather than gain more at greater risk. He was content. He would adventure nothing. He had won the credit of defeating his enemy; he lost the chance of destroying him.

Meanwhile, on the 3d, the bulk of our cavalry had taken post on the right of our entire line, a few miles east of Gettysburg, to hold head against Stuart, who had, after his long and useless circuit, reported to his chief for duty. Stuart had received orders from Lee so to manœuvre as to strike the Union right if, in case of Confederate success, it should retire, as it probably would do, towards Westminster. He therefore made a stout attack upon Pleasonton, to seize if possible the Baltimore road, and create a panic in our rear. This could have been made of greatest service to Lee. But after a combat of some severity, in which swords were repeatedly crossed, Pleasonton was able to balk Stuart of his purpose; and the latter soon found that he must himself retire to protect Lee's retreat rather than attempt further to disturb Meade's communications.

On the 4th Lee was still upon Seminary Ridge. His

lines had been drawn in, and were concentrated where he could best cover the Hagerstown and Chambersburg roads. His cavalry protected his flanks. It is probable that he would have received a Federal attack with alacrity, and the Army of Northern Virginia was, despite its losses and defeat, in condition to give a good account of itself.

Meade advanced his lines slowly into Gettysburg and on the left, and reconnoitred with his cavalry. He still believed a fresh attack by the enemy possible, and considered what would be his best course in the event that such an attack should be made, or what if the Army of Northern Virginia should retreat.

So passed our National Holiday. By daylight of the 5th the enemy had disappeared into the Cumberland Valley.

There were two roads over which Meade could undertake the pursuit. He could follow up Lee's army on its direct line of retreat *via* Chambersburg and Hagerstown, or he could move around by a circuit nearly twice as long east of the South Mountain range, and through the gaps to Middletown. The former route covered Gettysburg, and therefore Baltimore and Washington. The latter would take Lee in flank, if pushed with sufficient speed, for he was hampered with long trains. After some indecisive movements along the first, Meade decided on the second route.

Meanwhile, French, who had been at Frederick, had made a demonstration towards his old post at Harper's Ferry on the 3d of July, and finding Lee's pontoon-bridge at Falling Waters, just below Williamsport, but slightly guarded, he destroyed it. At the moment when Pickett was leading his men to what he deemed certain victory, the existence of the Army of Northern Virginia was compromised if it should be defeated and sharply followed up.

Lee's retreat was conducted with as much expedition as the tired, disheartened men and many miles of trains would warrant. Meade's pursuit was lamentably slow. On the 6th the Army of the Potomac was at Emmetsburg. On the 7th at Frederick. On the 7th and 8th it was concentrating at Middletown. Now that the enemy was on the retreat, Halleck hurried forward reinforcements from Washington; and Smith moved down with his Pennsylvania levies. But Meade made the utilization of these accessions the cause of still greater slowness. He would not believe that the enemy was vastly more disorganized than the Army of the Potomac by the fearful struggle at Gettysburg. He seemed to fear renewed attack by Lee. Finally, on July 13, he drew up in front of Lee's line along Marsh Creek near Williamsport, where the latter had been for nearly a week, and had strongly intrenched his army.

The elements were fighting for the Union army. The river had risen so as to be unfordable. Lee was absolutely trapped. Not but what the Army of Northern Virginia would have fought for existence as it had never yet fought for victory. But the Federals so largely outnumbered the enemy, that some action seemed to be demanded. The position might have been turned by way of Conecocheaque Run. Almost any course rather than inaction appeared advisable. In case of a disastrous assault, the Army of Northern Virginia would be scarcely ready to reassume the offensive. But at a council of his corps commanders on July 13, it was advised not to attack Lee's lines. This opinion, arrived at with all the then known facts before them, ought no doubt to modify to-day's criticism.

Meade, however, in spite of this advice decided to make an attack on the 14th. Too late. As morning dawned, it was discovered that the enemy had recrossed the Potomac. A new pontoon-bridge had been improvised, and as the water had largely subsided, the Williamsport ford could be used. The Army of Northern Virginia had merely suffered a defeat and beat an orderly retreat.

The numbers engaged and lost in this greatest of our battles have been the subject of much discussion. One of the best-read military men in the South, in a recent letter to me, honestly figures the Confederate effective at sixty thousand, and the Federal at ninety thousand. It is, of course, impossible to reach accuracy. But about sixty-eight thousand for the Army of Northern Virginia to eighty-four thousand for the Army of the Potomac seems approximately true, and is a generous enough estimate for the gallant men who attacked our lines on those three eventful days.

The loss was twenty-three thousand on each side,—all but one in three engaged.

Meade was a ripe, sound soldier. He fell short of greatness, perhaps, but few equalled him in precision and steady-going capacity. Under him the Army of the Potomac saw its greatest triumph, and its greatest humiliation. Gettysburg was Meade's victory; Cold Harbor was not Meade's defeat. While he was in command the army was always in safe hands; its discipline was excellent; its *esprit de corps* high. All his subordinates held him in great esteem. In minor stations Meade obeyed with alacrity; in supreme control he commanded with discretion. His qualities are not salient; but he was well rounded both as a soldier and as a man.

From this time on the South waged a strictly defensive warfare. Not but what Lee again and again attacked the Army of the Potomac, as Hood did Sherman in the West. But every intelligent man in the Confederacy saw that to conquer any kind of peace which would afford them independence was all but an impossibility. Not that they lost heart. Their efforts were still marvelous. But after Gettysburg the Confederates fought because it was not in them to give up,—not because they believed they could win.

It was upon this spot that the death-knell of slavery was tolled, and that the American Nation proved its right to be one and indivisible. No man who carried arms in this greatest of our country's battles but may tell the tale with glowing pride; no scar there won but yields its meed of honor; no life laid down upon this hard-fought field but inscribes his name who bravely gave it up on the roll of imperishable renown.

Rest to their ashes! Peace to that nobler part which dieth not!

THE BATTLE OF
CHANCELLORSVILLE.

THE BATTLE OF CHANCELLORSVILLE.*

In the "Lowell Institute" course of lectures, in Boston last winter, the following lecture was delivered by Colonel Theodore A. Dodge, author of the admirable book on Chancellorsville, which we had occasion to notice so favorably. In order that our readers may see clearly *who* it is that gives this able, clear, and very fair account of this great battle, we insert the following brief sketch of Colonel Dodge given by the Boston *Herald*:

"Colonel Theodore A. Dodge is one of the best known men in Boston military circles. He is now in his 43d year, having been born in Pittsfield, Massachusetts, in 1842. When quite young he went to Berlin, Prussia, where he received his military education under General von Froneich, of the Prussian army. When the civil war cloud burst in the United States he promptly returned home, enlisted and went to the front. He served constantly in the Army of the Potomac (in every volunteer regimental rank up to that of colonel) from the Peninsula, where he was with Kearney, through Pope's and Burnside's campaigns, and at Chancellorsville and Gettysburg, in which latter engagement he was with Howard. He was thrice brevetted for gallantry. After Gettysburg, where he lost a leg, he was ordered to duty in the war department. While there Secretary Stanton offered him a regular commission, which was accepted. Colonel Dodge remained in the war department until 1870, when he was, by reason of wounds received in the line of duty, placed on the retired list of the army, where he now is."

We insert with great pleasure the lecture, without note or comment of our

* Published in the Southern Historical Society Papers, 1886.

own, except to say, that while possibly we might find some statements in it
with which we might not fully concur, yet we hail it as a happy omen when
a gallant soldier who wore the Blue can give to a Boston audience so candid
and truthful an account of a great battle in which the Federal arms suffered
so severe a disaster.

COLONEL DODGE'S LECTURE.

Ladies and Gentlemen:—You have listened to an eloquent and able presentation of the main issues and
events of our civil war by one of our most distinguished fellow-citizens, a man upright in peace, zealous
in war.   You have heard a graphic narrative of a great
Southern victory from one of our late antagonists,
whose record, as one of Stonewall Jackson's staff
officers, stamps him honest and brave, as his presence
and bearing among us have stamped him thoroughly
reconstructed.   You have had spread before you an
elaborate and brilliant view of one of our glorious victories by a gallant soldier of two wars, who has beaten
into a ploughshare the sword he wielded to such good
purpose in Mexico and Virginia.   It has fallen to my
lot to tell you about one of our most lamentable defeats.   To tell the truth about Chancellorsville is an
invidious task.   Less than the truth no one today
would wish to hear.   Under Burnside the Army of

the Potomac suffered an equal disaster.   But Burnside
blamed himself alone.   No word but praise for his
lieutenants passed his lips.   After Chancellorsville, on
the contrary, Hooker sought to shift all the blame upon his subordinates, even to the extent of intimating
that they were braggarts, who would not fight.   Particularly Howard and Sedgwick were his scapegoats,
and for some years Hooker's views gained credence.
His course renders nesessary a critical examination of
the campaign.   But be it remembered that every word
of censure is uttered with the consciousness that Hooker's memory lies embalmed in our mausoleum of dead
heroes, and that in lesser commands his career was
patriotic and useful.

The disaster at Fredericksburg, in December, 1862,
had left its mark upon the ever faithful Army of the
Potomac.   It had lost confidence in its chief, but not
in itself.   Burnside retired in January to the satisfaction of all, but carrying away their affectionate regard.
Hooker succeeded to the command.   His sobriquet of
"Fighting Joe" aptly but superficially characterized
him.   Few men could handle a division—perhaps a
corps—to better advantage under definite orders.   None
gloried in the act of war more than he.   Lacking not

conduct, yet the dramatic side of the art-military was dearest to him, and his ubiquity and handsome bearing made him better known to the army at large than many of his more efficient brothers-in-arms. The troops accepted Hooker with the utmost heartiness. He had been identified with their history. He was bone of their bone. He seemed the very type and harbinger of success. Men and officers alike joined in the work of rehabilitation. Under well digested orders—for Hooker was a good organizer—the lamentable laxity of discipline soon disappeared; eagerness succeeded apathy, and the Army of the Potomac once again held high its head.

On April 30, 1863, the morning report showed, "for duty equipped," 131,491 officers and men, and nearly 400 guns in the camp near Falmouth. Confronting this overwhelming body of men lay the weather-beaten Army of Northern Virginia, numbering some 60,000 men and 170 guns. This force was posted from Banks' ford above, to Skenker's Neck below Fredericksburg, a distance of some fifteen miles. Every inch of this line was strongly and intelligently fortified. The *morale* of the Confederate army could not be finer. To numbers it opposed superior position and defences, and its wonderful successes had bred that contempt of danger and that hardihood which are of the very essence of discipline. Perhaps no infantry was ever, in its own peculiar way, more permeated with the instinct of pure fighting—ever felt the *gaudium certaminis*—than the Army of Northern Virginia at this time.

The Army of the Potomac could not well risk another front attack on Marye's Heights. To turn Lee's right flank necessitated operations quite *en evidence*, and the crossing of a river 1,000 feet wide in the very teeth of the enemy. Hooker matured his plans for a movement about Lee's left.

On April 12th the cavalry corps was ordered out upon a raid, *via* Culpeper and Gordonsville, to the rear of Lee's army, in order to cut his communications and to demoralize his troops at the moment when the main attack should fall upon him.

"Let your watchword be fight! and let all your orders be fight! fight!! fight!!!" was Hooker's aggressive order to Stoneman. The performance of the latter, however, was in inverse ratio to the promise of these instructions. The start was delayed two weeks by a rise in the river; and the movement was so weak from its inception that the cavalry raid degenerated into an utter failure, and the first step in the campaign thus miscarried. The operations of the cavalry corps scarcely belong to the history of Chancellorsville. They in no wise affected the conduct or outcome of the campaign.

In order to conceal his real move by the right, Hooker made show of moving down the river, and a strong demonstration with the First, Third and Sixth corps on the left, under command of Sedgwick. Covered by Hunt's guns, on April 29th and 30th, pontoons were thrown at Franklin's Crossing and Pollock's mills, troops were put over, and bridgeheads were constructed and held by Brooks' and Wadsworth's divisions. Lee made no serious attempt to dispute this movement, but watched the dispositions, uncertain how to gauge their value.

Meanwhile, the Eleventh and Twelfth corps, followed by the Fifth, with eight days' rations, marched up to Kelley's Ford. Here all three corps crossed the Rappahannock on the night of Wednesday the 29th; and on Thursday the two former crossed the Rapidan at Germania Ford, and the latter at Ely's, and all three reached Chancellorsville Thursday afternoon. Here Slocum assumed command. Gibbon's division, of the

Second corps, had been left to guard the Falmouth camps and do provost duty, while French and Hancock, after United States Ford had been unmasked, crossed at this point and joined the forces at Chancellorsville. The Third corps was likewise ordered from the left, by the same route, to the same point.

Thus far, everything had been admirably conceived and executed. Small criticism can be passed upon Hooker's logistics. They were uniformly good. Two of our corps had centred the enemy's attention upon his right flank, below Fredericksburg, while we had massed four corps upon his left flank, with a fifth close by, and had scarcely lost a man. Hooker's vaunting order of this day is all but justified by the situation. But one more immediate and vigorous push, and the Army of Northern Virginia would have been desperately compromised, practically defeated.

Lee had not been unaware of what the Federals had been doing, but he had been largely misled by the feint below the town, and had so little anticipated Hooker's movement by the right, that less than 3,000 of his cavalry were on hand to observe the crossing of the Rappannock and Rapidan. Stuart had not, until Thursday, fully gauged the importance of this move-

ment, and only on Thursday night had Lee ascertained
the facts, and been able to mature his plans for parrying Hooker's thrust. Anderson had received, on
Wednesday, orders to check at Chancellorsville, as
long as possible, our advance, supposed to be partial
only, and then to slowly retire to the Mine Run road.
This he had done, and here Lee's engineers were speedily engaged in drawing up a line of intrenchments.
Early was left at Hamilton's Crossing, Barksdale remained in the town, and Lee, with the bulk* of his
forces, hurried out to meet the Army of the Potomac.
At an early hour on Friday morning Jackson arrived
at the Mine Run line and took command. Hooker's
tardiness in advancing had already allowed the erection of a difficult barrier.

The headquarters of the Army of the Potomac had
remained at Falmouth till Hooker personally reached
Chancellorsville. After the transfer hither, the chief
of staff, for ease of communication between the wings,
was kept at the old camp. Hooker now announced
his plan to advance Friday, in force, and uncover
Banks' ford, so as to be within quicker reach of Sedgwick. It had been a grave error not to make this advance on Thursday afternoon. On Friday morning,

after reconnoitering the ground, he accordingly ordered an advance toward the open country to the east, while Sedgwick should threaten an attack in the neighborhood of Hamilton's Crossing to draw Lee's attention.

In pursuance of these orders, Meade advanced to within grasp of Banks' Ford quite unopposed. Sykes and Hancock on the turnpike, on leaving the forest, ran upon the intrenched divisions of Anderson and McLaws, whom they engaged. Slocum, with the Eleventh and Twelfth corps on the plank road, was arrested by the left of this same line. The opposition was nowhere serious. The troops were there to fight. Hooker should have carried out his programme in full by ordering up fresh troops, and by driving back the largely overmatched force of the enemy.

Every reason demanded this. The Army of the Potomac had just emerged from the Wilderness, in whose confines no superiority of force could be made available as it could be on the open ground toward Fredericksburg. It was essential that the two wings should be got within easier communicasion. The enemy had been surprised and should be followed up. The plan had succeeded well so far; to abandon it would create a loss of *morale* among the troops.

Suddenly every one concerned was surprised by an order from Hooker to withdraw again into the Wilderness. Here may be said to have begun the certain loss of the campaign. The proceeding was absurd. Hooker had reached Chancellorsville Thursday noon with forty thousand men, fresh, and abundantly able to advance toward and seize Banks' Ford, his first objective. To delay here until Friday noon was a grave mistake. Still, had the advance on Friday been pushed home by a concerted movement by the left, so as to seize Banks', and cover United States Ford, it was by no means too late to gather the fruits of the vigor and secrecy exhibited thus far in this flank march.

But the advance on Friday was checked by Hooker without personal examination of the situation, to the surprise of every one, and against the protest of many of his subordinates. A more fatal error cannot be conceived. Here first appeared Hooker's lack of balance. The troops retired, and Jackson at once took advantage of the situation by advancing his left to Welford's.

The Army of the Potomac on Friday night lay huddled in the chapparal around Chancellorsville, instead of occupying, as they might, a well defined position on the open ground in front of Banks' Ford. Gradually, during the night, the several corps drifted, weary and disheartened at this unexplained check in the midst of success, into the position which they had taken up after crossing the river, without any idea of fighting there. The line was thus a hap-hazard one, on the worst conceivable ground, where cavalry was useless, artillery confined to the roads or to a few open spaces, and infantry hidden or paralyzed.

Reynolds was now ordered from the left wing to Chancellorsville. The line lay from left to right—Meade, Couch, Slocum, Sickles, Howard. Hooker determined to receive instead of delivering an attack. He knew how vastly he outnumbered Lee; he could gauge the advantage he had gained from his initiative; he could not be blind to the wretched *terrain* around Chancellorsville, and yet he sat down as if already worsted. Nothing but a sudden loss of moral force can explain such enigmatic conduct. Hooker had come to the end of his mental tether. The march had taxed his powers to their limits. He had no more stomach for the fight.

During this night, while the Army of Northern Virginia was moving into position in front of its gigantic, but apparently unnerved enemy, Lee and Jackson developed a plan for an attack upon our right, which, though posted on high ground, was really in the air. Lee may have originated the plan, but it bears a distinctly Jacksonian flavor; and surely without such a lieutenant to execute it, Lee would never have dreamed of making such a risky move. The plan gave Jackson about 24,000 men with which to undertake a march around our right flank to a position where he might cut us off from United States Ford. It was ultra-hazardous, for it separated a small army in the presence of a large one. It was justifiable only on the ground that Hooker evidently meant to retain the defensive; that the movement would be screened from his eye by the woods; that there seemed no more available plan; that some immediate action was demanded. Had it failed it would have met the censure of every soldier. No maxim of tactics applies to it so well as the proverb "Nothing venture, nothing have."

Although Jackson's corps had been on foot and partially engaged for some thirty hours, the men set out on this new march with cheerful alacrity. They could always follow "Old Jack" with their eyes shut. Stuart's cavalry masked the advance. Jackson did not know that his column would have to pass some open ground in full view of our line at Dowdall's, until too late to have it follow a better concealed route. Early Saturday morning the movement was discovered by the Third corps, and a reconnoisance was pushed out to embarrass its advance. After some trouble and a slight and successful attack, Birney ascertained and reported that Jackson was moving over to our right. The conclusion which Hooker drew from this fact was, apparently, that Lee was retreating. Jackson, meanwhile keeping Sickles busy with a small rear-guard, advanced along the Brock road until, toward afternoon, he was abreast and in the rear of our right flank. While he was thus massing his men to take the Army of the Potomac in reverse, Hooker continued to authorize Sickles to deplete the threatened wing by sending a large part of its available strength (Barlow, Birney, Whipple, and Geary in part—some 15,000 men) out into the woods in the hope of capturing the force which had long ago eluded his grasp and was ready to fall upon our rear. Hooker's right flank, of barely 10,000 men, was completely isolated. And yet though scouts, pickets, and an actual attack at 3:30 P. M., proved beyond a peradventure Jackson's presence at this point,

Hooker allowed this flank to be held by an untried corps, composed of the most heterogeneous and untrustworthy elements in the Army of the Potomac.

This march of Jackson's might, at first blush, have been construed by Hooker to be either a retreat or strategic march by Lee to new ground, or to be a threatened flank attack. Either would have been accompanied by the same tactical symptoms which now appeared. If the former, Hooker had his option to attack at an early or late period more or less vigorously, as might appear best to him. Hooker afterward claimed that he believed in the flank attack. But the testimony of his dispatches at the time finds him riding both horses, and he acted on the retreat theory. At 9:30 A. M., he had notified Slocum and Howard to look out and prepare for a flank attack, and to post heavy reserves to meet one. He telegraphed Sedgwick at 4:10 P. M.: "We know that the enemy is flying, trying to save his trains." In the meantime he had removed the heavy reserves in question and sent them out on Sickles' wild goose chase to the front. He made no inspection of the right except one early in the morning.

Howard, commanding on the right, misled by Hooker's orders and apathy, held to the retreat theory. He had, on the receipt of the 9:30 order, disposed Barlow's brigade and his reserve artillery so as to resist an attack along the pike, but Barlow had been ordered by Hooker to join Sickles. General Devens made several distinct attempts to impress on Howard the danger of an attack, but the latter took his color, as well as his orders, from the commander of the army. General Carl Schurz, under whom I served that day, also held strongly to the flank-attack theory, and scores of men in the Eleventh corps, after the picket fight of 3:30, fully believed that another attack would be made in the same place. Common generosity to the memory of Hooker, who was a gallant and successful corps commander, leads us to think that at the time he believed that the enemy was retreating. His neglect of the right was otherwise criminal. In him alone centred all the information of constantly occurring changes. To him alone was reported each new circumstance. His subordinates knew but the partial truth. They relied on him for the initiative.

At 6 P. M., then, the situation was this: The left and centre lay as before. Howard held the right, the "key of the position," with 10,000 men, a half brigade

of Devens' only astride the pike, the rest of Devens'
and Schurz's facing south, and Steinwehr massed at
Dowdall's.   Howard's best brigade was gone, and
there was not a man to support him between Dowdall's
and Chancellorsville.   For this portion of the line under Sickles had been advanced into the woods nearly
two miles.   On the right flank of this little force lay
Jackson's corps of over 20,000 men, whose wide wings,
like the arms of a gigantic cuttlefish, were ready to
clutch it in their fatal embrace.

To cover Jackson's march, Lee at intervals during
the day tapped at the lines in his front, principally
where Hancock lay.

During all this afternoon, Hooker had a chance
handsomely to redeem his Friday's error in retiring into the Wilderness.   Whatever the *reason*, the *fact* that
that Lee had divided his army remained clear.   Lee,
with the right wing, had but 18,000 men.   Hooker
knew that he could not have more than 25,000.   He
himself had 70,000 splendid troops.   He could have
crushed Lee like an egg-shell, and then have turned on
Jackson.   But, with a knowledge of Jackson's habit of
mystery, of his wonderful speed and fighting capacity,
and of his presence on our right, with all the means of

knowing that this same right flank was isolated by two miles of impenetrable woods from any supporting force, he sat still, folded his hands, as it were for sleep, and waited events.

The Eleventh corps was cooking or eating supper. Arms were stacked. Breastworks looking south were but fairly substantial. Facing east were none. Some carelessness was apparent, in that ambulances, ammunition wagons, pack mules and even a drove of beeves were close behind the line. Every one was at ease, though a few were not wanting in anxiety. Little Wilderness Church, near by, endeavored to stamp a peaceful air upon the warlike scene. The general feeling seemed to be that it was too late to get up much of a fight to-day.

Jackson, in three lines, Rodes in advance, Colston next and A. P. Hill still coming up, lay close by. He had caught Hooker's right *flagrante delictu*. At 6 P. M. the order was given, and 22,000 of the best infantry in existence closed rapidly down upon the flank of 10,000 of the least hardened of the troops of the Army of the Potomac. No division in the Army of the Potomac, not the Old Guard, not Frederick's automata, could have changed front under the staggering blow.

The fight was short, sharp, deadly, but partial only. But the force on the right was swept away like a cobweb by Jackson's mighty besom. Some of Schurz's regiments made a gallant show of resistance under the terrible ordeal of friends and foes breaking through their hastily formed lines; some melted away without burning a cartridge. Bushbeck's brigade threw itself into some breastworks constructed across the road at Dowdall's and made a desperate resistance. It was here that Howard had asked leave to place his line, but had been refused. A ridge made the line well available for defence.

The whole situation was confusion worse confounded. The attack had been so sudden that the stampede of the regiments on the extreme right swept away many of those which were endeavoring to form near the fork of the roads. The drove of beeves, the frightened teamsters and ambulance drivers, officers' servants, and hundreds of camp followers were rushing blindly to and fro, seeking an escape from the murderous hail of lead. The enemy came on with remorseless steadfastness. Never was an army more completely surprised, more absolutely overwhelmed. Few, even among the old soldiers, preserved their calmness, but many did their duty. The higher officers were in the thickest of the fray. An occasional stand would be made, only to be again broken. Everywhere appeared the evidence of unpreparedness.

It is small wonder that the corps made no resistance worthy the name. Rather wonder that, under the circumstances I have detailed, the onset of Jackson was actually checked by this surprised and over-matched, this telescoped force, considerably more than an hour, at a loss of one-third its effective strength. Could more have been expected?

The worthlessness of Hooker's dispositions now became apparent. Jackson's small rear-guard had been playing with Sickles, while his main body had extinguished Howard. Nothing now lay between Jackson and the headquarters of the army except a difficult forest, through which a mass of panic-stricken fugitives were rushing in dire confusion out of range. Happily night was approaching, and Jackson's troops had to be halted and reformed, his three lines having become inextricably mixed.

Anderson had made a serious attack on our centre so soon as the guns of Jackson's corps were heard, so that Hooker had nothing at hand to throw into the gap but Berry's division of the old Third corps. Other troops were too far away. This division was now hurried into position across the pike. The artillery of the Third corps and many guns of the Eleventh corps were assembled on the Fairview crest. Sickles faced about the 15,000 men he had led into the woods, and disposed himself to attack Jackson in more practical fashion. Between good use of several batteries, and a gallant charge by a handful of cavalry, a diversion upon his flank was created, which, coupled to Berry's desperate resistance and the heavy artillery fire from Fairview, arrested Jackson's onset. It was after this check, while reconnoitering in front of his troops, that this noted soldier received, from his own lines, the volley which inflicted on him a mortal wound.

A midnight attack was made by Sickles upon Jackson. Sickles' claim that he drove the enemy back to Dowdall's is scarcely substantiated. The attack had no particular result. Sickles regained once more his old position at Hazel Grove, which he held until daylight Sunday morning, when he was ordered back to Chancellorsville by Hooker. The latter seemed unaware how important this height might prove in his own, how dangerous in Lee's hands. For, as his line

here made a salient, it behooved him to strengthen it
by just such a height, or else to abandon this line
of defence.

On Sunday morning at daylight Stuart, who succeeded Jackson, ranged his 20,000 men opposite the
Fairview crest, and supported them by batteries on this
same Hazel Grove. Fairview was crowned by our artillery and defended by about an equal infantry force
on the next ridge below, consisting of the entire Third
corps and Williams of the Twelfth corps. Anderson
and McLaws, with 17,000 men, still confronted Geary
and Hancock with 12,000. Reynolds had arrived during the night, but was posted on the extreme right,
away from the scene of actual hostilities. No other
troops were brought into action. Thus the superior
tactics of the enemy enabled him to outnumber us at
every point of attack, while an equal number of available Union troops lay upon their arms close by, wit-
nessing the unneeded slaughter of their comrades.

The attack of the Confederates began shortly after
daylight, with "Jackson!" for a watchword, and was
gallant in the extreme. Anderson pushed in on our
left centre, as Stuart did on the right centre, both con-
tending for the Chancellor House, which barred their

possession of the turnpike. No praise is too high for the staunchness of the attack or the stubbornness of the defence; but, after heavy fighting during the entire forenoon, the Army of the Potomac yielded to the Confederate pressure and retired to a new line already prepared by its engineers, and which had its apex at White House. Time does not allow the barest details of this struggle to be entered upon. Suffice it to say, that the loss of the Third, Twelfth and Second corps, of 4,000, 3,000 and 2,000 respectively, effectually gauges the bitterness of the contest. The Confederate loss was, if anything, higher than ours during this Sunday morning. Lee was reforming for an assault upon our new line, when rumors from Fredericksburg diverted his attention.

During this fight of Sunday morning, the general plan of the Confederates was to obtain possession of the direct road, by which they could keep to themselves the communications with Fredericksburg. Hooker's plan, after failing to attack one or the other of Lee's divided wings, should have been to retain this road, the key to which was the Chancellorsville crest and plateau. But he seemed to have no conception of using the forces at hand. The First, Fifth and Eleventh corps were not put into action at all, though of their 47,000 men, 30,000 could easily have been spared from the positions they held. Reynolds could have projected a strong column upon Stuart's left flank, and was eager to render this simple service. From our left, several divisions could have made a diversion against McLaws' right. Our force at Fairview could have been doubled at any time. But all that Hooker seemed able to do was to call upon Sedgwick, a dozen miles away, to perform an impossible task in succor of his own overwhelming force.

To be sure, Hooker was disabled for some hours by the falling against him, about 10 A. M., of a column of the Chancellor House, which was dislodged by a shell. During this period Couch acted as his mouthpiece. But this disablement cannot excuse the error which preceded it, and Hooker was beaten, morally and tactically, before this accident. For he had predetermined retreat by the erection of the new lines, and had taken none of the measures which ordinary military *nous* demanded, while he was able-bodied. There is no palliation to be found in this accident. There is nothing approaching tactical combination to be seen on our side in this campaign after Friday's withdrawal into the

It has been surmised that Hooker, during this campaign, was incapacitated by a habit of which, at times, he had been the victim. There is rather evidence that he was prostrated by too much abstemiousness, when a reasonable use of stimulants might have kept his nervous system at its normal tension. It was certainly not the use of alcohol during this time which lay at the foot of his indecision.

Let us now turn to Sedgwick, who properly formed the left wing of the Army of the Potomac, though, as the operations eventuated, his corps was rather a detached command. Sedgwick had lain on the Falmouth side, with one division across the river guarding the bridgeheads. During the afternoon of Saturday, Hooker ordered him to cross and pursue what he called the "flying enemy" "by the Bowling Green road." Sedgwick did cross, and began skirmishing with Early, to force the latter from that road back into the woods. After the Eleventh corps had been crushed, the same evening, Hooker ordered Sedgwick, at 9 P. M., to march to Chancellorsville, "destroying any force he might fall in with on the road." This order was received by Sedgwick at 11 P. M., when he was intent on pursuit in the opposite direction. Sedgwick sent out his orders to change these dispositions within fifteen minutes after receipt of Hooker's dispatch, but it was after midnight before he could get his command faced about and fairly headed in the new direction.

The Fredericksburg heights were held by Early and Barksdale with 8,500 men, and plenty of artillery. In December a few brigades had here defeated the entire Army of the Potomac. Hooker himself, with his battleworn veterans, had then pronounced the task impossible. It was after midnight, Sedgwick had fifteen miles to march, after capturing this almost impregnable position, and all this to be done before daylight— that is, within three hours, if he was to carry out his orders.

So soon as his head of column reached the town four regiments were sent against the rifle-pits, but were speedily repulsed, with considerable loss. Before Sedgwick had sufficiently altered the disposition of his troops to warrant an assault, day broke. Brooks still held the left of the line, Howe the centre, and Newton the right. Gibbon, who had been left in Falmouth, threw a bridge above Fredericksburg, crossed and filed in on Sedgwick's right. Both Gibbon and Howe made demonstrations against the enemy's flanks, but the

Sedgwick was now reduced to a general assault. Two storming columns were formed, one from Howe's front and one from Newton's. These dispositions were not completed until 11 A. M., after a delay, perhaps not justifiable, in view of the stringency of the orders. But their work was well done. Without firing a shot these columns advanced, rushed upon and over the intrenchments, and carried them at the point of the bayonet, with a loss of over 1,000 men. This cut the Confederate force on the heights in two, and gave Sedgwick possession of the plank road, the direct way to Chancellorsville.

If Sedgwick had captured the heights before daylight, and, leaving a strong rear-guard to occupy Early's attention, had advanced straight toward Chancellorsville, he might have reached Hooker by 9 or 10 A. M., the hour when his chief was worse pressed. And some of Sedgwick's subordinates think this could readily have been done. But while it is hard to-day to insist that this much might not have been accomplished, the probabilities certainly are that a night attack in force would have resulted either in defeat, or in giving Early, who was entirely familiar with the ground, a chance to deal some fatal blows at Sedgwick's moving column, which would be more or less disorganized by the night assault and march. Be this as it may, Sedgwick's movements were certainly more speedy than those of Sickles, and his work stands out handsomely when contrasted with any done on our side in this campaign.

Another delay now occurred in giving Brooks the head of the column in the advance toward Chancellorsville. Though technically proper, Brooks not having been engaged, the nature of Sedgwick's orders certainly did not warrant this delay. Newton followed Brooks. Howe brought up the rear.

By noon word reached Lee that Sedgwick had captured the Fredericksburg heights. Wilcox, cut off from Early, alone separated Sedgwick from Lee's rear. McLaws and part of Anderson's men were at once dispatched to sustain Wilcox. These troops arrived at Salem church by 2 P. M. Brooks and Newton shortly came upon the field, and endeavored to capture the position they had taken up, but though 1,500 men were lost in the attempt, our troops finally recoiled.

A pontoon bridge was now thrown across at Bank's Ford, and nearer communication was opened with headquarters. Up to this time, be it noted, Hooker in no-

wise reflected on Sedgwick's tardiness, though aware,
through Warren, who had been his representative with
Sedgwick, of all the Sixth corps had done or failed to
do.   His dispatches to Sedgwick are plainly couched in
terms of approval.

During Sunday night Lee concluded that he must
permanently dispose of Sedgwick before he could again
assault Hooker's lines.   Early had recaptured the Fredericksburg heights.   Gibbon had recrossed the river.
The balance of Anderson's force now joined McLaws.
With Anderson, McLaws and Early, some 25,000 men,
Lee thought he could fairly expect to dispose of the
Sixth corps, which was now reduced to 5,000 less, and
felt its lack of success.   After this he could turn again
upon Hooker.   Jackson's corps alone was left to watch
Hooker.

Here, then, we have the spectacle, happily rare in
war, of a slender force of 20,000 men, who had been
continuously marching and fighting for four days, pen-
ning in their defences an army of over 60,000, while
its commander cries for aid to a lieutenant who is miles
away and beset by a larger force than he himself commands.   And this slack-sinewed commander is the
very same who initiated the campaign with the watch-

word: "Fight! Fight!! Fight!!!" and with the motto: "Celerity, audacity, and resolution are everything in war."

Despite which lamentable fact, this same commander's after wit sought to lay half the blame of his defeat upon this lieutenant's failure to come to his assistance.   The other half fell upon Howard on equally invalid grounds.

So soon as Sedgwick became aware of the presence of the bulk of Lee's force in his front, he disposed his three divisions so as best to cover Banks' Ford, both from east and west, and to hold a footing on the plank-road. Substantially, Newton faced west, Brooks south, Howe east. Lee, after some hours' preparation, made ready to push in Sedgwick's centre. It is worth while, perhaps, to note the fact that Lee's delay in attacking Sedgwick was fully as great as Sedgwick's in forcing Marye's Heights. And yet his haste was quite as pressing, for at any moment Hooker might decide to move toward his lieutenant.

Many dispatches passed between Hooker and Sedgwick at this time. Sedgwick must, of course, be judged by the time of their receipt. At 4 P. M. of this day, Monday, he received word to "look well to the safety of his corps," and to cross at Banks' Ford to the north side, if desirable. These dispatches he answered, but he could not be sure that the answers reached Hooker. Later, Hooker ordered him to hold on to Banks' Ford, if possible. Then, again, on receiving Sedgwick's report of the insecurity of his position, Hooker ordered him to withdraw, and, still later, again to hold on. This last dispatch, however, was received by Sedgwick too late. For under the former authority to the same effect, he had determined to retire across the river as soon as night should fall.

At 6 P. M. Lee attacked. McLaws fell upon the corner held by Brooks; Early assaulted Howe. The latter's onset was very hardy. Our loss was over 2,000 men, but no serious impression was made.

During the night Sedgwick withdrew and took up his pontoon bridge. The corps had lost over 5,000 men. Lee, having acomplished his task, sent Early back to Fredericksburg and himself returned to Hooker's front.

While Lee was considering how he might again best attack the Army of the Potomac, Hooker called his corps commanders together to ascertain their feeling relative to advance or retreat. All except Sickles were in favor of a vigorous advance. Sickles thought that political reasons favored retreat, lest the Army of the Potomac should suffer an overwhelming defeat, which, at this time, might discourage the war party of the North. Moreover the rations brought by the troops had been exhausted and the river was now rising and threatening the bridges. Here, again, it may be noted that unless retreat had been actually predetermined, the past three days should have been used to revictual the army for a possible advance. For Hooker was, as a rule, careful in these matters. Under all the circumstances, and after hearing all opinions, Hooker decided to retire.

A new line was accordingly made to protect United States Ford, and during the night of May 5th the army recrossed, the last troops about 8 A. M. of May 6th. Lee did not interfere with this movement. He was glad to see an end put to his dangerous situation, for his army was absolutely exhausted. But had he known the precarious situation of our troops, huddled that night in the *cul de sac* at the bridgeheads, he might have inflicted terrible damage upon us.

The total loss of the Army of the Potomac was 17,200; of the Army of Northern Virginia, 12,300.

On arriving at its old camps, the Union army received an order tendering it the congratulations of its chief on the achievements of the last seven days. Lee recommended the Southern troops to unite in ascribing to the Lord of Hosts the glory due His name.

Two years later Hooker, in his testimony before the Committee on the Conduct of the War, stated that, in his opinion, there was nothing to regret in regard to Chancellorsville, except that he did not accomplish all that he moved to accomplish, and that he did not consider the campaign a defeat.

Up to Thursday noon, Hooker's manœuvre was a pronounced success. His subsequent defeat may be ascribed to the following tactical and logistic errors:

First—Failure to move his cavalry effectively. This is probably more Stoneman's fault than Hooker's.

Second—Failure to move the entire army out into the open country and to seize Banks' Ford on Thursday afternoon.

Third—This having been neglected, failure to make a vigorous push toward the same objective point on Friday morning.

Fourth—Weakness in withdrawing into the Wilderness to fight a defensive battle after a successful offen-

Fifth—Failure to order (after 9:30 A. M.) on Saturday, and personally to see, that suitable dispositions were made on the right flank to resist a threatened or possible attack at that point.

Sixth—Weakness, in allowing a partial, slow and ineffective movement against such a wily tactician as Jackson to produce a gap in his line, which robbed his right flank of all support.

Seventh—Failure to fall in force upon one or other of Lee's separated wings Saturday afternoon or early Sunday morning.

Eighth—Not having done so, failure to hold Hazel Grove as head of salient on Sunday morning.

Ninth—Failure to sustain the gallant struggle at Fairview with some of his unused divisions, which themselves outnumbered the enemy, or to attack the enemy's flank in its support.

Tenth—Failure to attack whatever was in his front in support of Sedgwick's advance and fight at Salem Church, and during Monday.

Eleventh—Failure to ration his army while his communications were open, so that he might have again advanced on Tuesday.

Twelfth—Failure to keep Sedgwick on the south

side of the river, so as to aid in a new joint advance.

The direct result of Chancellorsville was the second invasion of the Northern States by Lee, which culminated in the defeat of the Army of Northern Virginia, two months later, on the hills of Gettysburg.

Tried by the rule of brilliant success against vast odds, Lee's work in this campaign is scarcely open to criticism.

The hero of the campaign is Thomas J. Jackson, the most able lieutenant of our civil war.

While historical accuracy obliges us to place the *onus* of this lost campaign upon Hooker, and, while his own bitter perverseness toward his lieutenants may lend some asperity to our criticism, it will not do to forget Hooker's excellent services to the country. As a brigade, division and corps commander, previous to Chancellorsville, he had earned an enviable record in the Army of the Potomac. Subsequently, in lieu of retiring in dudgeon, he went to Chattanooga with the Eleventh and Twelfth corps, and there did worthy service. Hooker's efficiency was always weakened by his peculiar desire to work for the public eye, and by his characteristic shortcomings. But Hooker was a brave soldier, a true patriot, and, within his limitations, a reliable general officer. He did not, however, possess that rare combination of self-reliance, intellectual vigor and military common sense which enable a man to bear the strain laid upon him by the command of an army opposed to such a captain as Robert E. Lee.

Here, for the hundredth time, American manhood graved with steel its name upon the brazen shield of Fame. The Army of Northern Virginia, led as its valor deserved to be led, showed that resolution which can accomplish the all but impossible. The Army of the Potomac, held in the leash by blunders which bowed its head in shame, but which it could not repair, illustrated that fidelity which always shone forth from disaster with a refulgence which even a victory scarce could lend it. Every virtue which crowns the brow of the soldier was typified in the ranks of either army. The ability of the conqueror to-day elicits our admiration; the errors of the conquered leader have long since been forgiven. We hold the laurel wreath above the heads of those who fought here and still live; we lay it tenderly upon the graves of those from whose devotion to either cause has sprung that brotherly respect and love which best insures the perpetuity of the Union. Rest to their ashes! Peace to that nobler part, which dieth not!

A ROMANCE OF
CHANCELLORSVILLE.

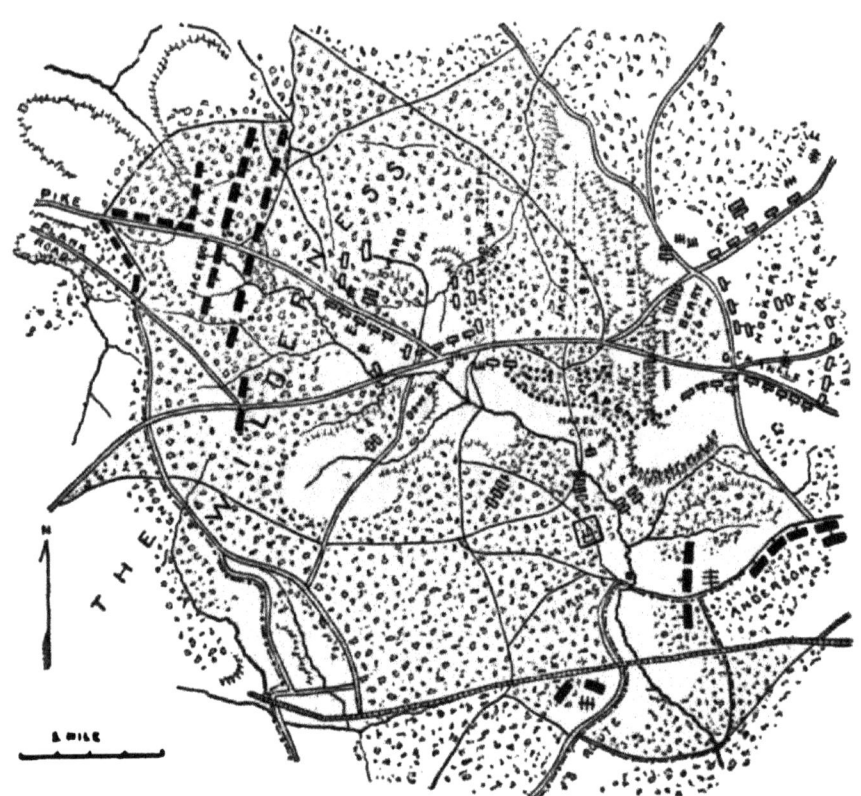

MY DEAR COLONEL:—

After having given several days consideration to "A Romance of Chancellorsville," which you were kind enough to send me for publication in the Cavalry Journal, I am compelled, very much to my regret, to return it to you, as, in my opinion, unsuited to the pages of the Journal.

Although I served through the campaign of 1863, from the battle of Beverly Ford until the end of the year, I never made the personal acquaintance of General Pleasonton, nor have I ever met him since the close of the war; but my regard for the man who commanded the Cavalry Corps in the most trying and successful cavalry campaign of modern times, who selected the ground on which to fight the battle of Gettysburg, and made the victory gained there possible; who made as energetic a pursuit afterwards as his superiors would permit him to make, is too high to admit of my assisting in publishing an article of so personal a nature, to his detriment.

General Pleasonton is not a member of the Cavalry Association, and therefore it is presumable that he does not receive its Journal. Suppose that some one who does, should show him a copy of it containing your article—perhaps long after he could have profitably replied to it, would he not be justified in thinking he had been stabbed in the house of those who should, at least, be his friends. Suppose he should never see it, his friends, through kindness—mistaken or not—concealing it from him, he would go to his grave, unconscious of leaving such an unfavorable criticism on record for the use of future historians.

You say "it is time the truth should be told." Very true, perhaps, but is it expedient, or for the best interests of the country? Certain it is that it will not be told in our day, nor for fifty years after the death of all the actors in the great drama of 1861-65.

Granting that Keenan's charge was unwise, ineffective, an utter failure even, still the story of it has been repeated until it has become so fixed in the minds of many that it would be impossible to convince them of the truth as you have told it, and believing it as they do, it may serve as an inspiration to later generations of soldiers who may, in attempting the same thing, accomplish something of real value.

If the truth, and the truth only, were to be told of the incidents of the battlefield; if, instead of the pictures of Detaille and de Neuville, we were allowed to study only those of Verestschagin, and from which, all romance, dash, and idealism are banished, nothing less than a powerful army could compel men to run the risk of encountering the horrors of war, even in defence of their homes and their country.

Pleasonton may have claimed more for himself than was his rightful due, and yet may have done so without the least intention of dealing unjustly by others. The range of vision on the battlefield of the present day is limited, as we know, to a very small space, and those engaged in a mortal struggle upon it, are very apt to become impressed with the idea that they, and they alone, are doing all the fighting—and reports written upon the spot, instead of being, as is generally supposed, the truest, are, in many cases, the most untrustworthy.

Now, my dear Colonel, I have written you at this length, to endeavor, in my lame way, to give you my reasons for declining to publish your paper. To decline a historical paper from an author so well known, and justly distinguished, whose name would be, upon the pages of the Journal, an honor to it, requires some amount of courage based upon convictions too well grounded to be easily shaken—but I feel justified in doing so, in the interests of the Journal, and, perhaps, yours also.

Very truly yours,

C. C. C. CARR,

Major 8th Cavalry,

Editor of Journal.

COLONEL THEODORE AYRAULT DODGE, U. S. A.

The Rocks, Brookline, Mass.

A ROMANCE OF CHANCELLORSVILLE.

IT is ungracious to destroy the inspiriting fiction
of Keenan's cavalry charge at Chancellorsville.
But fiction it is, and the truth is preferable at whatever sacrifice. In the effervescence of the movement,
a romance of which himself is the central figure was
constructed by General Pleasonton out of very simple
facts, and, appearing in his report of the battle, it grew
with time and came near to being accepted as history.
There was many a man on that awful evening of the
second of May, 1863, who imagined that it was he
who had stopped Jackson's victorious onset. Pleasonton not only imagined but asserted as much; General
Sickles, unaware of the facts, echoed his report; Hooker did the like. Everyone was misled, and for years
Pleasonton enjoyed the credit of having done a mas-
terly thing. When I first published my history of

Chancellorsville, I fell into the error of believing these reports, whose statements had been reïterated much more strongly before the Committee on the Conduct of the War. Nor was I the only author who did so. The other side was presented to me later, and the now well-proven facts are embodied in the second and subsequent editions of my history. In 1886 Pleasonton wrote some articles in the Century, renewing his claims, but these were roughly overhauled. So much has been said about this phase of the battle, that it requires study to unravel the snarl. Colonel Hermance's interesting article in the June Journal of the Cavalry Association shows that he has not had access to the evidence of the main actors in the Pleasonton drama. Mere repetition, even in good faith, is apt to give headway to error. This it is well to check.

The facts are these. They are not given in any spirit of antagonism, but solely to conserve the truth. The main facts are undisputed. The minor facts are substantiated by the testimony of the General Huey, who commanded, and Major Carpenter, who belonged to the Eighth Pennsylvania Cavalry (Keenan's regiment); by that of Major Huntington, who commanded the three batteries of Whipple's division, which were

supposed to have been trained on Jackson by Pleasonton, and by that of a number of other participants;
and they are sustained by official evidence and by
Pleasonton's own admissions.

On the afternoon of the second of May, 1863, the
right wing of the Army of the Potomac lay along the
Culpeper Pike and Plank Road, facing south. Howard
was on the extreme right; Sickles' position was on his
left. But as Jackson had been marching westerly
along our front all day, Sickles, at his own suggestion,
had been sent out to the front by Hooker, with Birney's and Whipple's divisions of the Third and Williams' of the Twelfth corps; and later Barlow's Brigade,
Howard's reserve, was detached from the right and
sent out to swell his force. Pleasonton with his cavalry and a horse-battery was also with Sickles, in the
clearing at Hazel Grove. Sickles' idea was that he
could strike Jackson in flank. The result was that
Jackson, with twenty-three thousand men, struck
Howard's eleven thousand men in flank, and demolished the right wing of the Army of the Potomac, because Sickles, instead of being in his proper position
on Howard's left, where he could sustain him, had by
his advance left a gap of a mile and a half in the

line, without a man to hold it. The result was inevitable.

Pleasonton's report and evidence before the Committee on the Conduct of the War assumes that it was he who stopped Jackson in his victorious advance. The fact is that only the extreme right of Jackson's advancing line could have been near Hazel Grove. The bulk of it was not within a half mile of the position held by Pleasonton.

What Pleasonton particularly misstates with regard to the charge of Keenan and the Eighth Pennsylvania cavalry, is that, in order to hold back Jackson's victorious and fast advancing lines long enough to enable him to get some guns in position, he ordered Major Keenan to charge upon the enemy in the woods; that Keenan dramatically did so, and, by the sacrifice of his life, gave Pleasonton time enough to put some guns in battery, whose destructive fire arrested Jackson's corps and thus saved the Army of the Potomac. The truth pares down Pleasonton's work to very small proportions.

Howard, when attacked at 6 P. M., had sent for some cavalry to help hold the right, and Pleasonton was ordered to send it to him, as there was with the

army at this time only his small cavalry brigade of
three regiments and one horse battery, the whole cavalry corps being on a raid on Lee's communications.
Major Huey, who, as senior, commanded the Eighth
Pennsylvania cavalry, was selected and ordered to report to Howard.   So far from the open space at Hazel
Grove being *at that time* filled with fugitives, caissons,
ambulances, etc., as alleged by Pleasonton, there was
not a straggler nor an enemy in front, and no appearance that Howard had been or would be driven back
by Jackson, except advancing musketry-fire more than
a mile distant.   To give Huey this order to report to
Howard was all Pleasonton did.   Major Carpenter indeed testifies that Pleasonton's last word of caution to
Keenan, who led the first squadron, was: "Don't blow
your horses, Major!"   In obedience to these orders,
somewhat after 7 P. M., Huey started with his regiment from Hazel Grove up the wood-road toward the
pike, so as to march to Dowdall's.   Jackson had meanwhile demolished Howard, and had advanced up the
pike so that the extreme flank of his three lines, now
pretty well mixed, was near the road Huey was on.
The bulk of the enemy was sweeping along from west
to east in a line from this point north.   The Eighth,

marching by the flank, unexpectedly ran across the rebel right. That the stream of Eleventh Corps fugitives had mainly kept north of the pike is shown by the fact that the Eighth had but short notice of the immediate presence of the enemy,—a fact which seems to be established by the evidence of many men engaged. As any cavalry officer would do, if only for the purpose of extricating himself from the dilemma, whoever was at the head of the column at once ordered: "Draw sabres; charge!" The charge was very irregular and ineffective, as it must of necessity be along a woodroad where they had been marching but two abreast, and the squadrons in the rear only imitated what they saw done by their leaders. Thus the whole body rode down into the rebel lines. The shock was only at one point, but it was gallantly given, and men and horses were tumbled pell-mell into the mass of rebel soldiery.

This charge had next to no influence in arresting Jackson's onset. This had already begun to spend its force, and was actually stopped by the Fairview Artillery, Berry's infantry line, and particularly by Jackson's death and the darkness. The charge may have prevented a part of the right of Jackson's column from moving down this wood-road to Hazel Grove, but that was all. The charge was without question a plucky one, but it was entirely accidental. The loss was some thirty men killed and three of the officers, Major Keenan, Captain Arrowsmith and Adjutant Haddick, who were riding at the head of the column. They all sacrificed their lives manfully—*but not at Pleasonton's behest*.

The explanation of Pleasonton's romancing is probably this. When he was summoned before the Committee on the Conduct of the War, he desired, as he did in his report, to make as good a showing as possible, inasmuch as he hoped for (and really shortly after obtained) his Major General's stars. It may have been lapse of memory which made him say that he ordered Major Keenan instead of Major Huey to make the charge in question; it may be that he knew that the dead Keenan could not deny it and thought that the living Huey might. Having once made the statement, he continued to repeat it, except when Huey on several occasions called on him for an explanation, when he promptly acknowledged that Huey commanded the regiment, not Keenan. Of late Pleasonton has stuck permanently to Keenan and thrown Huey overboard. He has obtained the statements of a number of men of

the Eighth Pennsylvania that they did not see Huey
head the charge, or that Huey told them that he did
not do so. Such statements, twenty years after the
event, are not unnatural; they proceed from mere for-
getfulness. But they fall short of proof. There is
Major Wistar, who was in the charge, who testifies
that Huey told him he was not in it himself; Captain
Goddard, also in the charge, who saw Huey sitting on
his horse on the roadside as the regiment filed by; Vet-
erinary Surgeon Wentz, accidentally in the charge, and
shot, who testifies to the same; Sergeant Payne, Quar-
termaster-Sergeant Ringgold and Private Payne, all at
the head of the column, who testify that Huey did not
lead the charge; and a number more, some rather
vaguely, testify to the same effect.

The best proof of such matters is the evidence of
writings made at the time. Huey is given in the Official Record as in command of the Eighth, and Pleasonton is on record in many places to show that Huey was
in command, not Keenan. He states this fact in his
report to the Adjutant General of the Army of the Potomac of May 18, 1863, where he says Huey is "entitled to mention." In neithor this nor his report to
Sickles is Keenan mentioned; it is in his testimony

before the Committee on the Conduct of the War that
Keenan first becomes the chief actor. He made no
protest to Huey's report of the regiment's operations,
dated May 9, 1863, but endorses its recommendations;
nor to General Devin's report of May 12, 1863, both
containing the statement that Huey was in command.
He wrote a letter to General Curtin June 2, 1863, com-
mending Huey for this very work, and complimenting
his general conduct in high terms. He wrote in similar terms to Secretary Stanton, February 25, 1864. In
an endorsement referred to General Rawlins, chief of
staff, May 29, 1866, he states Huey to have been in
command and to have charged the enemy by his direction. He makes the same statement as to Huey being
in command in a letter of March 23, 1881. In addition
to this Huey's oath is probably as good evidence as
Pleasonton's, and Huey states on oath that he was in
command and at the head of the regiment and gave
the command to draw sabres and charge. Moreover
Major Carpenter happened, May 5, 1863, three days
after the fight, to write a letter home, stating that
Huey and he were the only two officers who came out
of the head of column alive. I have seen no sworn
testimony supporting Huey's affidavit that he was at

the head of the regiment and gave the command to charge. The affidavits of others that they saw him watching the regiment file by is not incompatible with his having regained the head of the column. All this testimony is surplussage. It is not a question of how much or how little Huey did, but how much or how little Pleasonton·did, and the question is not worth following up. Keenan was unquestionably at the head of the column, and fell there, a gallant sacrifice to duty.

The whole Pleasonton-Huey imbroglio is a tempest in a teapot. But it goes to show the fiction of Pleasonton's services on this occasion, and that small heed can be paid to his testimony as a contribution to history. It would not be worth discussion, unless Pleasonton's work had been foisted into notice as one of the great feats of Chancellorsville, whereas it was but a supernumerary's part on a stage where seventeen thousand men bit the dust. So much for Pleasonton and the cavalry.

Now about Pleasonton and the artillery. Testimony is cumulative to the effect that at the time of the cavalry charge, there was no sign whatever at Hazel Grove of the wreck of the Eleventh Corps, let alone of Jack-

son's victorious column. There was no enemy to attack
nor fugitives to arrest. Pleasonton had under his command only Martin's horse-battery. But there did happen to be, in the corner of the clearing, three other
batteries, belonging to Whipple's division,—Huntington's Ohio battery and Puttkamer's and Bruen's New
York batteries,—which had been ordered to remain in
the open, while Whipple's infantry marched further
on towards the Furnace, where Birney already lay.
Everything was so quiet, and so little was danger
anticipated *at this moment*, that the horses had been
unbridled and were being fed.

When, after the lapse of some time, the firing of
Jackson's men began to approach, Captain Huntington,
being senior, assumed command of the three Whipple
batteries. These had been facing substantially south,
so that their right flank was exposed to the attack of
the enemy, whose fire showed him to be approaching
from an unexpected quarter. Huntington at once posted the batteries in position facing northwest; and it
was while he was doing this that the first batch of
fugitives put in their appearance. These runaways
shortly increased to a stream which threatened to
stampede the batteries, but by the efforts of all con-

cerned this was averted. The three batteries held
their ground, remained under command of Captain
Huntington, and Pleasonton had nothing whatsoever
to do with their movements or fire, nor attempted in
any way to exercise control over them. Upon the
heels of the fugitives came a small part of the right of
the enemy's line; and when it put in an appearance, it
was received by these three batteries with canister and
dispersed; but it was not under Pleasonton's orders
that this was done. No doubt Pleasonton ordered Martin, who was on the left of the Whipple batteries, to
fire at the same time, but this was but a small part of
the twenty-two guns in line. General Pleasonton mentions that a "Captain Frank Crosby" came to his aid
at a most opportune time with six guns,—like a *deus ex
machinâ*. This must have been First Lieutenant Franklin B. Crosby, Battery F, Fourth United States Artillery,
attached to Williams' division. Just how he happened
to be there does not appear.

As the rebel line continued to advance towards Fairview, a part of Jackson's column discovered the guns
on its flank and began firing from the woods upon the
right of the batteries, and Bruen's battery, being most
exposed, limbered up and withdrew. Huntington's bat-

tery then changed front and used shell and canister on the woods. Martin's horse-battery, and perhaps Crosby's, on the left of the three Whipple batteries, kept up a heavy cross-fire on the woods.

The engagement was confined to shelling the woods. Huntington, though in the front line, saw nothing of the desperate charge of the "immense body of men" mentioned by Pleasonton. The affair was over before Whipple's and Birney's infantry returned to the Hazel Grove clearing. The only guns Pleasonton could have got, in addition to his horse-battery, were these batteries under Huntington, and perhaps Crosby's. Birney, to judge from his report, had kept his artillery with the division. These guns are unquestionably the ones Pleasonton spoke of, as he mentions twenty-two as the number engaged.

It is a fact so plain that he who runneth may read, that Pleasonton had nothing to do with stopping Jackson's advance, nor indeed much with the Hazel Grove fight. It was the fire of the Fairview guns and their supporting infantry which, coupled to darkness, Jackson's death and exhausted effort, stopped the main rebel columns; for these were constantly north of the pike. It was the fire of the three Whipple batteries under command of Huntington, aided by the other guns under Pleasonton, which won whatever, fight there was, at Hazel Grove or Scott's Run, with the few Confederates who reached the clearing.

Pleasonton, probably for the reasons before intimated,—and to win promotion is no doubt a laudable ambition—appears to have magnified a simple affair into a pitched battle, and for the same reasons to have asserted that he had assumed command of all the guns. It seems, however, that over his own signature, General Sickles not long afterwards stated to the Adjutant General of the army that it was Captain Huntington who did the work thus claimed to have been done by Pleasonton. That he copied Pleasonton's statements in his report was, immediately after the battle, natural enough.

That the engagement was of no moment is best testified by the fact that there is no mention of it by any of the Confederate generals, except Iverson. Nor does it appear in magnificent colors anywhere except in Sickles' and Pleasonton's reports and testimony. The whole affair as generally quoted is imaginative. It would tactically have made no odds, in view of Hooker's inability to act, whether the enemy had captured

Hazel Grove that evening or not, except that Sickles' force might have been cut off.

Sickles, about 7 P. M., had an opportunity of battering Jackson's flank by advancing north; but darkness had set in before his infantry regained the clearing. His "midnight attack" made no grave impression on the enemy. Before next morning he was withdrawn.

Whoever will make himself familiar with the details and the topography of the battle-field of Chancellorsville, will readily see that Sickles bore no part in saving the Army of the Potomac on May 2. On the contrary, Sickles' advance towards the Furnace opened the very gap which robbed Howard of support on his left, as well as took from him his strongest and reserve brigade, Barlow's. This advance was made under Hooker's orders, to be sure, but at Sickles' suggestion. The claim so often advanced, that Sickles, or Pleasonton, or Keenan, "saved the Army of the Potomac," is frivolous. The advance of Sickles out to the Furnace was a grave mistake, which had much to do with the initial disaster of this battle. Had Sickles been in his original position along the pike when Howard was attacked, it is easy to imagine

that, with the splendid fighting qualities of the old
Third Corps, and Sickles' always gallant leadership,
the right would have been held and the result of the
entire campaign have been changed.

Hooker, as general commanding, is primarily liable
for permitting this advance of Sickles to be made;
but it was on the latter's part a mistake of discretion
similar to the one he made at Gettysburg, a more
fatal one, and one which a general of greater experience would not have committed.

Pleasonton had no connection with the charge of
the Eighth Pennsylvania, and bore a minor part in
the work of the guns at Hazel Grove. Gallant Keenan
was a true enough hero without making him an unconscious actor in a fabricated drama. Moreover, our cavalry was always gallant and efficient, and it has credit
scores enough to enable it readily to dispense with the
fictitious romancing of the Keenan charge. Pleasonton himself did excellent service during the war; he
should not arrogate to himself distinction he did not
earn.

WAS HOOKER AN
ABLE ARMY-COMMANDER?

WAS HOOKER AN ABLE ARMY-COMMANDER?

IN February and March, 1886, there was de
at the Lowell Institute, in Boston, a series
lectures upon the late civil war, by the followin
gentlemen:—

Feb. 16. Introduction. Gen. Charles Devens of Boston.
Feb. 19. Pope's Campaign. Col. Jed. Hotchkiss of Staunton, Va.
Feb. 22. Antietam. Gen. George H. Gordon of Boston.
Feb. 26. Chancellorville. Col. Theodore A. Dodge, U. S. Army.
March 2. Stonewall Jackson. Col. W. Allan of McDonough, Md.
March 5. Gettysburg. Gen. Francis A. Walker of Boston.
March 9. The Northern Volunteer. Col. T. L. Livermore of Boston.
March 12. The Southern Volunteer. Major H. Kyd Douglas of
town, Md.
March 16. Chattanooga. Gen. William F. Smith of Wilmington, Del.
March 19. The Wilderness. John C. Ropes, Esq., of Boston.
March 22. Franklin and Nashville. Col. Henry Stone of Boston.
March 26. The Last Campaign. Col. Fred C. Newhall of

These lecturers were well equipped for their tas

• Published in later editions of "The Campaign of Chancellorsville,"
Col. Theodore A. Dodge, U. S. Army.

Earnest study of their respective subjects had been attested by numerous volumes published by them relating to the war. The desire to have the truth told was apparent in the presence of three Confederate officers among the number; and the special feature of the course seemed to be, that not only was the truth spoken in the most unvarnished manner, but that it was listened to with marked approval by overflowing audiences.

Perhaps the most invidious subject fell to my lot. What I said was merely a summary of my published volume. But one point in my lecture aroused the ire of some of Gen. Hooker's partisans, and was made the subject of attacks so bitter that virulence degenerated into puerility. The occasion of this rodomontade was a meeting of Third-Corps veterans, and its outcome was a series of resolutions aimed at the person who had dared to reflect on Gen. Hooker's capacity, and to refer to the question of Gen. Hooker's habitual use of stimulants. The public mention of my name was as sedulously avoided as a reference to his satanic majesty is wont to be in the society of the superstitious; but the exuberance of the attack must have afforded unbounded satisfaction to its authors, as it very appar-

Following are the resolutions, which are of mild flavor compared to their accompanying seasoning of speeches:—

RESOLUTIONS.

The veterans of the Third Army Corps assembled here to-day, soldiers who served under Gen. Joseph Hooker in his division, corps, and army, re-affirm their lifelong affection for their old commander, their admiration for his brilliant achievements as one of the prominent generals of our armies, and protest against the recent revival of unjust assaults made on his conduct at Chancellorsville. Whether, after *one of the most noted tactical victories of modern times*, having placed the Army of the Potomac across the Rappahannock River on the flank of Lee, he might have gained a still farther advanced position; whether the failure of the cavalry to fully accomplish what was expected of it; whether the disaster to the Eleventh Corps and the delay in the advance of the Sixth Corps,—are to be attributed to errors of judgement of Gen. Hooker or of the subordinate commanders, are points which will be discussed again and again with profit to the military student. But we, who witnessed his successful generalship at Williamsburg, Glendale, Malvern Hill, Second Bull Run, and Antietam, have no language at our command strong enough to express our contempt for any one who, twenty years after the war, affirms that on any occasion in battle, with the lives of his men and the cause of his country in his keeping, Gen. Hooker was incapacitated for performing his whole duty as an officer by either the use of liquor or by the want of it.

We protest against oft-repeated statements that "Fighting Joe Hooker," while one of the bravest and ablest division commanders in the army, was possibly equal to handling a corps, but proved a failure as an independent commander. Assigned to the Army of the Potomac in January, 1863, after the disaster at Fredericksburg and the failure of oft-repeated campaigns, our army demoralized by defeat, desertions, and dissentions, Gen. Hooker re-organized his forces, stopped desertions, brought back to their colors thousands of absentees, and in three months revived confidence, re-established discipline, and enabled his army to take the field unsurpassed in loyalty, courage, and efficiency, as was shown at Chancellorsville and Gettysburg. We say Chancellorsville because, although not a victory for us, the campaign *inflicted on the enemy losses at least equal to our own;* and we say also Gettysburg because that victory was won by the army Hooker had re-organized, and led with such matchless skill from Falmouth to the eve of the battle.

Whatever ambition he may have had to command armies, it did not prevent his cheerfully serving his country under junior officers, giving them faithful support, and his record shows no instance of his removal from command by his superiors.

Here in his native State, amid the homes of so many of his old brigade, the survivors of the Third Army Corps, all witnesses of his genius, valor, and devotion to duty, indorse his record as a soldier, as a gentleman, and as a patriot, and sincerely believe that history will assign to Major-Gen. Joseph Hooker a place among the greatest commanders of the late civil war.

The italics are mine. "One of the most noted tactical victories of modern times," applied to Chancellorsville, is refreshing. Equally so is the exultant claim that "we inflicted on the enemy losses at least equal to our own." The infliction of loss on the enemy has always been understood by military men to be an incident rather than the object of war.

The following reply in "The Boston Herald" of April 11, 1886, explains itself:—

To the Editor of the Herald.

In the call for the meeting of the Third Corps Gettysburg Re-union Association, held at Music Hall on Fast Day, was the following clause:—

"Loyalty to the memory of our beloved commander, Major-Gen. Joseph Hooker, makes it a duty, on this occasion, to protest against unjust and uncalled-for criticisms on his military record as commander of the Army of the Potomac."

It having been intimated to me by some old brother officers of the Third Corps, that my late Lowell lecture on Chancellorsville was the occasion of this proposed protest, I wrote to the chairman of the committee which called the meeting, asking for an opportunity to reply to this protest, within such bounds as even-handedness and the purposes of the meeting would allow. The committee answered that it could not see the propriety of turning the occasion into a public debate, and referred me to the press. I do not object to their decision, made, no doubt, upon what appeared to them sufficient grounds; but as the occasion was turned into a public debate—one-sided, to be sure—I ask you for space to reply in your valued columns.

As an old Third-Corps man, I attended the meeting at Music Hall. The treasurer did not object to selling me a ticket to the dinner. I expected to hear some new facts about Hooker and Chancellorsville. I expected to hear some new deductions from old facts. I do not consider myself beyond making an occasional lapse even in a carefully prepared piece of work, and am always open to correction. But, to my surprise, (with the exception of a conjecture that Lee's object in his march into Pennsylvania was to wreck the anthracite-coal industry), there was not one single fact or statement laid before the meeting, or the company at dinner, which has not already been, in its minutest details, canvassed and argued at a length covering hundreds of pages in the volumes on Chancellorsville, by Hotchkiss and Allen, Swinton, Bates, the Comte de Paris, Doubleday, and myself, not to speak of numberless and valuable brochures by others. The bulk of the time devoted to talking on this occasion was used in denunciation of the wretch—in other words, myself—who alleged that Joseph Hooker was drunk at Chancellorsville, or at any other time. This denunciation began with a devout curse in the chaplain's prayer, culminated in a set of fierce resolutions, and ended with the last after-dinner speech.

One thing particularly struck me. There was no one, of all who spoke, who began to say as many things in favor of Joseph Hooker as I for years have done; and not in fleeting words, but printed chapters. There was plenty of eulogy, in nine-tenths of which I joined with all my heart. But it was of the soldiers' talk order,—cheering and honest and loyal, appealing to the sentiments rather than the intelligence. What I have said of Hooker has been solid praise of his soldierly worth, shown to be borne out by the facts. Barring, in all I say, the five fighting days at Chancellorsville, I have yet to find the man who has publicly, and in print, eulogized Hooker as I have done; and no one among the veterans gathered together Fast Day applauded with more sincerity than I, all the tributes to his memory. For though, as some one remarked, it is true that I "fought mit Sigel," and decamped from Chancellorsville with the Eleventh Corps; it is also true that I passed through the fiery ordeal of the Seven Days, and fought my way across the railroad-cutting at Manassas, side by side with Joseph Hooker, under the gallant leadership of that other hero, Philip Kearny. It was very evident that but few of the speakers, as well as auditors, had themselves heard or read what I actually said. The result of "coaching" for the occasion by some wire-puller was painfully apparent. Let

us see what was said. I give the entire paragraph
from my Lowell lecture:—

"It has been surmised that Hooker, during this campaign, was incapacitated by a habit of which, at times,
he had been the victim. There is, rather, evidence
that he was prostrated by too much abstemiousness,
when a reasonable use of stimulants might have kept
his nervous system at its normal tension. It was certainly not the use of alcohol, during this time, which
lay at the root of his indecision."

If that is an accusation that Hooker was then drunk,
if it does not rather lean toward an exculpation from
the charge of drunkenness, then I can neither write
nor read the English language. As is well known, the
question of Hooker's sudden and unaccountable loss of
power during the fighting half of this campaign,
coupled with the question of drunkenness, has been
bandied to and fro for years. The mention alone of
Chancellorsville has been enough, ever since that day,
to provoke a query on this very subject, among civilians and soldiers alike. In a lecture on the subject,
I deemed it judicious to lay this ghost as well as
might be. Had I believed that Hooker was intoxi-
cated at Chancellorsville, I should not have been de-

terred by the fear of opposition from saying so. Hooker's over-anxious friends have now turned into a public scandal what was generally understood as an exoneration, by intentially distorting what was said into an implication that Hooker was so besotted as to be incapable of command. What I have written of his marching the army to this field and to the field of Gettysburg is a full answer to such unnecessary perversion. Let these would-be friends of Hooker remember that this calumny is of their own making, not mine. I am as sorry for it as they ought to be. If the contempt expressed in the resolutions they passed had been silent, instead of boisterous, Hooker's memory would have suffered far less damage.

Gens. Sickles and Butterfield are doubtless good witnesses, though they sedulously refrained from any testimony on the subject, contenting themselves with declamation. But they are not the only good witnesses. After the loss of a leg at Gettysburg, I was ordered to duty in the War Department, where I served in charge of one or other bureau for seven years. I have heard this Hooker question discussed in all its bearings, in the office of the Secretary of War or Adjutant-General, by nearly every leading officer of the army, hundreds of whom had known Hooker from West Point up. I have had abundant opportunity of forming an opinion, and I have expressed it. Let him who garbles its meaning, bear the blame.

This action by many veterans of the Third Corps— even though procured by design from their thoughtless and open soldier's nature—is, however, much more sweeping and important. To the world at large it is a general condemnation of every thing which can be said in criticism of Hooker. It will reach far and wide, and in this light I desire to say what I do. The resolutions passed at the meeting explicitly protest against the statement that Hooker proved a failure as an independent commander. This needs notice at greater length than the question of sobriety or drunkenness. Few have studied the details of the campaign of Chancellorsville as carefully as I; but one other author has spread the facts so fully before the reading public. No part of my recent criticism before the Lowell Institute was new. It was embodied at much greater length four years ago, in my "History of Chancellorsville," the reception of which volume by press, public, and soldiers, has been its own best excuse. Gen. Hooker, though making no report, has put on record his explanation of this campaign. Before the Committee on the Conduct of the War, he stated his views as follows: "I may say here, the battle of Chancellorsville has been associated with the battle of Fredericksburg, and has been called a disaster. My whole loss in the battle of Chancellorsville was a little over seventeen thousand. . . . In my opinion, there is nothing to regret in regard to Chancellorsville, except to accomplish all I moved to accomplish. The troops lost no honor, except one corps, and we lost no more men than the enemy; but expectation was high, the army in splendid condition, and greater results were expected from it. When I returned from Chancellorsville, I felt that I had fought no battle; in fact, I had more men than I could use, and I fought no general battle, for the reason that I could not get my men in position to do so."

To speak thus of a passage of arms lasting a week and costing seventeen thousand men is, to say the least, abnormal.

In trying to shift the onus of failure from his own shoulders he said: "Some of our corps commanders, and also officers of other rank, appear to be unwilling to go into a fight. . . . So far as my experience extends,

there are in all armies officers more valiant after the
fight than while it is pending, and when a truthful
history of the Rebellion shall be written, it will be
found that the Army of the Potomac is not an exception."

This slur is cast upon men like Reynolds, Meade,
Couch, Sedgwick, Slocum, Howard, Hancock, Humphreys, Sykes, Warren, Birney, Whipple, Wright,
Griffin, and many others equally gallant.   To call it
ungenerous is a mild phrase.   It certainly does open
the door to unsparing criticism.   Hooker also concisely
stated his military rule of action: "Throughout the
Rebellion I have acted on the principle that if I had as
large a force as the enemy, I had no apprehensions of
the result of an encounter."   And in his initial orders
to Stoneman, in opening the campaign, came the true
ring of the always gallant corps commander, "Let
your watchword be 'Fight!' and let all your orders be,
'Fight, fight, fight!'"

I might here say that the only attempt, on Fast Day,
to exculpate Hooker for the disaster of Chancellorsville
was not of an order which can be answered.   When
one speaker asks, "If Gen. Hooker tells us that it was
wise to withdraw across the river, is not that enough

for you and me, my comrades?"—I can only say that
history is not so easily satisfied. To another speaker,
who states that when Hooker had planted himself on
Lee's flank by crossing the river, Lee ought, by all the
rules of war, to have retreated, but when he didn't he
upset all Hooker's calculations; that when Jackson
made his "extra-hazardous" march around Hooker's
flank, he ought, by all rules of war, to have been
destroyed, but when he was not he upset all Hooker's
calculations, and that therefore Hooker was forced to
retreat,—it is quite beyond my ability to reply. When
Gen. Sickles throws the blame upon Howard for the
defeat of the Eleventh Corps, by reading the 9.30 A. M.
order, without saying one word about Hooker's actions,
change of plans, and despatches from that hour till
the attack at 6 P. M., he makes any thinking man question seriously the sincerity of what he calls history.
When Gen. Butterfield indulges in innuendoes against
Gen. Meade, whose chief of staff he was, and insults
his memory in the effort to exculpate the Third Corps
from a charge no one has ever made, or thought of
making, against it, the fair-minded can only wonder
why he goes out of his way to call any one to task for
criticising Hooker. Not one word was spoken on Fast

Day which does not find its full and entire answer in the already published works on Chancellorsville. It was all a mere re-hash, and poorly cooked at that. To rely on the four reasons given by the Committee on the Conduct of the War as a purgation of Hooker from responsibility for our defeat at Chancellorsville, simply deserves no notice. It is all of a piece with the discussion of the Third-Corps fight at Gettysburg on July 2. No one ever doubted that the Third Corps fought, as they always did, like heroes that day. What has been alleged is merely that Sickles did not occupy and protect Little Round Top, as he would have done if he had had the military *coup d'œil*.

Now, I desire to compare with Hooker's recorded words, and the utterances of Fast Day, the actual performance, and see what "loyalty to Hooker," as voted in Music Hall, means. Chancellorsville bristles with points of criticism, and there are some few points of possible disagreement. Of the latter the principal ones upon which Hooker's formal apologists rely, are the destruction of the Eleventh Corps through Howard's alleged carelessness, and the failure of Sedgwick to perform the herculean task assigned to him in coming to Hooker's support. Allowing, for the moment, that

Howard and Sedgwick were entirely at fault, and eliminating these two questions entirely from the issue, let us see what Hooker himself did, bearing in mind that he has officially acknowledged that he knew, substantially, the number of Lee's army, and bearing also in mind that the following are facts which can be disputed only by denying the truth and accuracy of all reports, Federal and Confederate, taken as a body; and these reports happen to dovetail into each other in one so consistent whole, that they leave to the careful student none but entirely insignificant items open to doubt.

From Saturday at 8 A. M. till Sunday noon, some twenty-eight hours, Hooker with seventy-five thousand, and, after the arrival of the First Corps, nearly ninety thousand men, lay between the separated wings of Lee's army of twenty-four thousand and seventeen thousand men respectively, being all the while cognizant of the facts. Had ever a general a better chance to whip his enemy in detail? And yet we were badly beaten in this fight. Now, if loyalty to Hooker requires us to believe that his conduct of this campaign was even respectable, it follows that the Army of the Potomac, respectably led, could be defeated by the Army of Northern Virginia, two to one. Will the soldiers of the ever-faithful army accept this as an explanation of our defeat?

Again: from Sunday noon till Monday at 9 A. M., twenty-one hours, Hooker, with over eighty thousand men, was held in the White House lines by a force of twenty-seven thousand. If loyalty to Hooker requires us to believe that this was even respectable general-ship, it follows that the Army of the Potomac, well led, could be defeated by the Army of Northern Vir-ginia, three to one. Shall we accept this as an expla-nation of of our defeat?

Again: from Monday at 9 A. M. till Tuesday at 4 P. M., thirty-one hours, against the advice of all his corps commanders except Sickles and Couch (the latter agreeing to retreat only because he felt that the army would be defeated under Hooker whatever they might do), Hooker, with eighty thousand men, was held in the White House lines by a force of nineteen thousand, while the rest turned upon and demolished Sedgwick. If loyalty to Hooker requires us to believe that this was even respectable generalship, it follows that the Army of the Potomac, well led, could be defeated by the Army of Northern Virginia, four to one. Shall we accept this as an explanation of our defeat?

If there is in the world's military history a parallel to this extraordinary generalship, for which any one who has even pretended to study the art of war is able to pen an excuse, I have failed to find such an instance in the course of many years' reading, and shall be happy to have it pointed out to me. Hooker's wound cannot be alleged in extenuation. If he was disabled, his duty was to turn the command over to Couch, the next in rank. If he did not do this, he was responsible for what followed. And he retained the command himself, only using Couch as his mouthpiece.

I have always maintained, that, man for man, the Army of the Potomac was at any time the equal of the Army of Northern Virginia, and that, man for man, the old Third Corps has proved itself good for Jackson's in its palmiest days. When, therefore, the Army of the Potomac was, as here, defeated or bottled up by one-half, one-third, or one-quarter its force of the enemy, my loyalty to that army demands that I seek a reason other than Hooker's allegation of lack of heart in his subordinate officers. And this reason is only to be found in Hooker's inability to handle so many men. All the resolutions in the world, passed under a *furore* of misstatement and misconception, even by such a noble body of men as Third-Corps veterans, will not re-habilitate Joseph Hooker's military character during these five days, nor make him other than a morally and intellectually impotent man from May 1 to May 5, 1863. Loyalty to Hooker, so-called, is disloyalty to the grand old army, disloyalty to the seventeen thousand men who fell, disloyalty to every comrade who fought at Chancellorsville. I begrudge no man the desire to blanket facts and smother truth in order to turn a galling defeat into a respectable campaign; I begrudge no man his acceptance of Hooker's theory that Chancellorsville was not a disaster; I begrudge no one his faith in Hooker as a successful battle-field commander of the Army of the Potomac. But let it be well understood that this faith of necessity implies the fact that the Army of the Potomac was unable or unwilling to fight one-quarter its number of Lee's troops. I prefer my faith in the stanch, patient army, in its noble rank and file, in its gallant officers, from company to corps; and I refuse to accept Hooker's insult to his subordinates as any explanation for allowing the Army of the Potomac to be here "defeated without ever being fought."

The Army of the Potomac was better than its commanders from first to last. It was, beyond speaking, superior to its commander during the fighting days at Chancellorsville. As a corps commander, Joseph Hooker will always be a type and household word. In logistics, even as commander of the Army of the Potomac, he deserves high praise. But when it comes to fighting the army at Chancellorsville, let whoso will keep his loyalty to Hooker, without protest from me. I claim for myself and the bulk of my comrades the right, equally without protest, sneers, or resolutions, to express my loyalty to the rank and file, my loyalty to the officers, and my loyalty to the army as a whole. And I claim, moreover, the right, without protest, sneers, or resolutions, to show that on this field it was the general commanding, and not the army, whose lapses caused defeat. Not that I object to these Fast-Day resolutions. I believe that I can still struggle onward in life, even under the contempt of their authors. But partisanship in matters of history is a boomerang which always flies back to whack its thrower. And Fast Day's performance was baldly partisan.

I am satisfied to abide the verdict of all soldiers, of all citizens, who ever studied the facts of this campaign. Whatever the action of any meeting of old soldiers may be under partial knowledge of facts, under the influence of heated or sectional discussion, or under the whipping-in of a member of Hooker's staff, I do not believe that, with the issue squarely put before them and the facts plainly stated, any but a very inconsiderable fraction, and that not the most intelligent one, of the men of the Army of the Potomac, will give their suffrage to what has been suddenly discovered to be loyalty due to Gen. Joseph Hooker, as against loyalty to the Army of the Potomac.

The recent course of lectures at the Lowell Institute was intended to be a purely military one. There was no intention of bringing politics or sectional pride into the discussion, and it was thought that the lectures could to-day be delivered without rousing a breath of ancient animosity. If there was any campaign during our civil war which was especially, in a military sense, a glorious one for the rebels, and an ignominious one for us, it was Chancellorsville. It is indeed a pity that the skill of the one side and the errors of the other cannot be once again pointed out, that the true and only possible explanation of Hooker's one hundred and thirty thousand men being defeated by Lee's sixty thousand cannot be once again stated, without eliciting from a body of veterans of the old Third Corps a set of condemnatory resolutions. There has been some very heated criticism of the recent lectures, and not a little fault-finding with the lecturers. I presume that none of the gentlemen who participated in the course would feel like denying the inference, so often suggested, that the censors might have done much better than they were able to do. Such censors generally can. These dozen lecturers have all been earnest students of our civil war, as is abundantly testified by the twenty odd volumes on the subject published by them since the reports of operations became available; and they keenly feel that modesty which is always bred of study. Such as they had, they were glad to give the public; nor do they in any wise shrink from generous disagreement or courteous criticism. I submit, however, that some of the carping which has been indulged in is scarcely apt to lead to the correction of errors, or the elucidation of truth. It is passing strange, that, at this late day, one may not criticise the military operations without arousing the evil spirit of the war. Can we not aim at truth, rather than self-gratulation, which will live no longer than

we do? Criticism has always been indulged in, always
will be. If a Frederick may be dissected by a Lloyd,
if a Napoleon may be sat on in judgment by a Lanfrey,
may not the merest tyro in the art of war be par-
doned for reviewing Hooker? The gallant soldier who
helped make history rarely writes history. The same
spirit which sent him to the front in 1861 generally
keeps him busy to-day with the material interests of
the country. Despite the certainly novel fling of Fast
Day at one who went into service as a mere boy, it
remains a fact that rank, without the devoted study of
years and a single eye to truth, will not enable any
one to write history. It was proven beyond a peradventure, on Fast Day, that the command of a corps, let
alone a division, will not of itself breed a historian.
Partisanship never will.

Truth will get written some day. I myself prefer
to write as an American, forgetting North and South,
and to pass down to those who will write better than
any of us, as one who tried to speak the truth, whom-
soever it struck. It is not I who criticise, who condemn Joseph Hooker: it is the maxims of every
master, of every authority on the art of war. Not one
of Hooker's apologists can turn to the history of a

master's achievements, or to a volume of any accepted authority, without finding his pet commander condemned, in every action, and on every page, for the faults of the fighting days at Chancellorsville.

It was assumed on Fast Day that one should criticise only what he saw. I have never understood that Gibbon's "Decline and Fall of the Roman Empire" is any the less good because he did not live in the first few centuries of the Christian era, or that Jomini could write any less well of Frederick than of Napoleon. Service certainly helps a man in his researches or work, but it only helps. The best critic may be one who never served. I think I was the first officer to whom the Secretary of War permitted free use of the rebel archives for study. I have had good opportunities. How I have used them, I leave to others to say.

It is easy to capture a meeting of honest-hearted veterans by such lamentable prestidigitation as was exhibited on Fast Day, and to pass any resolutions desired, by appealing to their enthusiasm. I prefer to be judged by the sober after-thought of men who are neither partisans, nor ready to warp facts or make partial statements to sustain their theories.

THEODORE A. DODGE.

Boston, April 10, 1896.

ROPES'S NAPOLEON.

ROPES'S NAPOLEON.* †

THE unbiassed history of one who enacted so gigantic a role as Napoleon I. cannot well be written until the children of the men who fought under or against him have passed away. Jomini has gauged the Emperor's worth as a soldier in a fashion never to be equalled. But as a monarch, statesman, citizen, man, he has been hitherto measured by a standard of unreasoning, if not wilful, misrepresentation, or by one of fulsome eulogy.

Putting aside the deification of the Little Corporal by the masses of the French as a natural ebullition of

* THE FIRST NAPOLEON. A Sketch, Political and Military. By John Codman Ropes, Member of the Massachusetts Historical Society. With Maps. Boston: Houghton, Mifflin & Co.

† Published in The Dial, January, 1886.

the national love of glory, it is difficult to understand why English writers should to-day continue to treat Napoleon solely as the embodiment of wickedness. "Boney" still plays the part of black bogey to English children, still figures as the loyal Briton's evil genius. He can have done nothing well. He can have been nothing good. The Muse of History, with her modern training, need not conceal the shortcomings of Napoleon. They were too grave not to be universally admitted. But the two sides from which to view every historical figure—personal character and life's work,—should each have due weight.

Napoleon was as legitimately the outcome of the French Revolution as our own Constitution was of ours. We built upon a solid basis of inherited intelligence. The French structure was reared on the rotten foundation of the ignorance of ages. Anarchy, pure and simple, can never last long. There was not sufficient education in France for rule by the people. It was merely a question of who should seize the reins. The Revolution overthrew the rule of the privileged classes; it began a new era; but it left no healthy scheme of government to take its place. Bonaparte, happily for France, elbowed his way to the head of affairs, and, in the "Code Napoleon," first gave to a modern Latin race the recognition of every man's equality before the law. Admitted that he may have done this, not because he was by nature a philanthropist, not because the sorrows of the down-trodden appealed to his sense of justice, but because his sudden rise had made him characteristically the opponent of the existing customs of Europe. Admitted that his motives were selfish, and that he saw in this course alone the means of erecting a new Empire to which he could urge no other claim. The fact remains that he did do this thing; and he thus became the chief factor in preserving to the countries which fell under his rule, in a definite form, and to all of their neighbors as an aspiration, that for which the French masses rose in their horrible might in 1789.

Mr. Ropes's book consists of the Lowell lectures delivered by him in Boston in March, 1885. He disclaims the writing of a new history, but indicates the lines upon which a new history might be written. He gives us some broad military criticism, but does not deal in the detail of Napoleon's campaigns. The ever-new drama of Waterloo alone is prominently sketched. The interest of this study centres in his insistance on

Napoleon's value in moulding the chaotic ideas of the new departure into a definite form. Napoleon's scheme was by no means, as the English still aver, the conquest of Europe. He was not so weak as to believe it possible to do this, still less to cement the heterogeneous mass into one durable empire. His aim was to erect in Western Europe a confederation based on such liberal laws as, contrasted with the despotic rule of Russia, Austria, and Prussia, should preserve the balance of power in the hands of France and enable her to keep what she had won with so much blood. The basis of this liberality was the Code. The English assertion that Napoleon was not a jurist, that others made the code, is puerile. Napoleon caused it to be made. He stamped upon it much of his own individuality. And this Code was such as to outlive the Empire, and even to struggle through the Restoration. This alone is enough to stamp its author one of the benefactors of mankind.

Mr. Ropes devotes, perhaps unnecessarily, some space to showing that Napoleon was not naturally a cruel man; that his slaughter of so many thousands in his wars had nothing to do with a personal lack of humanity. But he does very properly contrast such a wanton act as Nelson's hanging Admiral Caraccioli from the yard-arm, in clear contravention of the terms of the capitulation of Naples, or even Wellington's failure to protest against the execution of Ney, a direct violation of the convention of Paris, with Napoleon's seizure and the execution of the duc d'Enghien. Nor does Napoleon suffer by the comparison. The one act by no means palliates the other; but it shows the turbulence of the times.

In discussing his campaigns, Mr. Ropes brings out strongly the fact that, as a soldier, Napoleon was a gambler, and that he often subordinated the result to be obtained to the technical perfection of his military art. However we may admire the ideal completeness of a campaign when this contributes to the result, the equities of war dictate that the ultimate practical ends alone shall be the guiding rule of the commander of an army. Perhaps this gambling spirit is the worst flaw in Napoleon's character.

Mr. Ropes does not pretend to exonerate Napoleon for his course in Spain. What he had done in Italy and Western Germany was justified by the striving of the people for better government, and by their eager acceptance of what he really gave them. But to force upon the Spanish people even a better system than their own, was clearly unjustifiable; though indeed it would have been well for Spain to have accepted the new régime. And his defeat in the Peninsula was a prime cause of Napoleon's eventual failure. The divorce of Josephine is condemned on moral grounds; the act being unextenuated by the existing political necessity for an heir to the throne of France.

Mr. Ropes shows, with some acumen, that Napoleon was by no means the attacking party in most of his wars, and argues from this that he was consistent in his endeavors to liberalize Europe. But surely Napoleon was the constant disturbing element—the man whose restless existence alone was a continuing threat to the established order of things; and Mr. Ropes frankly admits that he was unable, even for the good of France, to accept personal mortification. This is instanced in his refusing to buy off Austria from the triple coalition in 1813, and in his refusal of peace on fair terms after Leipsic. The character of Emperor and Frenchman was liable to be lost in that of soldier, and a gambling soldier at that.

In 1815, Napoleon's clearly defined policy should have been to conduct a defensive campaign. Home politics should have been kept in the background until success had come to justify his return from Elba. "France, at this crisis of her fate, needed a Frederick rather than a Napoleon. With a man of the iron temper of the king who carried his country through the seven years' war, France would have maintained her independence." This tribute to the Last of the Kings is just and gracious.

In the campaign of Waterloo, Napoleon's mind was no doubt as unclouded as at any period of his career. But his body had no longer that elasticity which enabled him on his early fields to rely so largely upon himself for his knowledge of the situation. Perhaps the fact that he did not absolutely ascertain the direction of the Prussian retreat after Ligny, and thus divided his army, was the proximate cause of his defeat.

Too many diverse authorities are agreed in ascribing to Napoleon great weaknesses of character; too many contemporary diaries describe acts and quote expressions of his, for us to doubt that the Emperor was indeed a man of failings as marked as his talents. But much of the perverseness of his nature was called to the surface by his being of necessity the antagonist of all that Europe had inherited from the dark ages;

and a view of what he really accomplished may lead us to look with more forgiveness upon his vices than upon those of princes whose asserted divine right should have crowned them with virtues to which Napoleon could make no claim so exalted. To view history from a standpoint of strict morality is well. But there are few of the agents in the upward progress of mankind not open to censure on some score. Perfect men have never done the world's work.

Our American ideas are still apt to be warped by the English perversion of everything Napoleonic. While it is not worth while to notice gratuitous affronts to his personal character, it cannot be denied that Napoleon, politically, gave France much; that he took nothing from her liberties; that every country which ever came under his rule benefitted by that rule; and that the strength of what he built was the prime reason that the liberty gained by the Revolution was not sooner swallowed up in the restoration of the Bourbons. The results of our own Civil War will lead us to appreciate the fact that even the fearful drain of men and material to which his wars subjected France may perhaps not have been all too great a price to pay for what Napoleon gave her.

No such crisp resumé of this question has been put
in print. In Mr. Ropes's discussions, the lawyer's even-
handedness has kept in check the intense admiration
for the great soldier which, as one of the best read
military critics of the day, he naturally harbors. The
public is indebted to this sketch for leaven which may
haply aid to leaven the whole lump. Its pages teem
with suggestiveness, and though one may not agree
with all Mr. Ropes's conclusions, there is food for
reflection in every one of his pages.

ADDRESS

AT THE

UNVEILING OF THE MONUMENT

OF THE

119TH REGIMENT
NEW YORK VOLUNTEERS

ON THE

BATTLE FIELD OF GETTYSBURG
JULY 4, 1888.

ADDRESS

AT THE

UNVEILING OF THE MONUMENT .

OF THE

119TH. REGIMENT NEW YORK VOLUNTEERS

ON THE

BATTLE FIELD OF GETTYSBURG
JULY 4, 1888.

COMRADES:—Ever since tradition first handed down a record of the deeds of men, the history of the world has been a continuous recital of wars. A few only have been such as to affect the conditions of mankind. Almost all the struggles of which we have any knowledge, beginning with the ten years' siege of Troy, as sung to us by Homer, have arisen from the arrogance, selfishness or ambition of princes. Temporary gain has been won for the few, by such loss and suffering to the many as we to-day can scarce conceive. Only a few of these wars of the world, and only a few of the battles in these wars, have been such as permanently to affect the welfare of mankind. Had the historian Creasy brought his list of the decisive battles of the world down to our day, he would have added, to the twelve he has given, one more,—the victory we have come here to celebrate. And why do we call the victory of Gettysburg the thirteenth decisive battle of the world? I will tell you.

While the populations of Europe have been struggling, all but in vain, during the past two hundred and fifty years, to wrest a small quota of personal and political freedom from the one-man power which holds them down, there has been going on in America that life and growth to which the future historian will point as the germ of the liberties of the twentieth century. The symptom of this life and growth is the idea of self-government,—the abilty to hold a town meeting,—as yet a quality resident only in America. The motto of this life and growth is, "The greatest good to the greatest number." And while, in every other part of the habitable globe, the doctrine obtains that the many must work that the few may refrain from working, that some may do or have what other men may not, that society may so remain organized that the greatest good may flow to the select few, the American has boldly worked on the theory of manhood's rights, and of so operating the government that not only shall it be "of the people, by the people and for the people," but that its results shall show the greatest good to the greatest number. This is the watchword of all social and political progress.

A quarter of a century ago, there was danger that the nation which had given birth to, and preached, this doctrine, would lose its unity, its identity; that the people who had promulgated to mankind the rule of conduct which will yet make the whole world free, could not insure its own stability. This was indeed a grave danger. It is not essential to inquire how this danger came about; but the danger I have referred to already existed. For two years the Southerner had fought to break up the Union, the Northerner had struggled to preserve it; and here on this field it was decided that the Union should be preserved. From and after the first three days of July, 1863, the tide of secession receded, until, after other two years, a million and a half of soldiers melted back into the population from whence they came, and the Union was, for the eventual and now well-recognized good of all concerned, pronounced one and indivisible. It is for this that the battle of Gettysburg, which preserved to the world the integrity, the homogeneity of the people which had promulgated this doctrine of the greatest good to the greatest number, will always be one of the decisive battles of the world.

But, comrades, what have we here of personal recollections? Our well-loved regimental leader has asked me to speak to you to-day. I am scarcely the one to be selected for this task. You, all of you, saw strewn like leaves upon this spot, twenty-five years ago to-day, many of our comrades: some never to rise again, to whom, thanks to the munificence of the State of New York, we have assembled to dedicate this graceful monument; some soon again to join their fellow-soldiers, and to fight with you on other fields; some not again to hear the martial trump of war. Among this last number, I, your ancient comrade, was. I had stood beside you on the murderous field of Chancellorsville, where fell the noble Peissner in his maiden fight. I stood beside you here. On both these fields the 119th New York Regiment lost all save honor. We marched through yonder town out here to the front, a bare quarter of the gallant body of men which, less than a year before, had flaunted its banners down Broadway. But three hundred men were under the colors as we filed out into the orchard, rested a few minutes, and then fell into line and moved across fields and fences to this spot. The enemy advanced upon us, and in a brief thirty minutes, so deadly was the fire, less than half that handful (one hundred and thirty) were on hand to answer when the roll was called. Surely this is a record of which all of us may well be proud. I have always been sorry, comrades, that my lot was not cast with you in the more successful career of the regiment in the West and the Carolinas. Fain would I have fought with you at Wauhatchie, and have stormed with you up Missionary Ridge; gladly would I have joined with you in the arduous march to save the army at Knoxville from starvation. I could wish to call up to memory the stirring events of Rocky-faced Ridge; the bold charge at Reseca, when gallant Lloyd laid down his life, and everready Lockman headed the forlorn hope; the constant bickering of out-post duty and flanking movements, and the sharp and bitter fights of Cassville, Dallas, Pine Hill,

Kolb's Farm, Kenesaw Mountain, Peach Tree Creek
and Atlanta.   I fain would feel that I, too, had
marched to the sea and through the Atlantic States to
the rear of Lee with William Tecumseh Sherman.
But all this was denied me; and, while you were gar-
landing your brows with laurels on fresh and constant
fields, I was compelled to rest on the few I had already
won, in the less heroic duties of the War Department
at Washington.   It is because of this that I feel that I
am not the proper one to address you to-day.   But I
can speak to you, comrades, with heartfelt warmth, of
the brave souls who here sealed their devotion to the
Union and the country a quarter of a century ago.
Who are they?   Not professional, not mercenary soldiers.   These were men who took up arms in defence
of what to them was dearer than life or fortune.
Among them was the pale-faced lad of eighteen summers, who exchanged book for bayonet, to graduate in
the school of war instead of under the shady elms of
his alma mater; who, looking all too weak to carry
his heavy load, of musket, cartridge-box, knapsack and
rations, yet trudged bravely on beside his sturdier
brother, an example and encouragement to all around
him.   Among them was the handsome, hearty fellow

in early manhood, who had left behind him at home a wife just wedded, and had given up all which is dearest to man, and comes to man but once in life, for the sake of country. He fell here, pierced to the heart by a bullet, which, to reach its mark, tore its way through the last letter from the loved one at home. Among them was the sturdy father of a family, whose sons were too young to bear arms, but who felt that some one must repay to the fatherland the benefits he and his had reaped. Among them was the gray-bearded man, just within the years of enlistment; and beside him stood two of his sons, while in the ranks of the drum corps, at the head of the regiment, plodded a third, the youngest scion of a noble, patriotic tribe. Among them was the light-haired, large-limbed Teuton, who sought to make up to his adopted country those gifts which she had so lavishly poured into his lap,—those gifts which he never did and never could have found in the home across the sea. Among them was the dark-haired, active Celt, who had come from the oppressed shores of the fairest island of the ocean, and made his home in a land where he was a man; and for the sake of that manhood he fought his last fight here.

All these, comrades, and many more of the same grand stamp, have here mixed with their native sod. We are here, not to a feast of the living, but to honor the memory of the gallant dead.

> "Their bones are dust,
> Their swords are rust,
> Their souls are with the saints, we trust."

Not a virtue which man may boast, but is illustrated on this field by the brave and true who fell before our eyes. From the star of such as Reynolds, the pattern officer, a man of intellect unclouded, far-seeing, bold, faithful soldier in every fibre, true to the end, down to the simple blue blouse of the humbler private, who knew no more than to face death because it was duty, every grade of quality and devotion has been made illustrious; and it is to these noble traits of head and heart, comrades, that we here to-day dedicate this monument.

But a single thought more, my comrades. Happy as may be our circle of family and friends that each of us was here preserved, and that we are still spared to them, there will be a time, not many years hence, when our feet shall also have gone tottering to our last resting-place in the lap of Mother Earth, that the coming generations shall say, in praise of you and me, "He fought at Gettysburg."

But of each of those comrades whom we here to-day, with uncovered heads and grateful hearts, do honor with reverent earnestness, that far greater badge of honor shall be uttered, "He fell at Gettysburg."

For each and every one of these heroes, comrades, join me in the creedless prayer: Rest to his ashes, Peace to that nobler part which dieth not.

VALOR AND SKILL IN THE
CIVIL WAR.

VALOR AND SKILL IN THE CIVIL WAR.

WAS EITHER THE BETTER SOLDIER?

THERE appears to have been gathered, by many of the readers of the war literature of the day, a distinctly erroneous impression to the effect that the South fought better than the North; or, to put it in another way, that the Southerner was the better soldier. Those who have well studied the subject, or who intelligently served through the war, do not share this opinion; but there is, in the events of the war, superficially considered, a certain basis for the assumption. This has, however, its very clear limitations.

The South had a certain task to accomplish, and certain means to accomplish it with. The North had its larger task, and larger means. If we will carefully

* Published in the Century Magazine, May, 1890.

consider what these respective tasks were, and the manner of their working out, it will appear as a result that the North performed its gigantic undertaking not only in a creditable and businesslike manner, but in a manner which will stand the test of historical comparison.

It is not difficult to state the task of the South. It was simply to conquer its independence. No student of the war, no old soldier, no American, but harbors the warmest admiration for what the Southerner did. He began the war with a vow to win or to die in the last ditch. He did not win, but he did actually do the other thing. He gave up the struggle because he had practically used up his last man and fired his last cartridge. Nor he nor any other could do more.

What was the task of the North? In 1861 the population of the South was five and a half millions, including slaves. As some part of the population had, of necessity, to raise breadstuffs, cotton and beef, and the slaves did this work, so that nearly all the whites could bear arms, the blacks can fairly be counted as a part of the population, so far as this question is concerned. The suggestion of a constant danger of servile insurrection is best answered by the fact that there was no such insurrection, and that the South was never called on to deplete the ranks at the front to forestall one.   The total population of five and a half millions may thus, with perfect fairness, be taken as a factor in the proposition. The population of the North was under twenty millions, that is, but three and a half times as great. From this had to be drawn all the men and material with which to suppress this greatest of the rebellions of history.

If we will turn back to our own Revolution, we shall find that the population of the United Kingdom alone was five times as great as that of the colonies.   And yet, Great Britain was unable, after seven years of stanch effort, to reduce these revolted colonies to obedience.   If we will go back a half generation further, to old Frederick, we shall find that, in the Seven Years' War, the population of the allies was twenty times as great as that of Prussia.   And yet the allies failed, in those seven years, to wrest Silesia from the iron grip of this "Last of the Kings."   Parallel cases might be multiplied, but the above suffices to illustrate the query advanced and its answer.

If a hundred years ago Great Britain, with more than five times their population, failed in seven campaigns to subject the colonies; if Austria, Russia, France, Sweden, and the Imperial forces combined were unable, in seven campaigns, to overwhelm that grim old Brandenburg monarch, surely we may feel that our work was not ill done, if in five campaigns, with a population of but three and a half to one, we succeeded in crushing out the rebellion of 1861.

And though Frederick, while equally brilliant in victory, was assuredly greater than any modern captain in reverse, it might, perhaps, be claimed that, in Virginia, Lee was all but as much superior to most of the generals opposed to him as the Prussian king to Prince Karl, Field-Marshals Browne and Daun, and the others with whom he had to do. Such superiority was not as marked in the West as in the East; but the average general officer of the South won his stars by service and not by political scheming, and he certainly largely outranked the average general of the North. At all events the Southern management of military affairs was sufficiently better than ours to warrant the above parallelism as a reasonably fair one.

Another point is noticeable. Frederick rarely had in the field more than one-quarter of the force of his enemies; but on the battle-field, by superior strategy, central position, interior lines, and nimble legs, he usually managed to oppose to them one-half as many at the point of actual contact.   Owing to its extraordinary exertions, the South had under arms, until the last third of the war, an average of about three-quarters of the force of the North.   And we shall see that at the point of actual contact the forces of the North and the South were not far from equal up to 1864.

TABLE OF NORTHERN AND SOUTHERN FORCES
UNDER ARMS.

Date.	Federals.	Confed's.	Per cent.
January 1, 1861	16,000	. . . . Arming	
July 1, 1861	186,000	 150,000	 80
January 1, 1862	576,000	 350,000	 60
March 1, 1862	637,000	 500,000	 80
January 1, 1863	918,000	 690,000	 78
January 1, 1864	860,000	 400,000	 47
January 1, 1865	959,000	 250,000	 26
March 31, 1865	980,000	 175,000	 18
May 1, 1865	1,000,000	. . . . None	

Moreover, out of this none too great margin the North was compelled, partly by the nature of its task, and partly in consequence of its frequently absurd political strategy, to keep a much larger number than the South on detached service.   Compared, then, with what other nations have accomplished, it may be claimed that the statistics of our war abundantly demonstrate that the North did the business of suppressing the Rebellion in a workmanlike and respectable, not to say handsome manner, leaving, under the circumstances, no great room for adverse criticism. In yielding our sincerest admiration to the splendid efforts of the South, we must not lose sight of the noble work of the North, nor of the conditions under which it was accomplished.

Again, to take up the impression prevailing that the Southerners were better fighters than the Northerners. This is also disproved by the figures. As has been frequently pointed out, the Southern troops throughout the war were a homogeneous body. The Northern troops were never so much so, and after the first two years were largely made up of "rag, tag, and bobtail." The Southerner felt that he was fighting for his home and fireside. This greatest of all inspirations we lacked. He fought with an intimate knowledge of the *terrain*, with the aid of every farmer—indeed, of every woman—as a spy. He was more in earnest, as a rule, as will be every soldier whose fields and homestead are being wasted and burned. Until the end, there was in the South never a day when there was actual danger of the war being stopped by political opposition. How was it in the North? The South had only the North to fight. The North had the South, and the most unreasonable part of its own population besides, to contend with.

I think it will be generally admitted, even by Southern soldiers, that some of the troops of the Army of the Potomac were always as good as any equal number in the Army of Northern Virginia. I am rather inclined to think that, estimating arms, rationing, and material, fifty thousand men of the three arms could have been picked out of the Potomac army superior to any fifty thousand in Lee's. It is certain that out of the two an army of one hundred thousand men could have been selected, of as high a grade in every characteristic as, and of a higher grade of intelligence and adaptability than, any troops that ever bore arms. The Army of the Potomac was always weakened by the admixture of poor material, far more than its gallant adversary. If the old *cadres* could have been kept full, instead of reënforcements coming in the shape of new regiments, that army, at two-thirds its average strength, would have been a far better fighting machine. Grant's Virginia campaign illustrates this fact.

I have no disposition to discuss the political conditions which necessitated our system of recruiting or the management of the armies. My question is purely a military one. But how many of us there were who for months carried about empty commissions to the grades we had honestly earned, but on which we could not be mustered, because by hard fighting our regiments had been reduced below the prescribed standard, and who gazed, heart-sick, at the brand-new shoulder-straps of the men who, at the eleventh hour, had helped to raise a new regiment. Such was rarely the case in the Southern armies.

The Army of the Potomac always had some of the best corps commanders. Not so with its chiefs. Certainly that army never enjoyed the advantage of having the same commander and practically the same generals of corps, divisions, and brigades, duly promoted, year in and year out, as did the Army of Northern Virginia. All these facts militated as much against the efficiency of the Northern as they contributed to that of the Southern troops. And yet, barring errors in command, what stanch work the much-tried Potomac army did through its four years' life. Whatever is said about the forces in Virginia applies, though modified by the difference in conditions, and often by the difference in commanders, equally to the Western armies.

It is no doubt true that the Southern advantage of defensive war, interior lines, knowledge of the topography of the theatre of operations, and superior strategy, enabled them, from smaller means, to oppose us at the point of actual contact with equal numbers. But it is not true that, at the point of contact, man for man, the Southerner fought better. Look at the following items of numbers actually engaged. The figures cover the years 1861, 1862, and 1868, the period before the South was quite overmatched. They have been diligently compared with the best authorities, and are as accurate as such comparison can make them. The numbers have been taken without bias, and were computed in each case without an idea of what their tabulation would show. While there is occasionally exhibited by some critics a disposition to trim statistics, or to deny the accuracy of even the Official War Records, it is thought the fairness of the following items will be generally admitted. Certainly no reasonable or admissible variation will alter the conclusion which must be drawn from them.

JULY 21, 1861.—At Bull Run, Virginia, McDowell had 28,000 men; Beauregard, 25,000. The result of the day's fighting was an apparent Union success, until, late in the afternoon, Johnston came in on the Union flank with 5,000 fresh troops, when victory changed to defeat.

AUGUST 10, 1861.—At Wilson's Creek, Missouri, Lyon had 5,000 men; Price and McCulloch, over 10,000. In spite of these great odds it was a hardly won Confederate victory.

OCTOBER 21, 1861.—At Ball's Bluff, Virginia, Baker had 1,900 men; Evans 3,200. Though the Federals fought bravely, their defeat was of the worst.

NOVEMBER 7, 1861.—At Belmont, Missouri, Grant had 3,100 men. The enemy at first had but 1,000, but Polk gradually reënforced this body up to 5,000 or 6,000. Confederate victory.

JANUARY 19, 1862.—At Mill Springs, Kentucky, Thomas, with about 6,000 men, utterly defeated Zollicoffer, with an equal number.

FEBRUARY 14–16, 1862.—Grant attacked Fort Donelson, Tennessee, garrisoned by 20,000 men, with a force not exceeding 15,000. He was subsequently reënforced up to 25,000 men. Brilliant Union success.

MARCH 6–8, 1862.—At Pea Ridge, Arkansas, Curtis, with 12,000 men, won a handsome victory over Price and Van Dorn, with a force of over 26,000, of which 16,000 were of good quality, and the rest raw levies and Indians.

MARCH 23, 1862.—At Winchester, Virginia, with 7,000 men, Shields won a victory over Jackson, who had about 4,200 on the field.

APRIL 6–7, 1862.—At Shiloh, Tennessee, Grant, with 40,000 men, was driven into a desperate corner on April 6, by A. S. Johnston and Beauregard, with an equal number. Next day, Buell, with his fresh troops, and with Grant in reserve, probably 50,000 men in all, defeated Beauregard, whose 30,000 men still left fought, nevertheless, most handsomely to retain their advantage.

MAY 5, 1862.—At Williamsburg, Virginia, Hooker, with some 10,000 men, bore the brunt of the fight, against Longstreet's equal force, from early dawn till late in the afternoon, when Kearny relieved him. Later, Hancock's and Peck's brigades came into action. In all, some 20,000 Union troops engaged, probably, 12,000 to 14,000 Confederates. Longstreet held his ground till night, and then

MAY 8, 1862.—At McDowell, Jackson, with some 8,000 men, badly defeated Milroy and Schenck, with 3,500.

MAY 25, 1862.—At Winchester, Jackson, with some 18,000 men, defeated Banks, with 5,000.

MAY 27, 1862.—At Hanover Court House, Fitz John Porter, with 10,000 men, won a handsome victory over Branch, with 9,000. Branch's forces at the beginning of the fight were quite scattered.

MAY 31, 1862.—At Seven Pines (or Fair Oaks), Virginia, Keyes fought alone, but unsuccessfully, against great odds till after 3 P. M., when Kearny came up. Then Keyes and Kearny, 19,000 against 39,000, held their ground till Sumner came in on their right flank. The Union force was then some 32,000 men; the Confederates, under G. W. Smith, Longstreet, and D. H. Hill, were some 40,000. Huger's forces were not actually in the fight until the following day. The next day, June 1, the Union forces recovered a part of the lost ground, and during the night the Confederates fell back towards Richmond.

JUNE 8, 1862.—At Cross Keys, Virginia, Ewell, with 5,000 men, defeated Frémont, with 12,000.

JUNE 9, 1862.—At Port Republic, Tyler and Carroll, with 3,500 men, held their ground against Jackson's

JUNE 26, 1862.—At Meadow Bridge (or Mechanicsville), McCall, with 9,000 men, inflicted grievous loss on A. P. Hill, with 14,000. McCall held his ground till night, and then retired.

JUNE 27, 1862.—At Gaines' Mill, Porter, with 35,000 men, held the bulk of the Confederate Army—at least 60,000 strong—at bay all day, retiring after night fell. The victory remained with Lee, but Porter's fighting was magnificent.

JUNE 29, 1862.—At Allen's Farm, Richardson and Sedgwick, 16,000 men, easily held head against a brilliant attack by McLaws and Griffith, with 7,000, retiring at night.

JUNE 29, 1862.—At Savage's Station, Sumner and Franklin, with 26,000 men, held back four brigades of Magruder and McLaws, with about 10,000, retiring at night. These two actions were affairs of the rear guard of the Army of the Potomac. The Confederate attacks were handsomely made.

JUNE 30, 1862.—Franklin, with a part of Sedgwick, some 18,000, held the approaches of White Oak Swamp against Jackson, whose corps was about 36,-000 strong. There was no chance in this defile for Jackson to attack.

JUNE 30, 1862.—At Glendale, Hooker, McCall, and part of Sedgwick — 18,000 — held their ground against the stanchest efforts of Longstreet, A. P. Hill, Huger, and Magruder, some 20,000, retiring at night.

JULY 1, 1862.—At Malvern Hill, McClellan had about 60,000 men at hand; Lee, probably 50,000 men. The Confederate attacks were confined to fifteen brigades of Magruder, D. H. Hill, and Huger, say 34,000 men, against Porter, Couch, Morell, Kearny, Caldwell, Sickles, Meagher, say 40,000 men. This was a clear Union victory.

AUGUST 8, 1862. — At Cedar Mountain, Virginia, Banks's 7,500 men made so smart an attack on Jackson's force of 21,500, that the Confederates retired from the field at night. Banks also withdrew. Much the larger part of Jackson's force was engaged.

AUGUST 28, 1862.—Near Gainesville, Virginia, the brigades of Gibbon and Doubleday, with 5,000 men, made a gallant fight against Ewell and Taliafero, with six brigades, some 7,000; but accomplished no result. The Federals held the field till 1 A. M.

AUGUST 29, 1862. — At Groveton, Reynolds, Sigel,

Reno, Heintzelman, and Stevens, 26,000 men, attacked Jackson's 25,000, but without result. On the same day, Hatch, with 5,000 men, had a sharp fight with two brigades of Hood's, some 3,800 men, without definite result.

AUGUST 30, 1862.—At the Second Bull Run (a continuation of the two preceding battles), Pope had about 58,000 men to Lee's 51,000. Practically, the whole force was engaged on both sides. Brilliant Confederate victory.

SEPTEMBER 1, 1862.—At Chantilly, Reno, Stevens, and Kearny, 11,000 strong, held A. P. Hill, with 8,000 in check.

SEPTEMBER 14, 1862.—Two divisions of Reno, Meade, Hatch, and Ricketts, 22,000 strong, forced Turner's Gap, on South Mountain, Maryland, defended by D. H. Hill and two divisions of Longstreet, all but 14,-000 strong.

SEPTEMBER 14, 1862.—Slocum and Brooks, with 6,500 men, drove McLaws, with 4,000 to 5,000, from Crampton's Gap.

SEPTEMBER 16-17, 1862.—At Antietam, Maryland, Lee's 40,000 men fought a most stubborn battle against McClellan's 75,000 men, of whom some

25,000 were not engaged. Lee put in his last man, and though forced to retire, he did so at his leisure.

SEPTEMBER 19, 1862.—At Iuka, Mississippi, Price's 13,000 men defeated Rosecrans's head of column, Hamilton's division, of 5,000 men. But, as Ord was approaching from the north, Price deemed it prudent to retire.

OCTOBER 3–4, 1862. — At Corinth, Mississippi, the forces were about 22,000 on a side, and Rosecrans defeated Van Dorn.

OCTOBER 8, 1862.—Buell, with 20,000 men, defeated Bragg, with an equal number, at Perryville.

DECEMBER 7, 1862.—At Prairie Grove, Arkansas, the Federal general Blunt defeated Hindman. Forces about 10,000 each.

DECEMBER 13, 1862.—The numbers in contact at Fredericksburg, Virginia, are impossible to estimate; nor was this a ranged battle. It was a gallant, but wrong-headed, attempt to do the impossible.

DECEMBER 31, 1862.—At Stone's River, Kentucky, Rosecrans, with 43,000 men, though at first driven back by Bragg's 47,000, managed to hold his own, and retain the field of battle. No praise is too high for the fighting on both sides.

MAY 2–5, 1863.—Chancellorsville was the most brilliant of Lee's victories. Here, by his splendid tactical dispositions, with 6†,000 men, he defeated Hooker with twice the number. But looking only at the actual fighting, on May 2, at Dowdall's Tavern, Jackson, with 22,000 men, defeated Howard, with 10,000; on May 3, at Fairview, Stuart, with 37,000 men, drove in Sickles and Couch, with 32,000; on the same day, at Salem Church, four Confederate brigades of 10,000 men defeated Brooks, with 9,000; on May 4, at Banks's Ford, Lee, with 25,000 men, defeated Sedgwick, with 20,000. The fighting of the Confederates was as superb as Lee's tactics. Whereever engaged, the Unionists fought with equal credit, but pluck was unavailing against Hooker's hebetude.

MAY 16, 1863. — At Champion's Hill, Mississippi, Grant had 15,000 men actually engaged, against Pemberton's 16,000. The latter suffered a disasterous defeat.

JULY 1–4, 1863.—Gettysburg, Pennsylvania. There is much dispute as to the numbers engaged, but 68,000 Confederates against 82,000 Federals is not far from the mark. On the first day Hill and Ewell much outnumbered as well as defeated the First and Eleventh Corps; on the second day the fight of the Third Corps, with some some reënforcements, against Hood and McLaws was about an even thing as to numbers and result, and the same applies to the fighting on Cemetery Hill; on the third day that part of the column under Pickett, Pettigrew, and Trimble which reached our line was speedily outnumbered by the forces which rushed in towards the threatened point.

SEPTEMBER 19–20, 1863.—At Chickamauga, Georgia, Rosecrans, with 55,000 men, was badly defeated by Bragg, with 65,000. But the stand here made by Thomas on Horse-shoe Ridge, against the repeated assaults of vast odds, will be forever memorable.

NOVEMBER 23–25, 1863.—At Chattanooga, Grant had about 60,000 men; Bragg, over 40,000. The defeat of the latter was overwhelming.

This list of fifty battles gives twenty victories to the Confederates, an equal number to the Federals, and leaves ten which may fairly be called drawn. In these fifty battles, at the point of fighting contact, the Confederates outnumbered the Federals by an average of about two per cent.

As regards brilliant assaults upon regular works, the Confederates were never called on to show such devotion as was manifested by the Federals at Fredericksburg, the several assaults at Vicksburg and Port Hudson, Spottsylvania, Cold Harbor, and Petersburg. Few trials of fighting qualities, in any war, go beyond some of these.

As will be seen from the table of forces, after the winter of 1863–64 the Union forces so vastly outnumbered the Confederate, that comparison of the merits of actual fighting becomes more difficult. We can deduce little from the battles except stanch purpose on the Federal, and brilliant courage, coupled with marvelously able military management, on the Confederate side. But if one will take the pains to tabulate the numbers actually engaged during all but the last months of the crumbling away of the Confederate armies, there appear plainly two facts: first, that the Confederates, by superior management and better position, opposed to the Federals fully equal numbers at the point of fighting contact; and secondly, that of the combats during the entire struggle the Federals had their full share of the victories.

It is certain that the statistics of the war rob the

wearers of the blue and the gray of the right to boast one at the expense of the other. Neither can claim superiority in actual battle. The case bears enough semblance to Greek meeting Greek to satisfy the reasonable aspirations of either "Yank" or "Johnny."

And in this connection it may not be amiss, once more, to give our national self-esteem a *bonne bouche* in the following table:

TABLE OF LOSSES IN SUNDRY BATTLES OF THE
EIGHTEENTH AND NINETEENTH CENTURIES.

	Percentage of killed and wounded of number engaged.
Prussians.—Up to Waterloo, in eight battles	18.42
" At Königgrätz	8.86
Austrians.—Up to Waterloo, in seven battles	11.17
" Since in two	8.56
French.—Up to Waterloo, in nine battles	22.38
" Since in nine	8.86
Germans.—Since 1745, in eight battles	11.53
English.—In four battles	10.36
Federals.—In eleven battles	12.89
Confederates.—In eleven battles	14.16

From this table it is manifest that, excepting only the troops of Frederick and of Napoleon, the American volunteer has shown himself equal to taking the severest punishment of any troops upon the field of battle.

The wonderfully pertinacious tactics of those two great captains, rather than the discipline of their troops, explains the excess of loss of their battles. And while the capacity to face heavy loss is but one of the elements which go to make up the soldier, it is perhaps of them all the most telling.

OPEN LETTERS.[*]

"VALOR AND SKILL IN THE CIVIL WAR."

IN the Century for May, 1890, there appeared an exceedingly interesting article entitled "Valor and Skill in the Civil War." The article was divided into two parts, the first written by Colonel Theodore Ayrault Dodge of the United States Army, the second by Charles A. Patch of the United States Volunteers. The whole article is in so friendly a spirit that we are obliged to believe in the intention of the writers to be fair. Yet in the part written by Colonel Dodge occur some very misleading and erroneous statements. It is the purpose of this article to call attention to some of these statements, but without any design of discussing the question "Was either the better soldier?" In arguing that the Southern Confederacy was not as

* Published in the Century Magazine, July, 1890.

greatly overmatched as some nations that had been more successful, Colonel Dodge says:

If we will turn back to our own Revolution, we shall find that the population of the United Kingdom alone was five times as great as that of the colonies. And yet Great Britain was unable, after seven years of stanch effort, to reduce these revolted colonies to obedience. If we will go back a half generation further, to old Frederick, we shall find that in the Seven Years' War the population of the allies was twenty times as great as that of Prussia. And yet the allies failed in those seven years to wrest Silesia from the iron grip of this "Last of the Kings." . . . If a hundred years ago Great Britain, with more than five times their population, failed in seven campaigns to subject the colonies; if Austria, Russia, France, Sweden, and the Imperial forces combined were unable, in seven campaigns, to overwhelm that grim old Brandenburg monarch, surely we may feel that our work was not ill done, if in five campaigns, with a population of but three and a half to one, we succeded in crushing out the rebellion of 1861.

Colonel Dodge seems to overlook the fact that the

broad Atlantic, separating Britain from her revolted colonies, was worth to the cause of America thousands of men. He also leaves entirely out of the count France, Spain, and Holland, which powerful nations all combined against Great Britain. At Yorktown the allied armies of France and the United States more than doubled the effective force under Cornwallis, and, besides, a powerful French fleet made certain the victory which secured American liberty. In the war of the Revolution Great Britain was the party over-matched and not the United States. Again, in the Silesian or Seven Years' War Frederick had as his allies Britain, Hanover, and Hesse, whose combined army, under the able leadership of Duke Ferdinand of Brunswick, did splendid service for the Prussian king. When at the close of his sixth campaign all subsidies from England were stopped by the Earl of Bute (after George II.'s death), Frederick was reduced to as great straits as was the Southern Confederacy at the close of 1864. Prussia was at her last gasp; but the death of the Czarina converted the most powerful of Frederick's enemies into a fast friend, and the Czar Peter III. joined his army to that of Prussia, while Sweden also retired from the alliance against him. Thus by timely help when all seemed lost Frederick was saved. Alone and unaided the Confederacy struggled for four years against a foe whose population outnumbered its own in the ratio of three and one-half to one, and whose armies were swelled by thousands of recruits from the nations of Europe. Again, Colonel Dodge says:

Owing to its extraordinary exertions, the South had under arms, until the last third of the war, an average of about three-quarters of the force of the North. And we shall see that at the point of actual contact the forces of the North and the South were not far from equal up to 1864.

To prove this statement he introduces the following extraordinary

TABLE OF NORTHERN AND SOUTHERN FORCES
UNDER ARMS.

Date.	Federals.	Confed's.	Per cent.
January 1, 1861	16,000	Arming	
July 1, 1861	186,000	150,000	80
January 1, 1862	576,000	350,000	60
March 1, 1862	637,000	500,000	80
January 1, 1863	918,000	690,000	78
January 1, 1864	860,000	400,000	47
January 1, 1865	959,000	250,000	26
March 31, 1865	980,000	175,000	18

From what source did Colonel Dodge get the above figures? In the greatest war-history ever published, viz. "Battles and Leaders of the Civil War," we find, Vol. IV., p. 767, an article entitled, "Notes on the Union and Confederate Armies." In these notes we find, taken from the official records, a table showing the number of men enlisted in the army and navy of the United States during the civil war. This number amounted to 2,778,304. There is another table, also taken from the official records, showing the whole number of men enrolled—present and absent—in the active armies of the Confederacy on each 1st of January:

Jan'y 1, 1862	Jan'y 1, 1863	Jan'y 1, 1864	Jan'y 1, 1865
318,011	465,584	472,781	439,675

The writer of the "Notes" adds:

"Very few, if any, of the local land forces, and none of the naval, are included in the tabular exhibit. If we take the 472,000 men in service at the beginning of 1864 and add thereto at least 250,000 deaths occurring prior to that date, it gives over 700,000. The discharges for disability and other causes and the desertions would probably increase the number (inclusive of the militia and naval forces) to over

Now, every one knows that the Confederate armies were much smaller in 1864 than in 1862 or 1863, and in 1865 they were smaller still. Hence it is evident that the absent list included sick, disabled, prisoners of war, and deserters. Every soldier knows that in an active campaign the absent from proper causes soon number a large proportion of the force enrolled, and that in garrison duty there is always a large proportion of sick. On page 290, Volume VII., Southern Historical Society Papers, Adjutant-General Cooper, of the Confederate army, says: "I can only state from general recollection that during the two last years of the war, the monthly returns of our armies received at my office exhibited the present active force in the field nearly one-half less than the returns themselves actually called for, on account of absentees by sickness, extra duty, furlough, desertions, and other casualties incident to a campaign life."

Of the 439,675 *present and absent* on the first of January, 1865, the Army of Northern Virginia is credited with 155,000 and the Army of Tennessee with 86,995. Now it is a well-known fact that at that very time the Army of Northern Virginia had less than 60,000 effectives for the field and the Army of Tennessee could not have mustered 20,000 effectives. At this rate the total available force of the Confederacy at that time must have been less than 150,000 men. Now the official records show conclusively that the Confederacy never at any time had 690,000 men, enrolled present and absent; 472,000 present and absent is the largest number enrolled at any time, and that, too, on the 1st of January, 1864, when everybody acquainted with the facts knows that the Confederate armies were smaller than in either of the previous years. The writer of Notes on the Union and Confederate Armies, as we have seen, estimates that, inclusive of the militia and naval forces, there were enlisted in the Confederate armies from first to last more than a million men. When we consider that the militia consisted of old men, boys, and disabled soldiers who had already been once enrolled, 100,000 would be a liberal estimate for the militia and naval forces of the Confederate States, which would bring the total number of enlistments considerably below a million. But suppose we concede the correctness of the estimate of the writer of the Notes. Then, if 2,700,000 enlistments in the Union armies give as the largest force under arms at any one time only one million men, surely 1,000,000 total enlistments in the Confederate armies ought to give as the largest force under arms at any one time only a little over 370,000 men, inclusive of militia and naval forces.

We also think that Colonel Dodge's list of battles contains several mistakes. At Fort Donelson the Confederates did not have over 15,000. Grant brought against them about 27,000, of whom, he claims, 6,000 or 7,000 were guarding trains.

At Cedar Mountain, Virginia, Banks had on the field from first to last 17,900 men instead of 7,500, and he was driven entirely from the field. Jackson, who had 20,000 men with him, held the field and buried the dead, and on the second day after the battle retired behind the Rapidan to wait the arrival of Lee. At Perryville, Kentucky, Buell had, according to the official records, 54,000 men, about half of whom were actually engaged, and Bragg 16,000. Each side claimed the victory, but Bragg's loss was only three-fourths that of Buell. At Murfreesboro', or Stone's River, Tennessee, according to the official records Rosecrans had 43,000 men, while Bragg had 37,000 instead of 47,000. At Antietam, or Sharpsburg, according to McClellan's report the Union army numbered 87,000, and about 60,000 took part in the actual fighting. According to Lee's report the Confederate army numbered less than 40,000. If Malvern Hill, from which the Union army retired at night without waiting for the renewal of the Confederate attack, was a Union victory, then most assuredly Antietam, where Lee repulsed nearly twice his numbers and offered battle all the next day without being attacked, was a Confederate victory.

Colonel Dodge also makes the following statement: "As regards brilliant assaults upon regular works, the Confederates were never called on to show such devotion as was manifested by the Federals at Fredericksburg, the several assaults at Vicksburg and Port Hudson, Spotsylvania, Cold Harbor, and Petersburg."

How about the persistent and successful assaults of the Confederates upon McClellan's fortified lines at Richmond, their successful attack upon Hooker's entrenched lines at Chancellorsville, their attack upon a force equal to their own behind strong field-works at Corinth, their brilliant but hopeless assault at Knoxville, and their brilliant and almost successful assault upon superior forces strongly posted at Gettysburg?

The aim of this article is merely to get at the facts

of history. The Union and Confederate soldiers made each a noble record of heroic deeds, of which all Americans may well be proud.

Joseph T. Derry,

Formerly of the 1st and 63d Georgia Regiments.

COLONEL DODGE'S REJOINDER.

I did not suppose that my article would provoke controversy; I awaited criticism. Mr. Derry has stated his objections fairly. They are hard to answer, because, whether he is right or wrong, my conclusion remains unimpeached. What I sought to show was that, after all is said, the business of suppressing the insurrection of the South was fairly well done by the United States, compared with the military work of other times and countries; and that, taking the actual fighting done, there was not much to choose between Yankee and Southron. Suppose the table of forces under arms to be corrected to conform to that in Vol. IV. of the "Battles and Leaders of the Civil War," it will not change the conclusion that, "compared, then, with what other nations have accomplished, it may be claimed that the statistics of our war abundantly demonstrate that the North did the business of suppressing the Rebellion in a workmanlike and respectable, not to say handsome, manner, leaving, under the circumstances, no great room for adverse criticism." Suppose each emendation Mr. Derry makes to the list of battles to be allowed, it will not alter the percentages so as to invalidate the conclusion "that first, the Confederates opposed to the Federals fully equal numbers at the point of fighting contact; and second, that of the combats during the entire struggle the Federals had their full share of victories." If we should allow that statistics exhibit an excess at the point of fighting contact of ten per cent. on the side of the Federals, it does not seem to me that the conclusion would be altered one jot. What I wrote and my statistics tend to show *substantial equality*. In such a case, ten per cent. might be disregarded. We should call two armies of ten and eleven thousand, or fifty and fifty-five thousand men, respectively, substantially equal; and had my figures, when tabulated, shown an excess of ten per cent. in favor of the Federals, I should have considered the case proved, as I should if, out of fifty battles, either side had an excess of three or four.

My article was written in Florence early in 1887, without ready access to records or statistics. I think that Vol. IV. of "Battles and Leaders of the Civil War" was not then out. I had not seen the War Records table. It must of course be taken as accurate, and mine, made some years ago, as faulty. I could not now exhume the sources of the Southern items of my table. The Northern items are from the Provost-Marshal-General's accounts. My table was first published in 1883. The table referred to in Vol. IV. of "Battles and Leaders" does not include "local land forces" of the Confederacy. Taking these at ten per cent. of those at the front, "the South had under arms, until the last third of the war, an average of about three-fifths the force of the North," and not "about three-fourths," as stated in my article. Or, throwing out "local land forces" entirely, "the South had about fifty-five per cent. of the force of the North." While this error in my figures is not thereby excused, the argument is in no material degree weakened by the variation. By a fair allowance for garrison work which the North had to do and the South had not, the original statement of three-quarters would stand.

At the time of making my battle-estimate I corresponded with the War Records Office, asking it to make for me the figures of men at the point of fight-

'ing contact in the battles tabulated; but the Bureau was practically unable to do so without taking indefinite time and more pains than I could ask. No official records, that I am aware of, have been made of the men at the point of fighting contact. I made mine by taking the brigades and divisions known to have been engaged, and estimating their force as well as possible when it was not given by some good authority. The numbers were set roundly. My premise depends strictly on estimates of men *at the point of fighting contact*, and I think my estimates are very close. For instance, if Chancellorsville were taken as an example, we would have a total of one hundred and thirty thousand men pitted against about fifty-eight to sixty thousand. But the men who actually fought were, not to count the assault on Fredericksburg Heights:

May 2d, at Dowdall's,	22,000 Confederates	against	10,000	Federals.
" 3d, at Fairview,	37,000 "	"	32,000	"
" 3d, at Salem Church,	10,000 "	"	9,000	"
" 4h, at Banks's Ford,	25,000 "	"	20,000	"

This makes a very different showing. Every Northerner who fought at the front recognizes the brilliant gallantry of the South. Many of us carry ever-present mementos of their hard fighting. The higher the Southern capacity to fight, claimed or proved by statistics, the better the work done by the North in carrying the war through to a successful issue. I do not insist on every item of my figures being beyond dispute; but it still seems to me that "no reasonable or admissible variation will alter the conclusion which must be drawn from them."

Mr. Derry points out fairly the difference between the conditions of the contestants in our Revolution and in our Civil War. There can be no exact historical parallel found. To illustrate my point, the one I chose remains good, especially as Anglo-Saxons were concerned in both wars.

Is not Mr. Derry inaccurate in what he says of Peter III. and Frederick? The Russian alliance with Frederick was terminated by Peter's death some four months after it was made. The help was timely and useful, but it was neither that which saved Frederick, nor the withdrawal of Sweden from among his enemies. The work of Ferdinand of Brunswick, while excellent, was of negative value in the campaigns of Frederick. Mr. Derry is right in saying that neither the Revolution nor the Seven Years' War is a close parallel; but each is illustratively good.

Mr. Derry's rule-of-three estimate of forces is ingenious, but I doubt if it will work in practice. Very slight difference in the methods of organization or of raising troops North and South would throw out this calculation.

While it is "impossible to argue the question to a satisfactory conclusion on theriories and opinions," and while I owe an apology to the readers of the Century for not correcting my table of forces up to date, the primary value of the statistics is to prove or disprove "either to be the better soldier." *Quoad hoc*, I do not see wherein the figures given have been falsified, nor do I think the premises capable of alteration so as to draw any other than my conclusion.

I thank Mr. Derry for his frank and kindly criticism.

Theodore Ayrault Dodge.

VON MOLTKE
AND FUTURE WARFARE.

VON MOLTKE AND FUTURE WARFARE.*

WAR is wont to be associated with the physical rather than the intellectual or moral qualities. The idea of youth and strength and ardor is coupled with the military profession. Alexander at the Granicus, Scipio at Zama, Napoleon in '96, McClellan in '62, represent to the popular fancy the typical soldier. But war, from the standpoint of the captain, is primarily an intellectual process. The successful conduct of a campaign requires, first, exceptional mental powers; next, moral qualities of high order; and, last, a physique to withstand the drain of unremitting mental and nervous tension. The gladiatorial courage which prompted the little Roman legionary to close in on the burly Teuton with the sword, or the prize-fighting pluck which carried the Guards through the day at

* Published in The Forum, June, 1891.

Waterloo, are not as essential to the captain as the moral force which on the broad strategic field helps him to push his own scheme home despite the threatening manœuvres of his opponent, which on the narrower field of battle enables him to risk the lives of thousands of his men upon the result of a calculation, or to watch with equipoise the compromising movements of his adversary, or to hold back his battalions for the supreme moment; are not as essential as that self-reliance which prompts him to great undertakings and sustains him through their performance.

Though there have been notable examples of great achievement by men under middle age, they are rather the exception than the rule. The most brilliant work is not usually done early in life. Alexander destroyed the Persian Empire at twenty-six; but Hannibal was in the forties when he held head against Fabius, Marcellus, and Nero; Cæsar was in the fifties when he defeated Pompey and his lieutenants; and Frederick was of equal age at the close of the Seven Years' War. Intellectual activity in peace is sometimes exhibited at an age which saps the physical powers to the core. But this is not the power called for by the kaleidoscopic changes of the drama of war. While the greatest military feats have as a rule been performed in middle life, it is rare that strength—mental, moral, and physical—is preserved to the biblical limit of years; and in military annals there is perhaps no one who has shown the ability to handle vast problems, to conceive and execute perplexing operations, to so great an age as the distinguished German captain who has recently passed from among us.

Helmuth Karl Bernhard von Moltke was born in the first year of the century which was to make Prussia a great power and to erect upon a sound pedestal the structure of the German Empire.   His father had been in the Prussian army, but when the pride of Frederick's kingdom was humbled at Jena, he had entered the service of Denmark. Helmuth's youth was one of poverty. Without the assistance of the government he could not have accomplished his studies at the Copenhagen Military Academy, and his genius might have been lost to arms. At the age of twenty-two von Moltke entered the service of Prussia, and ten years later he was assigned to the general staff with rank of first lieutenant. Here he remained, affording the spectacle, natural enough to the student of war but strange to him who associates war only with the clash of arms, of a man who never commanded troops, was never in a great battle until past sixty, who devoted himself solely to the administrative part of the profession, and yet who became one of the greatest strategists of modern times, and is perhaps the father of the coming system of war. From 1835 to 1839 von Moltke was given leave to serve in Turkey, where the army was being reorganized on a Prussian basis. During this period he exhibited great engineering and administrative talent and wrote a volume on Oriental matters which is still an authority.

For many years succeeding the desolation of the Napoleonic wars, the nations of Europe lay fallow to recuperate from the drain to which, for either attack or defense, the great Corsican had put the entire civilized world. During all this time, which covered the period·of Moltke's life from early manhood well into middle age, the Prussian staff officer was unremitting in his labors. He had become an adept in all the details of his profession, had assimilated the lessons of history, had utilized in arms the modern talent for invention, had mastered the language of every country of Europe and learned its capacity for war; and though at forty-two he was only a major of the general staff, he was known as one of the most accomplished men of the Prussian service. Still no one gave him credit for the wonderful resources that he was to be called on to display at a period of life when in our army an officer has long been retired for age.

In 1845 von Moltke had the opportunity of going to Italy on the staff of Prince Henry, who resided in Rome for several years, but on the death of the prince he returned to his former duties. In 1858 his abilities finally earned him the position he had honestly won. He was made chief of the grand general staff, and a year later he was promoted to be lieutenant-general. What he has done as such is the history of the man, of Prussia, and of Germany.

Field Marshall von Moltke was of slender build and appeared taller than he really was. Unlike the heavily-muscled Teuton, he more nearly resembled an American Anglo-Saxon—spare, but active and alert and of great endurance. His habits were simple, his dress was plain, his manners were quiet and reserved. He was "silent in seven languages." Nothing could excite him or throw him off his equipoise. Of the numerous decorations conferred upon him, he habitually wore only the Iron Cross. His habits were methodical, and he was able to apply himself continuously for a great number of hours. No man was ever more familiar with every detail of the service than he. His one work in life was to make the Prussian army perfect as a fighting machine, and every study, all accumulated knowledge, tended to this end. He was married in 1843, and his happiness centered in his home life until his wife died in 1868. He then sought labor as a relief from sorrow, and the result of his retirement was shown in the mobilization of 1870.

Moltke was the legitimate successor of Scharnhorst and Gneisenau. The astonishing victories of Frederick and the efficient army he left behind him were mainly due to the genius of this "Last of the Kings." The splendid army inherited from his father had been ground into powder during the Seven Years' War. What he left was not a Prussian army, but an aggregation of all nationalities organized and disciplined to an exceptional state of effectiveness. When the lamp of Frederick's genius went out, the army was left in darkness, and it was speedily disintegrated. Half a generation later the national movement of France gave the world the keynote of the modern system of war; Bonaparte appeared and carried it forward to perfection, and at Jena showed the world that Frederick's army without Frederick, albeit governed by his rules, was powerless against the mighty blows of a new genius backed by a people in arms. After repeated disasters, the Treaty of Tilsit limited the army of Prussia to 42,000 men. But the bitter lesson proved of use. The great minister, Stein, began to evolve financial order from the wreck, and Scharnhorst conceived the system by which each recruit entered service for a short instead of a long enlistment, and, once made a soldier, was sent back to the plow or the counter, ready in case of need. The patriotism and homogeneity of the Prussian people, stung to the quick by humiliating defeats, admirably seconded this plan, and such men as Gneisenau and Clausewitz carried forward the work. In six years a complete transformation had been effected, and the Prussian armies, which in 1813–15 contributed to the overthrow of Napoleon, were national to the pith. Thenceforward the organization of the Prussian army ripened. Compulsory personal service of three years with the colors and further terms with the reserve and *landwehr* became and remained the law. To this day there has been no cessation of army discipline, and the campaigns of 1866 and 1870

A genius in war can do much with raw recruits. Hannibal quickly moulded new levies into the form of seasoned troops. Napoleon, with a rabble under lax discipline, by crisp strategic combinations achieved astonishing results. But the best general is handicapped with an army unfit to second him. Perfect appointments, organization, and discipline under the colors are more essential than ability in the commander. Better a perfect army with fair generals than an untrustworthy army led by a genius. You are sure of the one; not so of the other. The work of the Prussian general staff was based on this fact. The kings of Prussia have always kept the best of talent in high places. The four corner pillars of the Prussian structure which made one Germany possible were Kaiser Wilhelm, Otto von Bismark, Theodor von Roon, and Helmuth von Moltke. All bent their energies toward the same end—to produce perfect tools with which to do the work which European jealousies were cutting out.

The unquestioned strategic ability of von Moltke was thus supplemented by the peerless army at his disposal. The Prussian officer has been the hardest-working man in his profession. He has drilled his men himself. He has become familiar with handling his command under all conditions apt to occur in actual war. Its personnel, armament, health, and efficiency are matters of every-day concern. There is a constant interchange between line and staff duty, so that the directing becomes associated with the fighting element. He has been prepared by constant study, lectures, manœuvres, and the application of theory to practice. In the field, every superior and staff officer, squadron and battery commander has special maps of the country he has to operate in. His independence has been fostered to the fullest extent, and his judgment is relied on to take advantage of every changing phase. The enlisted man is equally strong, and perhaps no army has ever placed in line so large a proportion of those "present for duty" as the Prussian. Details on extra or special duty are not permitted, and it is known with certainty how many men will appear in the fighting ranks of a regiment.

Under the watchful eye of von Moltke all the elements bearing on army efficiency were elaborated. The railroads and telegraph lines were public servants first, commercial ventures next. The artillery was thoroughly equipped. Every horse in the country was listed and liable to be taken for military duty; every man was subjected to some service and knew his place when called on. The infantry weapons were not only better than the enemy's, but there were plenty on hand. Without having to claim that the Prussian was a better man than the Austrian or the Frenchman, it may distinctly be claimed that he was a better soldier, if arms, equipment, drill, discipline, readiness, and an unusual sense of patriotism are considered as well as physique. When war came, Moltke could report the number of men, horses and guns which could be massed on any given point at a given moment, and could control the means of putting them there.

Such was the condition of the Prussian army in 1866. Von Moltke had borne his part in the preparation, and he was called on to direct the manœuvres of the Prussian columns. While he always deferred to the king, he was actually an autocrat. Let us see how he did his work.

The active army of Prussia was 335,000 strong. This could be increased to a war footing of 600,000. That of Austria was 384,000 men, capable of being raised to 700,000. In two weeks the Prussian mobilization was completed and the troops were on the frontier; the Austrian had begun much earlier, but the war was decided before the mobilization was as complete. The Prussian soldier was well educated, personally and as a soldier; the Austrian was ignorant and but half trained. The Prussian infantry carried the needle gun, and the batteries were mostly of breech loaders; the Austrian foot soldier was armed with the muzzle loader; the batteries were of the old pattern. Despite this the Austrian army was a splendid body.

The problem before Moltke was awkward. Prussia was not a compact territory. Westphalia and the Rhenish Provinces were separated from the rest of the kingdom by Hanover and Hesse-Cassel, allied to Austria. If Prussia advanced into Austrian territory, her rear was subject to attack. Saxony, likewise allied to Austria, was a salient thrust into the Prussian dominions from which the enemy could debouch at will on Berlin or Breslau. The plan of Moltke was comprehensive and simple—to neutralize Hanover and Hesse-Cassel, and then to throw the entire body of Prussian troops on the Austrian army in its own territory.

The main Prussian army of about 225,000 men was in three grand columns. The army of the Elbe, under General von Bittenfeld, was massed at Torgau, covering Berlin. The First Army, under Prince Friedrich Karl, took post at Görlitz. The Second Army, under the Crown Prince, stood at Neisse, covering Breslau. The flank armies were over 150 miles apart, but the central one was designed to sustain either. Sufficient forces remained at home, and Generals von Manteuffel and von Falkenstein, from Altona and Minden respectively, threatened Hanover with a division each; while General von Beyer with a division stood at Wetzlau ready to invade Hesse-Cassel.

Confronting these armies stood the main Austrian line, about 240,000 strong, massed near Prag, Brünn, and Olmütz, ready to concentrate at any point selected. Saxony had 25,000 men, Bavaria 50,000, and at Frankfurt stood a mixed force 40,000 strong. Hanover and Hesse-Cassel had each mobilized its army, some 25,000 effectives, and stood on the defensive, ready to fall on the rear of the Prussian armies if the opportunity offered. Italy, allied to Prussia, called away some Austrian forces, but their operations do not concern us.

Napoleon's favorite plan of attack was to move upon his enemy in one mass on one line, so that when brought to battle he might outnumber him, and from such a direction that he might compromise him. The campaigns of Ulm and Jena illustrate this method. It is unquestionably the soundest theory, but there are circumstances which render the plan unavailable. In the present case uncertainty of where the Austrian blow might fall, the necessity of protecting Silesia on the east and Westphalia and Rhineland on the west, as well as the impossibility of moving so many army corps on one line over the roads then existing, forbade an operation in one mass and justified the division of forces. Moltke knew and relied on his superior speed, as well as his better armament, and felt that whatever the manœuvres, he could concentrate before the great battle which is the outcome of all strategic combinations should take place.

The Austrian general, Field Marshal von Benedek, an able and distinguished officer, had expected to gain the initiative and invade Prussia. He confessed himself no strategist, but felt confident of his powers on the battlefield. He utterly misjudged his adversary. He held cheap the bureau-working, silent, studious Prussian chief of staff. But bureau work had prepared the way for operations far too rapid for von Benedek. The speed of the Prussians was Napoleonic. War was declared June 15. The Prussian columns advanced like an avalanche. In two weeks Hanover was brought to the verge of ruin, her king was dethroned, and her army surrendered. Hesse-Cassel met a like fate, and the elector was taken prisoner. The rear of Prussia was free; her communications with Westphalia and Rhineland were open. At the same moment Saxony had been invaded by the army of the Elbe and the First Army. In three days Dresden was taken, the King fled, and before the end of the month of June, all Saxony was in Prussian control. A fortnight had sufficed to settle the minor problems of the war, to cut off Bavaria and the Frankfurt forces, and to put Prussia in possession of the salient of Saxony which had been so marked an advantage to her antagonist. The army of the Elbe and the First Army were now joined, under command of Prince Friedrich Karl.

We have here a manifestation of the basis of Moltke's success—preparation, precision. For years the quiet man had bent every energy to detail. He had devoted no time to show work; he cared naught for the outward parade of efficiency. He had made sure that what the army was on paper it was in effect; that every man and officer was ready, and knew his place and duty; that mobilization should mean actual assem-

bly. Every uncertain element was eliminated. So far
as lay within human power, the war had been reduced
to a mathematical calculation, However sound his
strategy, it was of less importance than readiness; however able his opponent, the initiative gained by the
promptness of Prussia had placed him at a disadvant-
age. Moltke had won the first innings; the war was
to be waged on the enemy's soil; the *morale* of the
Prussians was high.

But the greater problem was far from solved. The
Crown Prince was separated by over 120 miles from
Prince Friedrich Karl. This position had been a polit-
ico-military necessity; but apart the two bodies were
in peril. How could they act in unison? If Benedek
should only be delayed in his advance for a few days
more, all would be well. Great captains always gauge
their adversaries and adapt themselves to their probable action. Moltke knew he could move the faster,
and relied on Benedek's natural and constrained slowness.

Prince Friedrich Karl was promptly advanced into
Bohemia, and the Crown Prince was ordered from
Silesia toward Gitschin, where the armies were to join.
The battlefield was manifestly to be on Bohemian soil.

To meet the Prussian lunge, Benedek slowly concentrated in the vicinity of the left bank of the Elbe, south-east from Königgrätz. He was thunderstruck at the turn affairs had taken. But he was a typical fighter and welcomed the approaching battle, for the result of which he had no fears. The two Prussian armies were still dangerously far apart. There was a chance for a Napoleon to interpose between them and beat them in detail; a Benedek could not do so. Moltke's idea on this subject was that Benedek had neither space nor speed enough to essay this bold game; that if he did so and attacked either army, the other would be able, by superior alertness, to take him in flank and rear.

A glance at the map of Bohemia will show that it is surrounded on north, west, and east by bold and rugged mountain chains. These were a difficulty to the Prussians and an advantage. Should they be defeated in the approaching battle, they had an excellent line of defense to fall back on, still on the enemy's territory. But meanwhile the Riesengebirge lay between their sundered armies.

The Crown Prince had before him a serious operation in crossing the mountains in the presence of Benedek's threatening and much larger force, but he did so successfully. To facilitate the operation, Prince Friedrich Karl was ordered to attack the Austrian left. There were isolated exchanges, almost rising to the dignity of general engagements, in which each side won some advantage, but Moltke's strategic plan was gradually nearing completion—the Prussian armies were fast approaching. Meanwhile von Benedek was pluming himself on his interior position and planning to hold back one Prussian army while he annihilated the other. He was far too slow. The Prussian heels were of more avail than their needle guns. Benedek had two chances. He could with a small force intrench the mountain passes against the Crown Prince, as the lessons of our civil war plainly taught him to do, and delay the latter's advance, while with the bulk of his force he fell upon Prince Friedrich Karl. Or he might demonstrate against the latter and destroy the Crown Prince as he slowly debouched from the mountains. But Moltke was fortunate in his enemies, as many a great captain has been; Benedek delayed his action.

The armies came into each other's presence at Königgrätz July 3. The Austrians had on the field 206,-000 men and 770 guns. Prince Friedrich Karl had

124,000 men and 444 guns. The Crown Prince had 96,-
000 men and 348 guns, but he was not yet in touch.
Could he come up? Two days sooner the Austrians
might have had things their own way. Lest Benedek
should detach sufficient force to hold head against the
Crown Prince, Prince Friedrich Karl was ordered to
force the fighting on the Austrian left, which he did
with a will, but was able to make no impression. He
was, in fact, roughly handled. But the stubborn work
relieved the pressure on the Crown Prince. Like
Blücher at Waterloo, the Crown Prince at the last
moment came in on the Austrian right flank, the
Austrians were defeated, and Moltke's strategy was
made perfect by success.

A notable difference between the rival generals and
their armies is shown in the orders and dispatches.
Moltke gave broad directions in few words, and left
specific action to the judgment of his well-trained
generals. Benedek arrogated all power to himself; he
relied solely on his own knowledge and judgment; he
gave no discretion to his lieutenants.

Königgrätz decided this war. The success of the
campaign of 1870 was predicated on the same element
of preparation. The triumph of 1866 was far from

relaxing Prussian watchfulness. It was not only kept up to the mark, but advanced in effectiveness. How the French could have supposed, as they did, that they were to have a walk-over, it is hard to imagine. When, in 1870, Napoleon declared war, the Prussian mobilization was effected in twelve days, and a deluge swept over France. The events of this war are too fresh in all minds to need recapitulation. It was perfect preparation rather than superior generalship which decided the struggle.

That von Moltke struck the keynote of the warfare of the future is probable. Careful preparation has always been a characteristic of great captains. We are apt to think that genius overrides the precautions of every day, but the history of war proves that success is bred of forethought. Genius is more than the capacity for unlimited hard work, but the hard work is indispensable. Alexander inherited a matchless phalanx from Philip, but his scrupulous care of it and his just weighing of every factor was what made his handful victorious over hordes. Hannibal exhibited greater patience and skill in working up his plans than any other captain. Cæsar was sometimes careless, but good fortune saved him from himself, and for most of his campaigns he laboriously made ready. Gustavus Adolphus was the first of modern times to show method in preparation for war and to overlook no condition. Frederick, like Alexander, inherited an army, but he kept it up to the mark by incessant work. From him comes a distinct part of Moltke's inspiration. Napoleon's extensive preparations were as marked as his strategy was bold and original. The German chief of staff enunciated no new doctrine. But has carried out his system with more fidelity and brains than any other man of the century.

The French Revolution put a national army afoot, and the mercenaries of the last century disappeared. The Prussian army is more national still. It is the very marrow of the people that forms the rank and file. *"Für Gott, König und Vaterland!"* is no vain battle-cry. The Prussian soldier is truly patriotic, and everything is done to foster the sentiment. His uniform is an honor, not a badge of servitude. However poor the officer, he is a very Lucifer for pride. Nor is this mere vanity. He knows, and he is encouraged to feel, that his is the most honorable of professions so long as he works earnestly and honorably at it; that he belongs to the most splendid army of

modern days, and that in the army lies the true safety
of the country. This is an inheritance from Friedrich
der Einzige, and it does not slacken. Moltke's rule
was work, pride in the profession, patriotism; he
ground this into the very souls of the Prussians.
Germany has followed suit.

Such is the basis. The superstructure consists of
making everything—modern invention, railroads, telegraph, private and public enterprises—subsidiary to
the needs of the country. This has been done with a
resolute intelligence never before equaled. Whether
the efficiency of the German staff will suffer from the
death of von Moltke cannot be said, but on it rests the
the integrity of the Teutonic Empire.

Perhaps the art of war has never been so enigmatical as it now is. It is the x of the problem of nations.
Among the Greeks war was a simple affair. The
phalanxes of Athens and Sparta marched out to battle,
and by a sort of consensus a plain was selected
where the two bodies fought, much as two champions
would fight a duel, and the victor dictated terms.
Epaminondas with his Theban phalanx beat the Spar-
tans by a keen eye for tactics. Philip beat the Thebans
with the Macedonian *sarissa*. Alexander, by an aston-

ishing power of gauging his work, and unequaled strategic and tactical originality, headed Philip's army and
conquered the world. The Roman legion worsted the
phalanx; or rather the Roman citizen, organized into
a national legion much as the Prussian is to-day, beat
the phalanx of mercenaries to which Greece had degenerated. The armies of Cæsar and Pompey were alike,
save in reflecting the spirit of their leaders. After
their day the art of war languished, to be revived by
Gustavus. Upon him followed Frederick, who taught
Europe how speed and resolution can enhance small
numbers. And then, in some respects greatest of all,
Napoleon taught the world the modern system. Dur-
all these eras war possessed a certain stability which
only some great cataclysm, like the invention of gunpowder, could interrupt. The personal element weighed
for much, as it always must. But a given result could
with reasonable accuracy be predicted from given conditions. This is no longer so. War is the most inex-
act of sciences.

Naval warfare stands over a volcano. The race
between ordnance casting heavy projectiles at fabulous
velocities, and armor-plated ships, has resulted in the
building of unseaworthy floating fortresses, armed with

guns which work their own ruin when fired, and defended by such weight of metal that, though theoreti-
cally flotative, they scarcely dare cross the ocean;
indeed, cannot coal for so long a journey. A noted
eccentric of the day once said that he preferred absence
of body to presence of mind. It may be said that the
light-armed cruiser with two or three efficient guns,
which can steam more than twenty knots and get out
of the way of danger—that is, can manoeuvre to advantage—is worth more than the first-rate iron-clad.
The future naval battle will yield vast surprises and
will result in enormous loss of life. The iron-clad
which floats at the end of the next stubborn sea fight
will be a paragon. On land matters are not quite so
unpromising, but, owing to the fertility of invention,
they are quite as perplexing. Arms of precision upset
the calculations of the best tacticians; smokeless powder threatens to cripple all calculation. Preparation
will remain the sheet-anchor of nations, but no soldier
can tell what the next invention applicable to war may
be or how it can be met; and the armament or drill of
a million men cannot be changed or amended in a day.
Money alone will not do it. To make ready for a
campaign has always been one of the most complex

of problems; the difficulties are to-day increased many fold.

No inventions, no changes in arms, can alter the maxims of strategy. These are immutable. Their use depends on the character of the captains. But tactics change with inventions in firearms. The manœuvres of the battlefield must depend upon the weapons of the enemy, upon the danger zones of his fire. From close order we have gone to open order, only to find that scattered groups are apt to weaken discipline; and to-day more than ever before we need *morale* and cohesiveness on the battlefield. That commander who, despite the fearful decimation of modern artillery and small arms, can keep his battalions the longest in heart, will win the day. The Old Dessauer's "*Wenn Du gehst nicht zurück, so geht der Feind zurück!*" still holds good. It is tactics reduced to its lowest terms. Many intelligent essays are published to prove this or the other system to be the one to govern the manœuvres of the coming battlefield, but in truth no one knows or can argue out what is to be. A theory sound to-day is discarded to-morrow. But a few facts are patent. Reliance can be placed only on a strictly national army. That nation the breasts of whose citizens are bared for her defense with honest patriotism, and which has leaders who leave no stone unturned to keep abreast of the progress of war, will remain the strongest. No nation, in the present condition of armed expectancy which pervades Europe, will, by better arms or more recent inventions, be able to dispense with this foundation. The rule held good in the days of the burgess-soldier of Rome; it holds good now.

The losses in the next war will probably not be an increase over the losses of previous ones. Campaigns will be of weeks, not months, and sickness will not add its terrors to wounds and death. The proportion of men who perish will decrease; but there will be enormous losses in some commands. As at sea, where iron-clads will go to the bottom with all on board, so on land, battalions, brigades will be annihilated by the increased efficiency of the enemy's arms. But on the whole the loss of life will be lessened.

There is scarcely any theory of warfare in the future which may not be argued out from the peculiar existing conditions. But it is a sphinx riddle which has not yet been guessed. The work done by von Moltke is typical of what the needs of the future must be; the man himself is the type of the soldier of the future.

The swashbuckler has gone for good, driven out by modern invention, as that ancient bully, the knight in armor, was driven out by gunpowder. In his place has come the intellectual, hard-working student of war. If the life of the great Prussian soldier teaches anything, it teaches us that war is no longer the province of the rough, but is the theatre for intellect, moral courage, and honest patience. The lower forms of courage have ceased to have their old-time value. It is brain tissue and *morale* which will win in future wars.

THE NEEDS OF OUR ARMY
AND NAVY.

THE NEEDS OF OUR ARMY AND NAVY.* †

WE Americans are not a military people. In view of our having carved our way into the wilderness with sword as well as with axe, of our having won our independence by arms, of our having come with abundant credit out of all our wars, of having carried through one of the most gigantic struggles of modern days, in which were fought battles almost unequalled in tenacity, this may appear to be an unwarranted statement. But it is true. It requires more than courage, more than ability to raise, to equip, to ration, to move, and to command armies, to make a

* The matter herein summarized is constantly discussed by military men, and has been the subject of many reports to Congress and the heads of Departments. It has been canvassed with special authority in the "Journal of the Military Service Institution" and in the "Proceedings of the United States Naval Institute," to which the reader is referred for detailed treatment.

† Published in The Forum, October, 1891.

military people. The most splendid conduct in war for an all-absorbing cause does not suffice. Having many of the essential qualities, we yet fall short of what the Romans were, the Germans are. Some sections of the country approach nearer to the military standard; but, taken as a whole, our lack of interest in army and navy, our thoroughly unbusiness-like way of handling our national problems of attack and defence, stamp us as the least military in our instincts of all the great peoples of the earth.

No nation so jealous of a standing army can claim to be a military people. Were it not a matter to bewail, it would be a fit subject for laughter, to see 60,000,000 self-reliant Americans looking askance at an army of 25,000 men as a possible menace to republican institutions—one blue-coat in every 144 square miles of our territory! And yet, after the cry of economy, this is not only the reason most commonly urged on the floor of Congress for its scant support of the army, but it is the feeling of the bulk of the population. A military people takes pride in its national defenders; it recognizes that it is the statesman who makes war, the soldier who secures peace; its uniform is an honor. With us the professional soldier is unconsidered and the enlisted man wears his army blue as if it were a badge of ostracism. The fact that our militia has its annual encampment with unstinted fuss and feathers is referable more to holiday skylarking than to any love of its military significance. If the encampment entailed sacrifices, it would soon be voted obnoxious.

We Americans are the most extravagant of economists. Statistics demonstrate that annual appropriations during the past hundred years for an army and a navy commensurate with our national standing and needs would have been twice saved in forstalling wars, shortening their duration, and preventing the destruction of incalculable amounts of private property. Indeed, the actual sums paid out for sudden and therefore costly levies in times of danger, not to count the losses incident to insufficient preparation, would have kept up a respectable force on land and sea, and have made a frequent saving in national disgrace. Despite the fact that when we put our hands to the plough we do not look back, our military history is one of blunders. Perhaps this is inseperable from our being "a nation of debaters." In time of peace we have never prepared for war. A war once ended, its lessons have been forgotten, and with true American assurance we have again turned to reliance on our isolated position and superabundant resources. To our population of arms-bearing men, unequalled in adaptiveness, we have given no opportunity to learn the duty to which, under the law, every American is liable. We educate our people compulsorily; but we do not so train them to arms. We have been wont to rely on crude militia, and have suffered the usual penalty.

The experience gained in the Revolutionary War was not lasting. Economy was a paramount reason for cutting down the military establishment; but not to speak of the wasteful method of its increase in 1798 on the threat of a war with France, and the peace we bought with Algiers, the parsimony of Jefferson and of Madison found us ready in 1812 to plunge into another war with England, with an army of 10,000 men (half of them raw recruits) and 17 vessels. The regulars were speedily increased by 25,000, but both the officers and the men were new and inefficient. All told, during the War of 1812, a quarter of a million of men were mustered into service, and yet such was the management that there were but three battles in which 5,000 Americans fought. The appointment of political generals and the conduct of the militia, some of which refused to serve out of its own State, brought about humiliations such as the surrender of Hull and the burning of the capital of a nation of 8,000,000 people by a force of 4,000 invaders. That militia did such good service at New Orleans was due to the Western riflemen in the ranks, the influence of a strong commander, and the excellence of the defensive position. The regulars, and the volunteers who were assimilated to them, uniformly fought well when once inured to discipline; and the conduct of our navy and privateers redeemed the struggle. The economies of Jefferson had reduced the national debt in ten years by $40,000,000; but the war cost $100,000,000 and 30,000 lives, not to mention the immense destruction of property. Had the money thus wasted been spent in a judicious fostering of army and navy, not only might the War of 1812 have been short and successful, but the national reputation would have been untarnished. That England had her hands full with the Napoleonic wars explains our escape from a more protracted struggle. Because American intelligence, enterprise, and gallantry saved us from disaster then, it will not do to rely upon it now.

After the War of 1812, the army and navy were for

some years kept on a higher level, and it seemed as if the army, instead of being a mere national police force, was really to be placed where it could play its proper *rôle* as a nucleus for a suitable reserve; but in 1821 both arms of the service were again cut down, and in 1835 the threatened war with France found us unprepared. The $20,000,000 spent on the Seminole War would have been more wisely disbursed in forestalling its outbreak by a suitable military force.

The Mexican War next surprised us without army and navy worthy the name. But though the regulars were promptly increased to 27,000, and 75,000 volunteers were raised, the war resulted in our favor mainly because we had a weak enemy. If Scott had been faced by good troops, would he have entered the city of Mexico with 11,000 men? His pluck and skill wrested success from the most desperate of ventures. Ability and heroism stood in inverse ratio to national management.

The usual reduction followed the Mexican War; and in 1861 the most terrible war of modern times burst upon us with an army of 14,000 regulars and a navy of 90 vessels, of which 42 were in commission. Except that the South had to create its military resources, and that the North rose as one man for the preservation of the Union, the result might have been even more costly. It demands small arithmetic to cipher out the difference in the cost of suppressing the Rebellion, if there had been a regular army, or reserves of respectable size, to put into the field at the outset, and a regular navy capable of commanding the Southern ports.

We are supposed to be a peaceful nation, but we have had our fair share of strife, foreign and domestic. Since the Revolution there have been wars with England and with Mexico, with Tripoli and with Algiers; broils with Paraguay and Corea, and a gigantic civil war; rumors of wars with France, England, Spain, and Italy. There have been the John Brown raid, the Barnburner and Fenian raids to Canada, many incursions across the Mexican border, and the filibustering expeditions to Cuba and Nicaragua. We have had the Whiskey and Shays rebellions, the election, draft, railroad, reconstruction, and sundry serious city riots; we have had well on to two hundred deadly Indian fights and many awful massacres. We have lost more men in active war since 1776 than any nation of Europe. This is a startling record for a peaceful people.

History demonstrates that the ocean is no preventive of imbroglios with foreign nations. It is scarcely probable that our national spirit of antagonism will decrease: it is bred in the bone. That we are not likely to be led into foreign complications is true; that we may be so has been recently shown by the New Orleans episode. The Monroe doctrine is capable of volcanic action, and there are many inflammable subjects on which we have no national patience. That no enemy could hold himself in the long run on American soil is indisputable; but can we afford to face the initial damage which a better prepared opponent could inflict upon us?

What is this damage? How can it be avoided? Is it cheaper to avoid it, or to take the risk of its occurring and keep our money for political log-rolling? We have got along so far without army or navy, it is said, and pretty well. Granted, but at high cost. Are we ready to pay in increased proportion in the future?

The probability of attack is remote—very remote. This is not the cry of an alarmist; it is an assembling of patent facts from which every one may draw his own conclusions. No European nation can well afford a war at arm's-length with constant danger at its own threshold. Such a war might furnish an occasion for jealous neighbors to assert themselves. England, for instance, is not only unlikely to become involved in serious variance with the United States, but we have the Geneva arbitration as a precedent to avert war under almost any circumstances; her people rely upon us largely for food; and her manufacturers, whose best customers we are, would suffer disastrously in a war in which, in the end, England would unquestionably be the greater loser. War is high priced. In these days, when every shot from a big gun consumes $1,000, the prudent nation, before declaring war, sitteth down and counteth the cost thereof. Few nations can afford our American extravagances. But if our wealth is a security to us, in it also lurks a temptation to others. Improbable as war is, in times of national excitement reason is often shelved. The improbable is constantly happening. War may come.

That the danger of fire to his homestead is but one in several hundred does not prevent a prudent householder from insuring it. For the same reason, and for the further one that a well-prepared nation is rarely attacked, is it not the part of wisdom to insure our commerce and our coast cities? The sum to be spent, practically to insure what is now open to destruction in war, amounts to but a small premium on the property covered, payable once for all. One per cent of what is at risk will pay for its permanent insurance by suitable defences, and a small annual outlay will keep up the protection.

There is another method of insurance which may prove cheaper. In all foreign complications, and these are sure to come if war does not, let us put our pride in our pocket, and stand and deliver whenever the demand is made by a well-armed opponent. This peace-at-any-price system may work; but, apart from the question of its economy, does it suit our national character? Can we Americans live with our eagle hooded?

That our frontier is at present open to easy attack no one attempts to deny. The facts are public property; but few people know just what this means. Not one of our national seaports has the means to resist the approach of a modern battle-ship. We no longer live in the age when hastily constructed earthworks and a few mortars and field-batteries might defend a city against vessels held under fire by *chevaux-de-frise*, booms, or chains stretched across the mouth of its harbor; when a town might stand a bombardment of many days, and yet suffer slight damage; when it took six weeks or longer for a fleet to cross the Atlantic. Means of national defence are no longer to be improvised: they consume years to create. Time is of the essence. The modern monitor cannot be put afloat in ninety days. Money, however lavish the outlay, will not accomplish it, nor ability of the highest order compass it; the nation, raising *en masse* to resist aggression, is powerless without time. Money and ability and patriotism are essential; in every American emergency they have come to the fore. But time cannot be cajoled. It is this truth that Prussia has so well understood.

To give an instance. In two weeks after a declaration of war, England could place 50 gunboats on the Lakes, and more than 30 armored vessels in the harbors of our leading cities, and could concentrate 75,000 regular troops in Canada, backed by a sturdy militia ready to march across our border; while in twice that time part of her Asiatic squadon could sail through the Golden Gate.

Our lake frontier is a cobweb. We are bound by treaty of 1817 to keep on the Lakes not exceeding four vessels of a hundred tons burden, each armed with one eighteen-pounder cannon! No land defences of such towns as Chicago, situated on the shore itself, could save them from bombardment. Neither do defences exist, nor, if they existed, have we suitable ordnance or forces to arm and man them. The best army could not protect Chicago against a mediocre modern fleet. Torpedoes are not available without shore defences to back them. Indeed, so much stress is not to-day laid on the efficiency of the torpedo system; torpedo-netting twenty-five feet from the hull of a vessel has been shown to all but nullify the danger of the explosion of the largest. Topedoes and submarine mines are excellent auxiliaries to big guns on land. Fear of them and the time taken in their removal hold the enemy under fire, but they do not stand alone. At best they are an uncertain arm.

If we are holden to this trivial force on the Lakes, say you, so is Canada. True; but Canada under the guise of commercial desirability, has built a strategic system of canals, along which England can float from the sea to the Lakes gunboats of considerable tonnage and heavily armed, and she has more than 100 such vessels available. The shipping and commerce of the

Lakes is attractive. The goods afloat and ashore suffice to pay a huge war indemnity. They are all at the mercy of an English flotilla.

Some people imagine that modern war has been humanized out of such measures as bombardment. But Paris was bombarded in 1870; so was Strassburg, and its beautiful cathedral spire was seriously injured. War has no æsthetic maxims. The occupation of a seaport leaves no alternative but submission and the payment of a heavy ransom—or bombardment. In a town like Chicago this would be followed by fire, and we all remember the $200,000,000 lost in the fire of 1871.

On our side not only are we by treaty bound to have no efficient war-vessels on the Lakes, but we have no means of placing them there. So far as land-forces go, the Canadian militia is as good as ours. We often hear of our vast army of veterans, forgetful of the fact that the youngest of the veterans of the civil war is a man of fifty to-day; that their average age is fifty-six. While between 1865 and 1880 we had a reserve of available veterans to call upon, to-day not only are all these men superannuated, but even the lads who were under age in 1861 are now graybeards. The fact is that we have but 3,000 regulars in the division of the Atlantic, plus the militia. England has a large number of regular officers to detail on such a duty. She has fast passenger-steamers in abundance (Cunard, Inman, White Star, and others) to transport troops, with battle-ships to back them. Military stores and arms are plentiful in Canada, or easily sent from home depots. In all these matters we are unequipped. Our northern frontier, *quoad* England, is absolutely open. Does the improbability of damage justify us in failure to provide against its possibility?

The remedy lies in our own hands, but it calls for time. We, as well as Canada, can build canals large enough to float gunboats, and hold these in readiness to be transported to the Lakes. We can buy or build guns and torpedoes. We can do what is feasible toward fortifying the lake-cities. We can erect works at such points as to prevent the passage of certain narrows by a fleet approaching the Lakes from the sea. "Fort Wayne on the Detroit River, if supplied with suitable armament well placed, could, with the assistance of submarine mines and torpedoes, prohibit a passage into Lake Huron," reports the Fortification Board; and "the fort at Rouse's Point is sufficient, with the aid of a few eight-inch rifles, to secure Lake Champlain from an inroad." Forts can be so placed on the St. Lawrence as to command parts of the Canadian canals and locks. Other parts of these canals are not to be reached except by a raid; but our people are apt at such work, and judicious preparation for such a venture could be made. We have built the nucleus of a fleet. So far as it goes, the White Squadron is a credit to us. Its presence at the mouth of the St. Lawrence in case of danger would have some effect. But it is small compared to the fleet England would send there, and cruisers are not battle-ships.

Our seacoat defences to-day amount to nothing. The works were designed long before the introduction of modern ordnance. Many of them have never been completed, or are falling to pieces for lack of repairs. Some of the earthworks were built in the last century. There are "gun-batteries without guns, and mortar-batteries without mortars. Barbette guns are old smooth-bores, and have no carriages except those which expose the gunners to the enemy's sharpshooters." Every harbor on the coast may to-day be captured by a small fleet of such vessels as all respectable powers in the world possess, saving only the

United States; and we own but the few armor-clads we have recently launched to defend them all.

What have our possible opponents in the way of navies with which to attack us? If we were near at hand, either England, France, Italy, Spain, Germany, or Russia, could throw upon us an irresistible fleet. But there are more than three thousand miles of ocean to traverse, and few war-vessels carry enough coal to be of value after such a cruise. Some, however, do.

Of sufficient endurance to operate from a home station as base, England has 17 battle-ships and 72 cruisers; Italy has 5 battle-ships and 6 cruisers; France, 14 cruisers; Spain, 10 cruisers; Germany, 10 cruisers; Russia, 8 cruisers. Of more limited endurance, such that they would require coal when they reached American waters, England has 30 battle-ships and 99 cruisers; France, 23 battle-ships and 18 cruisers; Spain, 10 cruisers. Here, then, we have 142 armor-clads capable of starting from a European port and of attacking our seaboard cities without re-coaling, and 180 capable of doing so by coaling on this side; a total of 322, all of them "ships of recent construction and of great power" reports the Policy Board of the navy. In addition to these there are many excellent armor-clads which were built before 1870, or which are not of the highest grade of efficiency, and other new and more efficient vessels are being constantly built.

All the vessels of any one nation could not leave home at the same time, but those having the requisite endurance might do so. The question of ammunition, of which no vessel carries a supply for long service, and which must be replenished, is serious. And there is the question of seaworthiness. While all these vessels are built to go to sea, there is no pretence that the battle-ships are seaworthy in the sense that a modern passenger-steamer is. Storms might entail disaster. Moreover, big guns are apt to burst, or to break their carriages, or to tear them loose, and a comparatively small number of shots measures the life of most big guns. No European power is anxious to put its precious craft at risk for any advantage to be probably gained over us. They are needed for home purposes. If a vessel is lost, even though indemnity be had, the time taken to build another leaves a gap for a while Every harbor is more or less difficult to enter in time of peace. In time of war it can be made a hundred-fold more difficult. The United States are the last nation which any foreign power would care to attack.

Herein lies our largest measure of protection. But it is not safe to count on this. If of a dozen battle-ships or cruisers but half succeeded in reaching our shores; if, on an average, each gun was disabled after even five shots,—what would it benefit us if one of our ports had been bombarded before failure, or a heavy ransom had been exacted?

The coal question is the most difficult one. So much of the flotative power of the big vessels is consumed by machinery, armor, guns, turrets, and ammunition, that there is not much left for coal. Hence the latter class of vessels is worthless for attack on our coasts, unless the nation owning them has on this side a coaling-station or an ally with one; or unless they can be coaled at sea (a possible but uncertain process), or can speedily capture a port where they can coal. In this respect the West Indies come into play. But, eliminating altogether this re-coaling class, there remains a formidable and constantly growing fleet able to hold our seas for some time, and to-day, and for years to come, able to enter any and every one of our harbors. With all saving clauses, the mere existence of these armor-clads, which vary between 4,000 and 13,-000 tons, is a fruitful source of thought.

What do we need to provide security? First, the navy, of which we now have the nucleus; second, sea-coast defences of the very highest order; third, an efficient militia, as a reserve to our small regular army.

That coast defences are first necessary, and a navy next, may be argued. For perfect defence they go together. To place a city beyond risk of capture there needs to be a fourfold line, the outer one of battle-ships; the second of attendant gunboats and cruisers; the next of torpedoes, stationary and movable, and torpedo-boats; the last a line of heavy guns mounted in turrets and casemates, and barbette and mortar batteries, and in some places floating batteries. The navy and coast defences are inseparable, if we would have a perfect system. Which alone is preferable is still a mooted question between army and navy experts.

The Policy Board of the navy, to whom the matter of a fleet has been committed, has laboriously accumulated the most varied information on this subject, and has made a comprehensive plan for a navy. It advises the construction of 92 all-steel armor-clads, viz., 10 battle-ships of 10,000 tons and of great coal endurance, which can steam up to 17 knots an hour, for carrying the war to the enemy's country; 25 battle-ships of limited coal endurance, in three classes of from 6,000 to 8,000 tons, able to steam nearly 16 knots an hour, for the defence of our coast and ports; 24 cruisers of from 4,000 to 7,500 tons, able to steam from 19 to 22 knots, for destroying the enemy's commerce, ravaging or blockading his coasts, scouting for the battle-ships, and protecting our own commercial fleets; 15 torpedo-cruisers of about 900 tons; 5 such cruisers of 1,200 tons, for service in the China and other distant waters; 10 rams proper of 3,500 tons; 3 torpedo and artificer's ships of 5,000 tons, able to steam 20 knots. These are exclusive of 100 first-class torpedo-boats for offensive war, and numerous second-class torpedo-boats such as are carried by battle-ships and cruisers. The largest ordnance on the battle-ships of this fleet will be 13-inch 60-ton guns 35 calibres long; most will be 12-inch 50-ton guns; the cruisers will carry 5 and 8-inch guns.

This will make a worthy fleet—when we get it. Including the vessels already built or appropriated for, the projected United States navy will boast of 120 armored ships of all classes, and 101 torpedo-boats, at a total estimated cost of $350,000,000. Truly a magnificent scheme and a costly. Our first impulse is to cry out at such extravagance. But in the past twenty years "we have wasted in patching old wooden vessels more than enough money to have built and kept in repair 19 ironclads like the British "Inflexible," 11 like the Italian "Lepanto," or 39 cruisers like the "Chicago," nearly half the proposed fleet. These old hulks are worthless; they have merely served their turn in affording employment to voters about election time. If we do not build the proposed armored fleet in whole or in part, how much "repairing" shall we do instead? This is a question of interest to every American.

Such a fleet would put us on a par with any power, and, coupled with coast defences, make us impregnable. Representing us in every harbor in the world, it would, with proper navigation laws, pay for itself in the one item of encouraging and building up our lost merchant marine. A generation ago the most beautiful man-of-war in any given foreign port was apt to float the stars and stripes. May it again be so! But all this is not the work of a day. To do it in the best manner will consume twelve to fifteen years. To do the work at home, we must first place the navy-yards at New York,

Boston, Norfolk, and Mare and League Islands in order, and by substantial orders encourage the laying-down of plants for plate-steel and guns by our large iron concerns. Though less time would suffice in case we bought material abroad, it is unquestionably desirable that we build our fleet at home.

This plan meanwhile would give us naval defences only so fast as the new vessels were launched and proven. What should be done in the line of harbor defences? This question has been committed by Congress to the Fortification Board, a body consisting of military and naval experts and distinguished civilians, who reported at great length in 1886.

Though our seaboard is so extensive, but 27 places need coast defence in order to shield it, and this number might be considerably reduced. By defending 11 of them, more than four-fifths of our entire commercial wealth may be protected. From their minor importance most seaboard towns are in no great danger. The high cost of a naval expedition makes a wealthy objective essential. No European fleet is apt to waste time on any but our largest cities, unless for coaling.

In New York both the entrance from the Ocean and the Sound should be fortified by armored revolving turrets, steel-armored casemates, barbette and mortar batteries, submarine mines, and torpedo-boats.   This requires 95 guns and 144 mortars, and will cost $8,-000,000 for the ordnance, and $14,500,000 for the defences in which to mount them.   In San Francisco there should be similar works, with 110 guns and 128 mortars, at a cost $7,250,000 for the ordnance, and $8,500,000 for the defences.   Floating batteries are needed at this point, which will add $10,750,000 to this sum.   In Boston 43 guns and 128 mortars will be needed at a cost of $4,000,000 for the ordnance, and $5,750,000 for the works.   The limit of the capacity of big guns has probably been reached; 18-inch guns are the largest which will float.   Such defences as these, mounted by superior guns, would be good for many years.

The other ports are far less costly to defend.   They are, in order of urgency, the lake-cities, Hampton Roads, New Orleans, Philadelphia, Washington, Baltimore, Portland (Me.), Narragansett Bay, Key West, Charleston, Mobile, New London, Savannah, Galveston, Portland (Ore.), Pensacola, Wilmington, San Diego, Portsmouth, Cumberland Sound, the Kennebec, New Bedford, the Penobscot, and New Haven.   The total for there ports would be $38,000,000 for guns, and $55,500,000 for works, or a total, including floating batteries, mines, and torpedoes, of $126,500,000. Again a protest against extravagance is in order.

The objections to this plan are its great cost, the time it takes to carry out, and the fact there is no "politics" in it. Is there not a cheaper means or a more speedy one? Yes. Certain works can be more rapidly constructed than others. The quickest way of affording a fair degree of protection to our harbors is by placing in each a well-devised line of mortar-batteries supplemented by torpedoes and mines. These can be made in one-fourth the time required for the same number of horizontal-fire guns in turrets and casemates and at a mere fraction of their cost.

A battery of 16 mortars can be made ready for service, including guns, carriages, and emplacement, for from $8,000 to $10,000 per mortar, according to location. The emplacement of a 12-inch gun costs about $150,000, and the gun and carriage will cost an equal amount. The fire of the recent mortar is not only accurate, but strikes an armor-clad at her most vulnerable point,—the deck. The 12-inch breech-loading mortar of to-day is a fine weapon. Its range is from three to almost six miles; and experiment shows that three out of four shells will hit a large vessel at anchor, and that a big battery will make it very dangerous for a moving vessel whose position is properly signalled. A battery of 16 mortars, each firing six times an hour, will give a shot ever 37 seconds. Moreover, these mortar-batteries can be placed where shells from ships which fire only horizontal guns cannot reach them. They are as effective from behind a hill as from any other position. For quick defence the mortar-battery system appears to be the most expedient thing to construct. With sufficient appropriations it would consume but a couple of years to place good mortar-batteries in all our harbors; and these, with an intelligent system of torpedoes and our growing navy, would be of unquestioned benefit. It is an excellent first step. Let the rest, if you will, come more deliberately. But we may not rest content with these. Alone they are not a perfect' defence. Mortars are intended to prevent a fleet anchoring at the mouth of a harbor: they are not the equivalent of horizontal-fire guns, which are necessary to destroy it, as rapid-fire guns are required to protect the mine-fields.

Now for the army. This paper is not a plea for a

vast increase of our military establishment. The proposed works have to be garrisoned and the guns manned. This, in time of peace, would be done by the regular army. In time of war the service of the coast defences has to be increased. The armies which take the field need increase, large and sudden. This is a more difficult problem. The naval increase comes about naturally. The general public sees the splendid cruisers which visit the various ports from time to time, and seems to take a proper pride in them. The old-fashioned love of a man-of-war has not died out among us. And as the navy gets additional ships, additional crews follow as of course. The army can make no such parade. The navy leaps into popular favor. The army is overlooked until it is needed. Coast defences as suggested require a moderately larger artillery force; but this would come about without friction when the defences were done. The addition to cavalry and infantry is not so easily provided. It is not wise to have a large increase, and it is not necessary; but it is of the highest consequence to foster what we have, and so to organize the militia that the army may occupy its true place as a nucleus for an effective reserve in time of war. As our militia system stands to-day, it is not to be relied upon.   In some States it is fairly good: in most States it is a farce.   That it is of higher quality than it was in 1861 is not doubtful.   But it is not such that it can be readily called into service in case of need, or be trusted to do serious work at the outset.

Apart from Indian warfare, the *rôle* of a regular army in this country is twofold.   In time of peace it should be a model on which a good militia may be patterned.   It is an educational body, so to speak. On the outbreak of war, its province is to bear the brunt of the first fighting, until suitable levies of volunteers can be made, or the militia or reserves can be mobilized.   By judicious training our militia can be made a reserve from which volunteers can be drawn in sufficient numbers; or, better still, a national reserve can be organized from the militia itself.   History has shown often enough, that, unless militia is sufficiently trained and by officers educated to arms, it is inefficient. Our volunteers in the Rebellion were comparatively useless against equally poor troops for more than a year.   They became good when they had had the same training as the regulars.   Education in the field is as rapid as it is efficient; but it is got at a terrible cost.

Neither of the duties mentioned has our regular

army ever been in a position to perform. While, putting aside the "menace" theory, a large standing army in the United States is unessential, such an army as could be represented by companies or regiments in each of the military divisions as a leaven for the militia is in every sense desirable. It has been shown to be so in recent cases where regulars have joined the militia in annual encampments. This opportunity has been too rarely afforded. Our little regular army since the war has indeed been too small to cope with the Indians in the "war of civilization." Give us an army sufficient to detail a regular company as a part of every militia regiment, and the militia would soon be a different body from what it is to-day.

There has been more than one system devised by which our militia can be made an efficient national reserve. Enlist such of the militia as choose to undergo extra drill and discipline; pay this force for time so spent; uniform and arm them. Many of the best of the militiamen would be glad to spend a month every year in regular military training. Of such a force the officers must be appointed by the State; but they could be subjected to an examination as to fitness, and could be given opportunities for study with regular troops at the military schools,—an advantage which would be eagerly embraced. Since the civil war no one doubts the advantage of a military education. If the Academy at West Point were doubled in size, so that annually there might be turned back into the population a num- of young men trained to arms, their effect upon the militia would be marked. Good officers mean good men: the best of men under poor officers are worthless.

There is to-day something more than 100,000 militia in the several States. It is possible to create out of this a strong and easily mobilized national reserve. But it must be done by men whose profession it is to organize troops. It must not be play. If the task were given by Congress to the army, and sufficient means were provided, two years would show a decided gain. It has been estimated that little more than $3,000,000 a year would be required to carry out an effective plan and to create a national reserve sufficient for our needs.

The danger has been indicated. The speediest means of partial protection as well as the most complete has been shown. How much of this shall be done it is for Congress to decide. *In medio tutissimus ibis:* erect partial coast defences and build a moderate fleet, say

most men. If we have too powerful a fleet, we may
be led into wars we should otherwise avoid. So far
the appropriations for the coast defences have been
sadly meagre,—$1,221,000 in 1890, and $750,000 in
1891. To the navy they have been more generous.
The building of ships calls on our iron manufacturers,
who in their turn influence Congress. Coast defences
do not seem to be so popular. A reasonable appropriation—$10,000,000—would erect mortar-batteries and
make in each of our harbors a torpedo system which,
though partial, can be rapidly erected.

The cost of complete coast defences and a navy, as
planned by the Fortification and Policy Boards, is all
but $500,000,000. To spread this amount over fifteen
years would make necessary an annual appropriation
of $33,000,000. Add to this sum $3,000,000 for militia
training, and we find that $36,000,000 a year will be
needed. There must also be a small appropriation for
experiments. The rapid advance of scientific discovery
requires constant testing of new devices. But this is
not large. We are spending vast sums on pensions, a
discreditable percentage of which are unearned or frau-
dulent. As the pension laws now stand, $140,000,000
will be required for the single year 1891. Is it not

wiser to spend something on protection from possible, even if remote, national disaster, than still greater sums on extensions of the pension system? With the defences indicated we should not fear attack, and could hold our own in foreign complications. It took but a few months during the civil war to spend $500,-000,000. Is it not possible, that, without defences, we may be called upon some day to spend even more than their cost on a disastrous war, on indemnities, or on ransoms of cities that some enemy may occupy? In any event, ought not lesser sums to be appropriated at once, to shield our naked harbors?

A GLANCE AT THE EUROPEAN ARMIES.

A GLANCE AT THE EUROPEAN ARMIES.*

O VER eighteen millions of men trained to arms stand ready for battle in Europe. The labor of the highest intellects is diverted from better channels to the details of war. National economics is no longer the single, if difficult, study of yore. It is complicated with a problem awful in its intensity. The noblest work of the world, from the philosophical or the humanitarian standpoint, is perverted to ignoble uses. A world in arms seems to enforce the truth of Martin Luther's odd dictum: "*Der Krieg ist an sich selbst etwas Göttliches, da er ein Weltgesetz ist.*"† In the past, war has in truth been the great civilizer; but it should to-day yield its province to education. War has been an incentive to progress; it now clogs its wheels. "*Die*

* Published in The Forum, July, 1892.
† "There is something holy in the very nature of war, for it is a law of the universe."

Waffen nieder!" * is no idle cry. If disarmament does not come by some process of arbitration now only dreamed of, it must come by starvation or by a cataclysm. Civilization marches fast, and in quite other channels than it used to do; war is now but its ally. We are approaching the time when the Geneva arbitration will become a leaven to the political kneading of the Continent. It was a difficult first step, even between peoples of the same blood; among the diverse tongues of Europe such a triumph of civilized common-sense is not yet possible. But the seed is sown, and the harvest, though not at hand, will be gathered in due time. Even Moltke, the great apostle of war, confessed to faith in eventual rarely-interrupted peace.

Meanwhile to what are these eighteen million soldiers looking forward? Europe has never been so perfectly prepared for war; nor, curiously, has she ever seen a time when soldiers were more loath to fight. There exists a marked and universal dread of war, coupled with an unexampled ability to wage it. Not that there is a lack of stomach; the *morale* of the leading armies is of the best. But Europe stands aghast at her own weapons. War is *quasi*-suicide; and Europe

* "Down with arms!"

gazes at the blade she holds against her vitals and shrinks from the thrust. The dread is born of the certainty that a war will be a general one, of the uncertainty of its issue. Even France, despite her unquenched thirst for revenge, will do nothing to provoke war. But an accident, the foolish demonstration of a mob in Paris or the ill-considered utterance of the German Kaiser, may precipitate war at any moment. Can we gauge the chances of any of the probable combatants?

There are twenty countries contributing to the eighteen millions of troops. Of these, two antagonistic groups monopolize the situation. In the centre of the Continent stands the German colossus, with its allies, Austria-Hungary and Italy. On either hand are France and Russia, a political Scylla and Charybdis between which the bark freighted with European peace must be steered. Possessing all they can properly claim, the members of the Triple Alliance are directly interested in steadying the helm, while France yearns for her old boundary, and Russia proposes—when the time is ripe —to seize the Golden Horn. The lesser powers, in case of war, can complicate the situation by joining either the Double or the Triple Alliance; but immediate danger lurks in the statecraft—one might say simply craft—of the five powers named. England, by the necessity of maintaining her supremacy in the Mediterranean, is drawn to closer relations with Italy. She looks askance at the encroachments in Africa of France and dreads the influence in Asia of Russia. The key of the situation has been thrust upon her. The substantial powers of Europe are three or four against two, in case of a general war. What are their relative abilities?

England stands by herself in not having adopted the rule of universal service. While still ruling the waves so long as there is no combination against her, Britannia cannot claim to be a military power. She alone takes herself seriously as such. Since the Napoleonic struggle she has had no war which has taxed her stanchness to the utmost, and this is the only test of military force. In view of the gigantic proportions of our Rebellion and of the Franco-Prussian war, is it not droll to see her "point with pride" to such pigmy operations as the Abyssinian, Ashantee, Zulu, Transvaal, Afghanistan, or Egyptian campaigns? Yet to the average Englishman these are clad with more splendor than the wars of the giants. This self-gratulation is much of a piece with the Balaclava incident, which poetry has placed at the head of all feats of arms. But however gallant that ride into the jaws of death, its prosaic statistics show that the loss in killed and wounded was less than 37 per cent, whereas more than sixty regiments during our Civil War lost in some one engagement over 50 per cent, one 82 per cent; yet few men have even heard of this fact. In like manner our Indian campaigns sink into oblivion unwept, unhonored, and unsung; but in this fight for civilization American heroism has been illustrated by a warfare more constant, more bloody, and more exhausting than any of England's campaigns for well on to eighty years. We are called and perhaps are a boastful people; but has not our cousin across the water retained a yet larger slice of this true Ango-Saxon inheritance? No one doubts that the English have kept intact the true mettle of our forefathers, nor that, when called on, the response will come promptly and in ample measure; but it has lain dormant so many decades that military pretensions on their part naturally provoke a smile on the Continent among peoples who know what the bitterness of war means, while Americans of this generation may fairly assert that we

have proved our claim to military stanchness as the
have not. It is for this reason that we look with mor
respect on the utterances of German critics, who, wit
their habit of war, study and understand our difficulti
and methods as the Briton is incapable of doing.

England has no army to-day in the sense of that
word in Europe. She can have none on a system of
voluntary enlistment. When the commander-in-chief
doubts her ability to mobilize quickly one army corps;
when officers of high rank and command testify before
a Parliamentary committee that there is not a single
effective infantry battalion at home, that no regiment
of the First Army Corps could be sent on service, that
50 per cent of the men at Aldershot are not fit to do a
day's duty even in England, that not 30 per cent of
the rank and file are equal to more than a two-hours'
sentry-go; when militia regiments out on manœuvre
refuse to sleep in tents as being too severe an exposure
—what is there left to say? The recruit of to-day is
not the time-honored Tommy Atkins. Out of 61,000
men who presented themselves for enlistment in 1887,
over 33,000 were rejected for unsoundness or dismissed
for vice. Medical experts declare the clothing, rations,
barracks, and habits incompatible with vigorous health.

The last decade repeatedly proved England's management of even a small army to be of the poorest, and her active service among savages is the worst of training for civilized war. It would really tax England to mobilize two army corps, say 50,000 men, and one cavalry division, with anything like Continental speed. Except as an ally who could make herself useful by landing a body of men on the enemy's coast as an opportune diversion, England is of positively no weight so far as her army is concerned. All this is said without for a moment forgetting Crécy and Agincourt, Malplaquet and Waterloo, with a faith, religious in its intensity, in the grit and honor of Old England.

On the sea it is otherwise. The British fleet is, despite the many errors which rapid advance in technical matters make unavoidable, the best afloat. But the other powers have not been idle. France possesses on her Atlantic shore and in the Mediterranean a powerful navy. By deepening the *Canal du Midi* she may be able to transfer quickly from one squadron to the other, while England must sail the long course through the Straits of Gibraltar; and her naval station at Biserta will be a threat to the road to India. France will before long be all but as strong in the Mediterranean as

England with Gibraltar, Malta, Port Said, and Cyprus. Small wonder that England leans toward an *entente cordiale* with Italy.

The gravest danger to England's position as a great power is not in Europe. It may be difficult for her to keep out of the next war, for France views with alarm her occupation of Egypt, yet redolent with the elder Napoleon's lustre; but this is a minor matter. It is in Russia's restless pushing across the great Aryan plateau toward the confines of the Indian empire that lurks the nearest peril. The Orientals have a cognate liking for Russia; they understand the stable autocracy of the czar; but a change in the British ministry is always an enigma. Were it not for the wonderful personal force of many English officials in the East, England could not long retain her prestige in rivalry with the insinuating policy of Russia. Since Turkestan fell under Russia's sway, Bokhara, Khiva, Kokhand, Merv, have slowly but surely followed. Just when Russia will feel strong enough to make an actual bid for control dangerous to England's holding in India depends upon many contingencies. But she can at almost any moment advance along the line Herat-Kandahar with a force sufficient to prevent England from interfering too seriously with her Bosphorus projects. By fortifying Quetta, England shows that she fears this. It seems as if Great Britain must side with the Triple Alliance and against France and Russia.

The aspirations of Russia in Europe extend only to the Balkan Peninsula. She cares little for the politics which sway the other powers. Her destiny pushes her toward a Mediterranean outlet for her potential commerce and toward the control of inner Asia. In whichever direction she can the more safely tread at any given time will be her path. She does not seek war, but she will not rest from encroachment. Her next step in Asia will be to control Persia, or she may attack the Turkish problem from Asia Minor. Russia is active in the Baltic, though in case of war the more mobile and active German fleet could probably neutralize hers. In the Black Sea she is not doing so much. As fearless of conquest as the United States, she is more troubled by her present finances than by fears of her future growth. She can bide her time, certain that she will gain ground to the south and east. But that a war which appealed to the restless element might quiet her internal politics does not make for peace.

Russia is rich in material for an army, since eight years ago she fell into line by adopting universal service. The material has excellent physical qualities, but it lacks intelligence. The Russian soldier has always been a dangerous opponent; Kunersdorf and Borodino tell a story of undaunted heroism. Brave, of wonderful endurance, uncomplaining, easily subjected to discipline, requiring little, he has been a pattern soldier. But to-day, when the intelligence of the enlisted man is so marked a factor in the efficiency of an army, it is a query whether the Russian can hold his own in Europe; for 73 per cent of the army in Europe can neither read nor write, of that in Asia, 82 per cent. The minor officers are, moreover, of low grade, a fact scarcely compatible with efficiency. The Russian army has always been proud of its ability to stand hammering at close quarters; but this is not of the essence of modern war—when actual annihilation may follow a false manœuvre. It is the intelligent intiative that keeps out of false positions which is demanded.

In a general European war the *rôle* of Russia, *quoad* Germany and Austria, is a defensive one, though she may look upon a sharp offensive as the best defence.

Her true line of defence against Germany is the Vistula, which she would seek to hold. As against Austria, she would probably advance into Galicia from the Polish salient. She has been fortifying of late years; but Russia knows enough not to depend on an inert line of strong places. She will put all her energy into active operations. Yet, despite some war-at-any-cost men who believe that, successful or not, it would increase the quota of the liberties they aspire to, Russia does not desire war. She will not have completed her new organization for two years. The lack of breadstuffs this year would seriously hamper her mobilization, though she has been moving troops to the westward. Some Hotspurs talk of huge cavalry raids into German territory like those of our Civil War, forgetful that our raids were made through a sparsely settled country, while eastern Germany is full of material which would quickly arrest a cavalry column of any size or destroy it if it penetrated too far. In other words, Russia is not prepared, and without some peculiar incitement will not venture on war this year. Far better for her quietly to increase her already growing influence in Afghanistan. That there are difficulties in the way of actual conquest too near

India, mainly logistic, is undeniable; but Russia uses true Oriental means, as do not the English. Samarkand is becoming Russianized; Peshawur is not a whit more English.

Russia's threat to India is a strong card. Great Britain must hold India, if only as a place for stray investments of men and money and as a means of keeping her trade-standing in the East. Nor is the threat an idle one. Russia now has steam communication across the Caspian with Samarkand and a respectable force *echeloned* along the way back to her reserves. Probably one hundred thousand men could be massed on the Afghan frontier in three months. England acknowledges that Russia in Afghanistan would lead to intolerable complications; with the czar's hand on Herat, the empress' influence over India would be forfeited; but as most of the troops now in India are urgently needed there, it is not probable that, as at present situated, England could put more than sixty thousand men along the Cabool-Guzni-Kandahar or the Peshawur-Quetta defensive lines; and to resort to a defence of her great subject empire along the Indus, however militarily sound in placing all the logistic difficulties on the enemy, cannot be thought of for a moment in view of its political hazard. India must be defended in Afghanistan. To sum up the case in the East, it is moral influence which will tell, and in this Russia is apparently gaining while England is not. This question bears more weight in European politics than at first blush appears.

The French army has never been in so prime a condition as it now is. Napoleon's, as an army, was at no time as sound throughout. It can pass almost any test. Even the best German authorities acknowledge this. *"Frankreich steht mit uns in den Waffen gleich,"* says General von Leszczynsky. Sir Charles Dilke's summary of the French armies goes too far—not in actual, but in comparative praise. The French army is not the best in Europe. It is highly commended when put on the same level as the German. There are still some serious points of criticism. The spirit which animates the army is the same as that which produces the restless ambition of the leaders and the changeableness of the people. Jealousies with many attendant evils come frequently to the surface. There is lacking the quiet pose of subordination to one central autocratic permanent power for which discipline,

* "France stands on an equality with us in military strength."

however severe, will not make up. No man is more
patriotic than the Gaul; but his patriotism is of a
different order from the *Vaterlandsliebe* of the Teuton.
No more splendid example of patient, intelligent, consistent work than the recent reorganization of the
French army adorns the pages of history. The infantry is excellent, the artillery of the best, and the
two arms work admirably together—the most important of modern demands. The cavalry did not show
its capacity in the last manœuvres, but it is well
mounted and taught. The engineers did remarkable
work; the telegraph and telephone service was perfect;
the balloon corps promised results; the train management was not to be criticised. But there was no
attempt to combine the workings of the three arms,
nor was the cavalry used in its proper *rôle*.

The manœuvres were none the less useful. The
beauty of the evolutions of troops on parade has ceased
to be a test of any value. Discipline as it used to be
understood must be supplanted by clear-headedness
and a power to act intelligently. Good education in
petty officers is far more valuable than ramrod precision of drill or set-up. That the French have gained
in the right direction was demonstrated by their ma-

nœuvres. What has always made the French army is
leadership, and however highly we may gauge the
French generals, which of them has demonstrated his
being abreast of the difficult problems of modern war?
This is everywhere the one treacherous factor in the
problem. In 1870 there was a ruling mind in the
European armies; there is no man of preëminent parts
to-day. And yet above the individual excellence of
the several armies, above every other consideration,
there is demanded sound strategical and tactical management. Whoever can guess where reside the highest qualities in the leaders may safely predict the
outcome of the next war. But where is the seer? To
all appearances the military talent of France is of a
high order. Whoever raised the French army from
the wreck of the last war has incontestable ability.
But is it of the order which can command as well as
organize?

The 1891 manœuvres in France proved the marching ability of the men, the excellence of their armament and equipment, the efficiency of the staff corps
and adjunct arms. But can a set of manœuvres,
planned out on paper and studied for months before
their execution, give the troops or their leaders any

training for the kaleidoscopic changes of actual war? There were confessedly a number of absurd errors and impossible evolutions—bodies of troops boldly marched over ground where they would have been annihilated by the enemy's massed batteries. All this is natural enough and proves nothing, as, indeed, the manœuvres themselves only proved certain excellences, without demonstrating the fitness of the troops and leaders for active operations. The troops were really better than the handling. The value of these great manœuvres end when the rival bodies reach fighting contact, so soon as they are deployed for battle. It is here, however, that for the ordinary spectator their interest begins; and the French dearly love the dramatic. You may learn something from the strategic work; the tactical cannot be so carried through as to demonstrate anything. The manœuvres should be for use, not show, though no doubt the self-confidence of the French army has been heightened by them.

Strategy for many ages aimed at the avoidance of battle. It now aims at immediate conflict. To keep a million men at work and in food is too difficult a problem to be long drawn out. Put every man you can mobilize on the frontier; seek your enemy at once;

compromise him by quick and skillful movements; beat him; cut off his retreat. Tactics is proportionately growing in value, and hence the individual ability of troops. The substantial equality of equal masses is no longer to be counted on, but numbers still tell. With the greater similarity in arms, discipline, and condition, whoever keeps his forces in hand, simplifies his manœuvres, is speedy in utilizing his tactical advantages on the battle-field, and then strikes with all his might will win. The French manœuvres could be no training for this.

Despite excellent preparation, the French are not eager for war. "*Revanche*" is not now as keen-scented a cry as it was ten years ago. Though his spurs are sharper, the Gallic cock's crow is less shrill. France recognizes the uncertainties of the situation, and though in better financial condition than Germany, is not going to war for a shadow. At an opening which promised success, however, she would immediately thrust. It is wiser for France not to strike for Alsace and Lorraine too soon; better use her means in developing her enormous African colonies and protectorates by the trans-Saharan railway. By and by she will be proportionately stronger than she now is. If her government remains stable, she will gain by every year's delay.

If the status of France is difficult to determine, that of Germany is a very maze. Those who in 1870 knew Prussia well had no doubt as to the issue of a war with France, though no one expected a walkover. The case to-day is different. The German army is not the superior of the French. Whoever estimates at their true value the homogeneous organization, the diligence, and the subordination of self to the general result which have always characterized the Germans, may cast his vote in their favor. But it is a narrow choice. The next war will call out national individualities. According as each views the qualities of the Teuton or the Gaul, each may divine results. Some conditions are to be noted. So long as an army is a despotic body, so long will service due to a single chief, which cannot be complicated by professional intrigues, be the better rendered. In the German army officers are put where they can do the work they are best fitted for. This is not always possible in France. The discipline of the French army is more severe; the training of the German is superior, and individual training is worth more in the field than severity. The latter work harder and more hours; they will go into a campaign more seasoned. All Germans work together; nation and army are interchangeable terms. Manœuvres lately introduced into France and Russia are a generation old in Prussia. The knowledge and individual initiative of the German officers of all ranks are higher than those which any body of military men has ever had; and they believe in and rely on the exceptional intelligence which permeates the ranks. That despite their penury the quality of the German officers does not slacken, speaks well. The Germans will bear up under initial disaster; a first defeat might dishearten the French—it might work a change in their commanders or even affect the government, a result which could not follow in Germany. Assuming that the armies are equal, it is method and race characteristics which will yield superiority. That army which has the best *morale*, other things being equal, will win. What may be said about the Germans in no wise detracts from the value of their opponents. No army can possess more *esprit de corps* than the French, nor be sounder through and through. And keen military observers have more than once expressed their preference for the present military status of *la belle France*.

There are other dangers to Germany. She preserves

her peaceful but resolute bearing under a serious financial and political handicap. She has a low treasury in proportion to her armament; the two-year-service law may prove a blunder; her people are ground down by taxes, cheerfully borne by the patriotic majority but galling none the less; trade is far from good. Worse than this, the people, loving and respecting the Hohenzollerns, are struggling with hearty purpose to keep from blemish the time-honored cry "For God, King, and Fatherland," while striving to hide and protesting with inward bitterness against the mediæval *dicta* of an immature would-be autocrat. These are beginning to work evil. Saxony, Wurtemberg, Bavaria, will not stand dictation, and the *Einheitlichkeit* of the German army is a *sine qua non* of continued Prussian hegemony, indeed of German safety. Already jealousies of "Prussian particularism" can be traced in the imperial structure. So far there is no question of the unity of command, but such questions are serious during a critical state of tension. A continuation of the emperor's course might provoke what would result in greater eventual liberties, but a disturbance of German homogeneity is fraught with danger greater than the gain.

I have conversed with hundreds of military men of every nationality in Europe since the year opened; I have found not one who did not shrink from war. Each seemed to have in mind what Vater Fritz once said: "*Der Schritt, einen Krieg zu unternehmen, ist so schwer und wichtig, dass es unbegreiflich ist, wie so viele Könige sich dazu so leicht entschliessen können. Ich bin versichert, wenn die Monarchen ein wahres und treues Bild des Elends sehen sollten, in welches eine einzige Kriegserklärung die Völker stürzt, nimmermehr könnten sie dagegen gleichgültig sein.*" * This was the real Frederick, who wanted not war, but would fight to the bitter end for what he deemed his rights. So now with all thinking soldiers. Never has warfare promised to be so terrible, so uncertain in its terrors.

Progress in warlike ability is to a certain extent retrogression. Bows and arrows lent equality to our savage ancestors; gunpowder modified hand-to-hand fighting, but none the less left a condition where relative forces could be estimated; modern science upsets all calculations. It thrusts its lever under and

* To wage war is so serious and weighty a matter that it is inconceivable how so many kings can undertake it so thoughtlessly. I am convinced that if monarchs had a true idea of the misery in which a mere declaration of war plunges a people, they could never be so indifferent to it.

upheaves our religious tenets; it makes capital an
ephemeral thing by multiplying means of production;
it drives out a new fighting equipment every decade;
it invents awful means of destruction, only to devise
more formidable methods of resistance. It is all
"bubble, bubble, toil and trouble." The penetration
of new arms of precision may perchance be met by a
new metal; smokeless powder suggests covering troops
by smoke artificially produced; ships are so heavily
loaded with armor that they barely float; ordnance
lives but a few rounds or tears itself from its emplacement. Uncertainty is universal. The men who have
proved their capacity are dead or in the sere and yellow leaf; by success or failure alone can the qualities
of the present leaders be gauged. Leadership is pre-
ëminently necessary, for strategy is immutable; business talent of the highest order, backed by untold
moneys, is called for to move and feed an army of a
million men, and becomes harder to get every year;
tactics is changed by every new invention. But a single factor remains—the personal equation—and it is
tactics which depends on the personal equation; the
troops longest kept in heart are the best. Early-morn-
ing courage has peculiar value. Where does it most

Germany can less afford a war than France. The receipt of a heavy indemnity does not foot expenditures; to pay one would grind her to powder. But she is ready. Her military standing is what it has always been. Her strategic railways to and along the French frontier are completed; to the Russian frontier Germany has ten and will soon have fourteen lines open, to but five of Russia's. She can mobilize in such a manner as to put in every armed man at the first call—which is the modern idea. The *fin-de-siècle* army is all but the migration of a people; even the "reserves" are now a part of the army in first line. But Germany is trammelled by the loss or shelving of her great men. She does not know when the Kaiser may fail her. All this is recognized, if not openly spoken, in Germany. The danger is omnipresent, so that a careless word of his may precipitate a misunderstanding which cannot be smoothed over. Germany is strong and self-confident; that she has a perfect army and the best average of officers, lesser and greater, is believed by many. But she no longer stands at the head of Europe. As with Napoleon toward the close of his career, her enemies have learned her method.

The Triple Alliance is strong. Austria has made a

great gain in her military status. Professional pride is higher, instruction is more diligent, discipline and *morale* are excellent, and the armament better than it has been. The intelligence of the troops is not as high as in Germany, but decidedly higher than in Russia. Her interests are identical with Germany's, but she fears no attack except from Russia, while Germany may have to meet Russia and France. Though with but half her force, Austria ought to be able to hold head against a Russian attack, especially as Roumania can lend a hand and keep at least two Russian army corps idle. Austria can more quickly mobilize, and is well placed strategically. She is strong in some arms. The cavalry and field artillery are all but the equal of Germany's; her infantry force is, however, on the whole, inferior of that of any of the greater powers. Her officers are poorly paid, and though the cadet school is gaining, are not so able as the French or German; and the non-commissioned officers are of lower grade. Little is done to make the soldier's life attractive or honorable. His pay, rations, and clothing are all poor, and the instruction cannot be called good. But a marked improvement is being scored every year. The magazine rifle and smokeless powder

will do wonders, and the new equipment is lighter and
better adapted to modern requirements.   There has
been added to the army-trains a system of portable
railways which can be quickly laid along otherwise
poor roads for the transport of army material, a thing
important in southeastern Europe; and field telegraphy
is now part of the staff equipment.   To fend off Russia's attack, Galicia has been strongly fortified and
garrisoned, but it has an open frontier.   Nothing short
of the Carpathian Mountains could well arrest a pronounced onset; but Austria could no doubt confine the
early campaign to the lowlands of Galicia, which
would act as a bumper for the nonce, while the second
line was coming up.

The value of Italy in the Triple Alliance is that she
holds in check all the French forces which lie in the districts of Lyons, Marseilles, and Nice, as well as the Al-
pine divisions.   To have Italy join with Germany and
Austria was imperative. The three are scarcely stronger
than France and Russia. Indeed, France believes that as
Germany must put up against Russia, on account of
her naturally open frontier, a much larger force than
France need put up against Italy, she can largely outnumber her old opponent with the sixteen army corps

she proposes to unleash in the Vosges region on the first cry of war. Italy adds no inconsiderable strength to the Triple Alliance, though despite severe economy she is financially bankrupt. Her army is very big on paper—a war strength of 2,700,000 men. But she cannot mobilize more than a portion of this force. Her coast lays her open to sudden and disastrous descents, and her length makes mobilization slow, despite the three railways running up and down the peninsula. France could put a large force on the Po before Italy could meet it. In twelve days several French corps could be at the defile of Stradella, while it would take Italy over twenty days to meet them. Such a movement is, however, highly improbable. France is led to expend her energy against Germany by every reason of pride and safety. Italy will not invade French territory; Germany will sweep over it as in 1870, unless France is on hand in overwhelming force.

The Italian army is fair. The men are notably brave; they are held under severe discipline and respond to it well; but that the individuality of the men can be relied on has been doubted by many Italian officers of good judgment. Some *élite* corps, such as the *bersaglieri*, are of the best. The new regulations are liberal, possibly too much so. They follow the new idea of leaving more to the intelligence and initiative of the officers and men. How the Italian regiments will respond to this remains to be seen. It is not probable that so much will be required of them as of the troops of their northern allies. The *bersaglieri* are not a fair sample of the whole, but the infantry of the line may do better than is anticipated. Italy's large and excellent fleet to-day is of greater importance than her army, however numerous; and when her new naval station in the island of Magdalena is completed, she will have still more to say as to the situation in the Mediterranean. Her fleet weighs heavier in the balance than it is usually understood to do.

It is, then, a question of France and Russia on exterior lines against Germany, Austria, and Italy on interior ones. And happily the powers holding interior lines most desire peace. There is some doubt as to whether Russia will join France in a fight for mere revenge. The Alsace-Lorraine question has no importance for Russia, said Prince Gortchakoff long ago, and the policy of Russia is not noted for unselfishness. The most important question is what England will do. All her leanings are, it would seem, to the side of the

Triple Alliance. What could induce her to side with France, the increase of whose fleet is a disturbing element, if not a subject of fear, it is hard to say; and as to Russia, England can be counted as certainly on the other side. England's neutrality would leave the scales very evenly balanced between the rival alliances; England's casting in her lot with the Triple Alliance would make this the stronger and tend toward peace, which England has also every motive to desire. Germany would like to feel herself abreast of the situation with England neutral, but she manifestly feels its doubtfulness as never before.

The part which other powers may play in the next European war is problematical. The Turkish question may become prominent through the act of Russia; otherwise the army of the sultan will remain innocuous. The Turks are in their way good soldiers. A youth is sent into the ranks in time of war with the inspiriting parental injunction, "May Allah make thee a martyr!" instead of, "May God preserve thee!" But though the Turk is fiery in a charge, he is not stable. Despite marked improvement over the last generation, the army is still ill-armed, ill-clothed, ill-equipped, and ill-fed; the pay is always in arrears or largely eaten up in the way of *bakshish* by those in authority, and the patient follower of the Crescent can scarcely be called intelligent.   The fatalism of the Turk will not take the place of instruction.   It is not many years ago since some officers of high rank could not read or write, that there was in the sultan's *entourage* only one officer who could correspond in French.   Lack of education keeps down the status of an army, but the green flag is still capable of evoking good work.   Until of late there has been no Turkish cavalry.   Now two light cavalry corps have been raised in Kurdestan, and more are on the carpet.   These will be much what the Cossacks are to Russia, and will help to stave off the czar's operations toward the Golden Horn from Asia Minor.

While the other European armies number many army corps, they do not count for much in to-day's situation.   As capable a military expert as exists in Europe, General von Leszczynski, draws from the situation no war-cloud for 1892.   There is a smouldering of the fire which may unfortunately be fanned into flame by some untoward accident, but the sensible, usually the governing men of every great power, are universally opposed to war, for every reason, political and financial. *"Pacem volo, bellum paro"* is the motto, now more full of meaning than ever. The relative strength of the several nations is gauged by the number of well-trained men each can quickest put into first line. *"Se multiplier par la vitesse"* is the method of to-day. The greatest capacity to do this resides in France and Germany. I am still inclined to yield the palm to the latter, though the scales hang very even between the two, and the peace estimate of France is 1½ per cent of the population as against 1 per cent in Germany. The best hope for peace lies in the fact that Germany unquestionably desires peace; France, though still smarting, does not welcome war, and Russia is scarcely ready. The Anglo-Russian situation may be the first to provoke it, but a European conflict seems improbable just now.

THE HORSE IN AMERICA.

THE HORSE IN AMERICA.[*]

A LTHOUGH the earliest known remains of the
ancestor of the horse are found in New Mexico, Wyoming, and Utah, there were, despite favorable
conditions, no horses to be found in the Americas at
the time of the arrival of the Spaniards. That the
climate and other circumstances were well fitted for
their development was abundantly proven by their
rapid increase from the few individuals abandoned by
or fugitive from the Spanish troops about the middle
of the sixteenth century. This is a curious but not an
isolated instance of such a failure in the equine race.
The original horse of northern Europe is thought to
have died out; he was at least entirely supplanted by
better specimens brought by man from Africa and the
East.

* Published in The North American Review, January, 1893.

The Spaniards had long used for war the light, handsome Moorish horse, and no doubt it was the Barb which came with them to America. The big Flanders or Norman mount, which alone could carry the knight in full armor, had been driven out, together with that wretched bully, his master, by the constantly extending use of fire-arms. The Barb was of the same race which is largely represented in the English thorough-bred, and upon the latter all civilized nations now rely to improve their stock. The beginning of the thorough-bred was in the native English racing mares, coming of mixed Spanish and English strains, the former being descendants of the Barbs, and both being impressed by the Arabian blood imported by the Stuarts. Thus by the earliest and by subsequent importation the horse of the Moors has become strongly represented in America, both in its wild and civilized states.

It is not probable that the grade of animal brought over from Spain three hundred and fifty years ago was high; but the climate of South and Central America was well suited to the creature whose original habitat was the sand of the desert, and it needed but a short space for large herds of wild horses to spring into being. These herds did not, however, very rapidly work their way north. It is always by man that the horse gets transplanted into colder climes. The Indians discovered his availability, and gradually domesticated him on our Western plains. There was no attempt among them to improve the breed; but the grass the ponies fed on was nutricious; the distance they had to travel to get their daily supply made them stayers; the frequent call to escape from wolves made them fleet; and their exposure made them hardy. These qualities have remained with the plains horse in ample measure. Many a pony has been lassoed and ridden a hundred miles on a stretch.

Colder latitudes are apt to stunt the wild horse. In Mexico it throve better, and there, to-day, many points of the Barb, particularly the oval face and teacup muzzle, may be distinctly recognized. For the rest, however, the pony has everywhere lost the beautiful lines of his ancestor. The noble crest and fine throttle, the round barrel well coupled to the quarters, the tail high set on, are no longer present. Grass has distended the belly for many generations, and has permanently injured the middle-piece and coupling in structure and looks, if not in usefulness. But the legs are as fine as a stag's, and in those points which make for service:

and not for show he ranks well. No amount of exposure or abuse will kill him, while his intelligence is marked.

Many of the ponies of the Canadian Indians do not come from the plains, but are offshoots of the civilized horse dwarfed by generations of exposure; and near civilization there is always some admixture of the plains with the domestic animal. But the horse of the plains remains a distinct creature. He is not the one which interests us at the moment. He has nothing to do with the horse of the Atlantic or Middle States, or, as he is called out among the cow-boys, the "American" horse.

Columbus, on his second voyage, in 1493, is known to have brought over a few horses. Cabeca de Vaca brought forty-two to Florida in 1527. But these all died out. De Soto's horses, abandoned on the Mississippi, bred on the plains and were lost to civilization. In 1625 Flemish horses were brought to New York; but the better blood later imported has gradually eliminated the Flanders character, unless it has survived in what used to be known as the Conestoga draught-horse. In 1629 horses were brought to the colony of Massachusetts Bay. Judging from their progeny, they were in all probability Cleveland bays and dray-horses.

The Canadian horse is a descendant of the Norman, imported shortly after 1600. The Norman is himself of a pure race (*i. e.*, one able to continue propagation in his own specific form), and possesses beauty of shape, great bulk, good endurance, and fine feet and legs. His docility has remained with him in his new home; he has kept most of his good qualities, lost bulk, and gained capacity for speed. The horse of the Eastern States exhibits traces of no particular race. While the richer planters of Maryland, Virginia, and the Carolinas, as well as the wealthy classes of New York and New Jersey, were able to import many and stanch thoroughbreds, the poor farmers of New England were fain to be content with the average specimens which they continued to bring over from time to time. Lack of blood and system in raising produced a haphazard breed of horses. These were distinctly useful for their purpose, remained sound in legs and feet on account of the dirt roads, and were good-tempered and able. But though the American was a good "all-round" horse, he did not improve without further infusion of blood. The South has always had a large proportion

of thorough blood.   There is a list of some three hundred thoroughbreds—horses carried on the Stud Book
—imported from England from 1729 to 1840, and
these went largely to the Southern States.

The good horse of the South shows more decided
marks of thorough blood than his equal in the North.
The common horse of the South is a weed; in the
North he has substance.   The draught-animal of the
South is the mule, as it is oxen which do the very
heavy work in the eastern country districts.   As a
rule, the western horses have come from the same sections as the population of the several Western States.
Upon the breeds carried beyond the Alleghanies from
the Eastern States there has been more or less impress
made by imported thorough blood.   Some heavy stock
has been imported from France and elsewhere for the
improvement, for draught purposes, of the native
horses.   But the cis-Mississippi horse has had his origin universally in the Atlantic States.

The trotting horse of the North, though great speed
was originally due to thoroughbred Messenger, has
drawn more largely on common strains than the racer
of the South, and in the Eastern States the saddle-
horse has never been cultivated as it always has been

in those States where bad roads restrict wheeled loco-
motion. Where snow lay three months in the year,
and roads were better cared for, the saddle-beast was
not a *sine quâ non*, and until fashion has again brought
riding to the fore there has been nothing worthy the
name since the extinction of the Narragansett pacer.
The form and capability of the horse always follow
the demand. In the North this demand has been for
a roadster; in the South for a saddle-beast. In each
section the horse has responded to the call in qualities
peculiarly suited to either duty.

Probably more and better horses are owned in America per thousand of population than in any other country, and the farmer or corner-groceryman, at least in
the North and West, can and does afford to keep as
good a roadster as the city nabob,—often a better one.
While the average horse lacks the distinctive characteristics of race, he has exceptionally good qualities.
American horses are, as a rule, sure-footed. There are
more broken-kneed nags in cabs and livery-stables in
England four-fold than here. Smooth roads and level
meadows uniformly breed horses less careful how they
tread than rough roads and stony pastures. The eastern granite soil produces safer steppers than the clay

of the South. Our horses are of even disposition; one rarely sees a brute, or a biting, striking, kicking devil in America. They are easily broken. In Kentucky the children ride the colts, often with only a stick to guide them. "I consider," said Herbert long ago, "the general horse of America superior, not in blood or in beauty, but decidedly in hardihood to do and to endure, in powers of travel, in speed, in docility, and in good temper, to any other race of general horses in the known world."

Except perhaps in the matter of trotting, the main distinction between the horse in England—as typical of Europe (for all Europe now is imitating England in matters equine)—and the horse in America, has lain in the lack of system in breeding. Of very late years there has been considerable attention paid in this country to breeding, and the admixture of different bloods, which has produced "nondescripts with which America is overrun," is being avoided. That breeds have been kept separate in England is due to the fact that the raising of horses has largely been in the hands of great land-owners or capitalists, and the farmers who raised horses had their intelligence as well as their stud to profit by; whereas in America, until of recent years, breeding of all but thoroughbreds was, with few exceptions, an entirely random affair. A farmer had a stanch mare. The only available stallion was in the neighboring village—perhaps on circuit. All he could see was that there were good qualities present in both, and he believed that these would be transmitted. Race was never dreamed of. Often the mare was not bred from until she was unfitted for work by something which equally unfitted her for breeding. No doubt the average produce of this lack of method may have been of excellent service in its way, but it was none the less "nondescript."

In England the thoroughbred or racer, the hunter, the hackney, the cob, the galloway, the Shetland, the carriage-horse, the gigster, the Suffolk Punch, Clydesdale and other cart-horses, the Cleveland bays and black Hanoverians, have all been kept distinct, and are regularly bred. One of the first things a horseman is struck with is the crisp distinction between the several varieties, in shape, qualities, and performance. In earlier days, in America, beside the imported thoroughbreds, a strain of which has always been kept pure, there were the Canadian Norman, the Narragansett pacer, the Vermont and the Conestoga draught-

horses, somewhat later the Morgan, the saddle-horse
of the South, and no doubt other more or less distinctive varieties. But these gradually became intermixed,
and lost their several characteristics. All horses grew
to look more or less alike. Within a generation greater care has again begun to be exercised to produce
horses especially adapted to certain classes of work.
Capital is put back of horse-breeding, and the results
are already noticeable.

Much has been written about and claimed for the
Morgan horse. By many he has been thought to be a
product of the Canadian Norman. But it is probable
that Justin Morgan, the founder of the breed, was of
excellent, if not thorough, English blood. Few horses
have been able to transmit their form and qualities as
did this remarkable little animal; and these were of
the best as regards beauty, intelligence, speed, and endurance. Though lacking size and "quality," Justin Morgan seemed to possess all the virtues associated
with the latter element. The Morgans have all but
run out to-day, but there have been some deserving
attempts to revive the breed, and for certain work they
were unsurpassed.

The special product of American horse-sense is the

trotter. So wonderful has been the result of our endeavors to produce a fast trotting horse that in true
national style we have distanced the universe. We
can easily place all the trotting horses of the world, as
Colonel O'Kelly did Eclipse—"the American trotter
first, the rest nowhere." The Orloff trotters brought
over here from Russia a few years since, though handsome and apparently of great endurance, were so lacking in speed that racing with them became a farce.
Not one of them could show a thirty-clip. To our dirt
roads is partly due the speed of our driving-horses. A
European turnpike would speedily use up a fast nag's
legs and feet. Dirt roads are apt to continue in the
country, and near cities there will always be a speed-
ing-ground provided so long as we drive fast horses.
Trickery on trotting-tracks has somewhat robbed this
sport of its good repute, and Anglomania, seasoning
the better breeding of the thoroughbred, has called up
running as the fashionable pastime. But whoso has
owned and regularly driven for pleasure a pair of fine
trotters or roadsters to the typical American light rig,
cannot fail to hope that the promised regeneration of
the trotting-track, with all its collateral usefulness,
may not be long delayed. The American roadster has

From the day, seventy years ago, when intelligent men laid their money against Boston Blue, who was matched to trot a mile inside of the then incredible time of three minutes, to the present year of grace, when the list of horses who have beaten 2:20 numbers many score, and the best trotting time is within less than half a minute of the best running speed, there has been such a marvellous advance in this problem, as well as in its corollary, fast road-horses, that it is doubtful whether there exists in the history of the horse, in any part of the world, its parallel. It took more than two centuries for the English thoroughbred to score a marked gain over his ancestor, the Arab. In a quarter of a century the trotter has made decidedly more marked progress in swiftness. The very anatomy of the animal has been changed by breeding. He is no longer what the original trotter was, but a fine thoroughbred creature, with as many of the points of speed and wind as the greyhound. He has, in fact, been bred too fine. He has lost his weight-pulling capacity. It is a curious fact that while the running thoroughbred has, since 1750, gained at least three inches in height, if not a full hand, the trotting horse, in some forty years, has lost in size and weight perhaps half as much. The average

of the speedy horses on the track are not capable of
pulling a heavy Goddard buggy in good style, let alone
a carry-all and four people, or a trap built on English
ideas. Our track sulkies have got down to forty
pounds and our road wagons to a hundred and twenty,
which equalizes the matter somewhat, but this decrease
in size is to be regretted, and is, to judge from the
racer, by no means a necessary sequence of trotting
speed.

But the endurance of the trotting-horse is as remarkable as his speed. Perhaps there is nothing in the
annals of the horse superior to Trustee, Lady Fulton,
John Stewart, and Captain MacGown trotting twenty
miles inside one hour; Ariel, Black Joke, and Spangle,
fifty miles in less than four; Conqueror, one hundred
miles short of nine hours; and Fanny Jenks, one hundred and one in nine and three-quarters. Fanny Mur-
ray and Kate are also on record as having done their
hundred miles in nine and three-quarter hours. And
the habit of trotting heats, best three in five, instead of dashes, proves the ability to repeat of the
American stock. The exertion called for by a mile
trotted in 2:10 is quite as great as that by a mile run
in 1:40.

In America we are going in the direction which speed always points out, and training and racing mere colts. The temptation to realize at an early age is, of course, great with breeders; but to see yearlings running and trotting in public races calls up a serious question. Two-year-olds and even yearlings have trotted at a speed which, forty years ago, was deemed impossible at any age. Yearlings have trotted quarters in thirty-eight seconds. It is claimed by breeders that this is natural speed; that the colts are not unduly trained or pushed, and that these trials are necessary to ascertain what colts have in them, and thus weed out those which will not pay to keep an extra year. But to produce a twenty-miler, or a horse which is sound and serviceable at twenty years, one would scarcely go to work after this fashion.

There is, perhaps, no establishment more typically American than Governor Leland Stanford's breeding-farm for trotters at Palo Alto, California. It has no equal anywhere. The entire ranch covers some eighty-five hundred acres, and it is here that the university is to be located. There were in April, 1891, in stables, paddocks, and pasture some eleven hundred colts and horses, counting yearlings being broken to harness, and weanlings daily exercised on the "kindergarten" track. This latter is a small oval enclosure, perhaps three hundred yards in circumference, around which the colts are daily exercised, a number at a time, under instruction of a trainer, who stands in the centre with a whip. The colts are allowed only to trot. If one breaks, all are stopped and started again. Here the colts gain strength, knowledge of what is required of them, and steadiness. Everything on the ranch is of the best, from blood down, and the system of reasonable treatment is enforced on a large scale. In the paddock a colt may "fool" to the top of his bent; but the instant a man approaches him he is taught that he will be kindly treated and that he must act in a business-like way. Teasing or playing with a colt, other than "gentling" him, is prohibited. So far from a groom being allowed to strike a horse, not even an ill-tempered word, much less an oath, is permitted. The result is apparent in the uniform tractability of the colts, or, in other words, their serviceability and value. They need no "breaking," as usually understood. As yearlings they are already well trained, and have such confidence in their attendants that most of them can be harnessed and driven without difficulty.

The running horse has always been the special pet of the Southerner, who has never taken kindly to trotting. Up to the fifties many of the very best racers came from the Northern States. None came from the East, for the camp-meeting Puritan would not countenance racing—though, indeed, it may be asserted that racing has done more for the good of the community by improving the horse than camp-meetings have ever done for religion by improving man. And many were the notable contests on the track, where dollars by the hundreds of thousands changed hands, which antedated the war. But the less amicable interchanges of civil strife drove horse-racing from the minds of every one and transplanted all but the choicest horses, and, indeed, many of these, from training-stables to cavalry barracks.

In the palmy days Northern racers fully held their own. Black Maria, than whom no stancher ever stood on four pasterns, was a Jersey mare; so was Fashion, by long odds the best racer of her day; Eclipse was raised on Long Island. What finer trio can be named? But the sport was more general in the South; and up to the outbreak of the war Virginia, followed by Kentucky, gained more extensive, if not better, results in runners, as their race meetings were more frequent and rivalry was stronger. A warm climate is generally most favorable to the thoroughbred. The blue-grass region is his paradise. Here, on the lower Silurian limestone, all mammals thrive. Men and women are of noticeable size and beauty. Cattle are huge. A paddock full of yearling colts or fillies gives you the impression of a lot of two-year-olds. The weight and height of the blue-grass thoroughbred average considerably more than elsewhere—even in California.

The relative speed and stoutness of the thoroughbred and the Oriental horse have been settled long ago. Two hundred years since, the fastest runners in the world were no doubt the Arabians. These are presumably to-day much what they then were, while their English progeny has vastly improved. This is due to more intelligent breeding and to tests on the race-course affording better selection of the fittest animals to breed from. Even with an allowance of as high as forty-eight pounds, the Arab has never been able to win an English race, while in Egypt, in the fifties, Fair Nell, who, though very well bred, was not proven thoroughbred, defeated all the best Barbs of Ali Pasha with ease, at all distances, on their own ground and on their

own terms. It is clear beyond a peradventure that
the thoroughbred possesses speed and endurance (or,
more properly, *endurance at speed,* for such is his peculiar inheritance) beyond any other horse, as he has
greater beauty. His feats of gameness and pace are
unmatched. To rehearse some of the old performances is worth while. Bay Bolton, at York, in 1710,
ran four miles in 7 minutes 43 seconds; Eclipse, at
Winchester, in 1769, in 8 minutes; Lady Elizabeth, at
Doncaster, in 1833, in 7 minutes 46 seconds; Stock-
well, at Newmarket, in 1854, in 7 minutes 29 seconds;
Lexington, at New Orleans, in 1855, in 7 minutes 19¾
seconds; Ten Broeck, at Louisville, in 1876, in 7 minutes 16 seconds; while Black Maria, on Long Island,
in 1832, ran her fifth four-mile heat in 8 minutes 47
seconds,—the whole twenty miles in 41 minutes 40
seconds! Not only do statistics show that the thoroughbred is superior to his ancestor, but that he is
gradually improving on himself; and this present process of improvement, due exclusively to the rivalry of
the turf, explains how he has gained on his Arabian
cousins, who have substantially stood still for centuries.

Another comparison may be instituted between the
marvellous performances which are related of ponies

on the plains and the well-known records of thoroughbreds. That the latter are invariably proven, and the
former rarely so, does not militate against the really
remarkable feats of the bronco. But the allegation
often made that the mustang can go further than the
civilized horse, let alone the thoroughbred, is very
wide of the truth. It is doubtful whether any wild
horse ever equalled the record of the little pony which
beat the mail from London to Exeter, one hundred and
seventy-two milēs, in twenty-three and a half hours,
or of the galloway who ran three hundred miles at
Newmarket in 1754 in sixty-four hours and twenty
minutes; while it can safely be claimed that no wild
horse ever went one hundred miles in nine or ten hours.
And one thing is especially to be noted: we not only
have no "record" of time and distance, but we never
learn whether the great feat quoted killed the bronco;
whereas the feat of the thoroughbred, to be of value,
must be accomplished without material injury. Any
game thoroughbred ridden until he stops will fall dead.
Not so the bronco. But the latter may be ruined, and
one hears of the performance, not its results. It is
very rare that the great performances of thoroughbreds permanently injure them.

The comparative stoutness and speed of English and American thoroughbreds is not a fruitful topic. The matter is so evenly balanced that the different methods of running, weighting, and timing horses produce statistics out of which one can prove arithmetically anything, actually nothing. In order to pronounce definite judgement between breeds or races of horses, there must be a perceptible difference. Between the thoroughbred of England and America the advantage is imperceptible. English turf records have been authoritative only since the St. Leger, Oaks, and Derby were established, a trifle over one hundred years ago. Those of the American turf are more recent. But excellent and perfectly reliable records were published in *The American Farmer* from 1818 to 1830, since when official records have been kept. But from the records no superiority can be shown.

Though the odds of percentage, climate, and accident are all against success in sending American horses over to compete on the English turf, we have no reason to be ashamed of our performances and trophies, from the days of stanch Prioress to Iroquois, winner of the Derby. A time-test will not serve. In America we race from start to finish. Many an English cup has been won where the stanchest horses have not extended themselves over a distance. But, judging from all facts, while there is perhaps no valid ground for asserting that the American thoroughbred is a better stayer than the English, or more speedy, it can be maintained with certainty that he does not fall behind him in any sense. On time-tests alone the American stands higher. It is to be regretted that friendly rivalry has not brought Englishmen over here with their studs as it has with their yachts, and that it is only Americans who have crossed the ocean to test their horses. This, however, is natural enough, for the home of the turf is the mother-country.

It is probable that the average of English breeding is more careful; until lately it certainly has been, and it has extended over a longer period than our own. It is also probable that the English trainers are more expert, certainly on their own soil, than ours, at least so far as preparing for mere speed and game is concerned. But a thoroughbred from a racing-stable rarely has manners. It is scarcely doubtful that the higher class of English jockeys are the more expert. America has produced no Archer. It is not intended to refer to the average of English jockeys. Many of these men who can find no occupation at home drift over here, and are in the same category with the majority of English grooms in American cities. But the jockeys who rise high in their profession in the larger field afforded by the English turf are artists, probably superior to any we have produced.

As fox-hunting is in America only an exotic, so we have no equivalent of the English hunter, a creature bred for his particular work, and no doubt at his best the most perfect of horses—bar none. Many of our well-bred horses turn out superb timber-jumpers; many are up to weight; but this alone does not insure success after hounds. There is too little variety in the obstacles of our country to make clever hunters. As a rule, thoroughbreds are flyers rather than high jumpers. Many of our horses have proven to be flyers, jumpers, and stayers under very severe tests. In leaping-contests we have done wonders. There has been no parallel to the high jumping at horse shows here and in Canada during the past few years. A number of horses have cleared six feet six of timber, while the abnormal height of seven feet has been cleared by one, if not more. These are not guess-work measurements, but accurately levelled, and the jumps have usually been made by artificial light and in cold blood. There are some traditional jumps in England, but no records equalling this. Still, mere high jumping by no means makes a hunter. These same horses were no better than many others after hounds. It will take years of cross-country riding in America to make either horse or man equal to the best English model. Our climate is neither suitable to the sport—hunting over snow scarcely sounds attractive—nor is the country such as to make it what it is in its true home in the midland counties. Too few men call for hunters here for us to expect to find the bone, courage, manners, cleverness, or strength of the English hunter, which is, without question, the animal best adapted to any and every use—except mere draught—to which a horse can be put. There is no work off the track for which he is not fit and which he is not able to do better than any other horse.

But we have none the less created in many sections of America a basis of very good sport. The obstacles are, as a rule, stone walls in Massachusetts; in New York, Pennsylvania, and Maryland, timber; in Canada, both. Hedges and water are rare. The stone walls are not high; the timber very stiff, but cleaner jumping. Probably no county in England affords such high timber-jumping as some localities regularly hunted here. Where the pace is not severe, the coarse horses do as good jumping as the thoroughbreds; trotting-stock produces fine jumpers; but in hunts where the pace is forced blood must be had. Hunting men here now ride American horses almost exclusively. Even the high-priced English and Irish horses, many of which have been imported, have done less well over our timber, and many have failed utterly. It seems to be the prevailing opinion that they showed endurance, but less jumping power than the American-bred horses, which, on the other hand, cost but a third of the money. Perhaps more good hunters come from the vicinity of Geneseo, N. Y., where is one of the oldest hunts in America, and from Canada, than from any other places at the present moment. Part of the thorough blood in this particular hunting-stock came from the South during or after the war. But (and this is a big word) there is in most places a plentiful lack of foxes. Our perseverance in hunting drags is certainly commendable. In Geneseo, Reynard has been longer cultivated and is more at home, and the drag is less essential. *Fox*-hunting there is common; else-

While saying everything in favor of English racing methods, and excepting always English hunting (for in this finest of all sports our British cousin is alone and incomparable), there is no doubt whatever that America furnishes the best saddle-horses. The type of hunter is so indelibly stamped on the Englishman's soul that his road-horse partakes too much of a similar character. In our Northern cities unreasoning imitation of the English type brings about the same result; in Canada a more natural process of imitation does the like; and riders, in their demand for a horse that can "gallop and jump," forget that south of Mason and Dixon's line—if there still be such an antiquated landmark—there are everywhere better saddle-beasts than any part of England can boast of to-day. Since the *manége* has been discarded from the old country, with lace ruffles and buckled shoes, the pendulum has swung too far away from the niceties of the saddle, and much that is admirable has been lost. The Briton recognizes but two gaits on the road—the trot and canter. The latter is uniformly *taboo* among men, and he is thus reduced to a simple trot. Our fashionables follow suit. Now, there is no more exhilarating, nobler gait than a square, open, sharp, elastic trot; nor, indeed, is there a better every-day wine than sherry. But to do nothing but trot on the road is on a par with a man's drinking nothing but sherry and discarding every other wine because sherry is good enough.

In the South it is usual to train horses to special gaits. Any horse can possess several distinct and well-settled gaits if a man will study to keep him pure in their performance. He may "walk," Southern style, or rack, five to eight miles an hour, single-foot up to twelve, trot from six to fifteen, and "canter all day in the shade of an apple-tree," or at a twelve-mile gait, at will. No man gallops on the road. The climate of the South naturally leads riders to prefer the easier gaits. But these are entirely consistent with an admirable trot if the rider desires it. And it is unquestionable that the Southern thoroughbred saddle-horse is by long odds a finer mount than anything which mere imitation of English style can produce in our Northern cities. This is no place to discuss riders. But the fact is undeniable that we have at home the *perfect saddle-beast*, and that our Anglomaniacs will not use him. When one is brought east (and many are), he is at once despoiled of his fine gaits and delicate training, taught to lug on the bit, and allowed only to trot, or on rare occasions to break into a gallop. Let us hope that time will cure this. To the English we of the North are indebted for very much in athlethics; especially for the new and capital habit of saddle-work. Let us look about us for the best means of keeping it up, and not despise what we have at home. Our own stock furnishes our best hunters. Let us stick to our own saddle-beasts as well, and learn from the Southerner what is best in his equitation, as shown us in the saddle-horses he can send us.

This superiority was well shown during the war in the cavalry service of North and South. For fully two years our cavalry could not compare with that of the South. Not only were our men poor riders, but the horses were not broken to saddle, and between them, as a rule, we made a sorry mess of it. But by-and-by we learned; good leaders came to the fore; our supply of animals lasted longer, and our cavalry became more than a match for the enemy. Old troopers will remember with pleasure the splendid mounts of "raider" stock which were occasionally picked up in Virginia, and how superior they were to the horse supposed to be quite fit for mounted service because he had "U. S." branded on his shoulder.

The Southern saddle-horse is of a distinct breed, having a marked strain of thorough blood. He may have originated in the Narragansett pacer. Some of these horses are known to have drifted to Tennessee. In Kentucky they speak of the thoroughbred racer, the thoroughbred trotter, and the thoroughbred saddle-horse. The first alone is of strictly thorough blood. The shape, gaits, and action of each are absolutely distinct. The racer and trotter we are familiar with. The saddle-horse has a much shorter, crisper, quicker gait. He does not extend himself. He is bred for the rider's comfort; and while he will gallop with a fine, open stride, and jump well, his peculiar value lies in the heritage of what we in the North call artificial gaits, but what to the Southerner, who rides fifty miles to our one, are the natural gaits. These rackers, or running walkers, can cover from six to eight miles an hour with such absolute freedom from motion to the riders that the feat is often performed of carrying a glass flush-full with water a mile or more in the saddle without spilling a drop. In the heat of summer this ease is essential where the saddle takes the place of wheels, and the gait is an exquisite one at all times. The horse does not tire on these gaits, though there is a general impression in States where these animals are not inbred that rackers or "walkers" cannot go a distance. In the South they go every day and all day. This suffices.

There is no special type of carriage-horse in America, but high prices are paid in the cities for handsome teams, and not even in the Bois de Boulogne can one count more superb matched pairs than are seen turning into Central Park on a fine afternoon in the season. So far we have avoided the ponderous family coach in which the dowager duchess takes her airing along the Serpentine; nor are the equally ponderous horses known; nor, indeed, the elaborate and heavy harnesses which cover many a straight shoulder and weak quarter. But for up-headed, high-stepping, speedy matched pairs from fifteen and a half to seventeen hands in height, which show quality in every point, our metropolitan cities have no superiors. We have found it of advantage to import English coachmen to teach us "style," as the best of them have really done; but the material was here ready to hand, and the means are poured out with lavish hand.

Perhaps the old-time coaching was as good a test of driving-horses as can be found. The annals of English coaching are well known. The testimony of Mr. Herbert, above quoted,—and he is a good witness, being an Englishman and one of the very best horsemen of his day,—is to the effect that, taking roads into consideration, the style of work which used to be done on the post-coaches in New England and New York, principally by Vermont horses, has never been approached elsewhere. This opinion was given from an almost unequalled experience, during the prime years of coaching, between 1825 and 1831, on all the flying-roads of the day in England. And he, moreover, adds that these Vermont mares are incomparably the likeliest from which, by a well-chosen thoroughbred sire, to raise the most magnificent carriage-horses in the world.

We have in America no equivalent of the big brewer's dray-horse of England, nor, indeed, use for him. The exceptional specimen of this overgrown animal is kept for purposes of show rather than utility. The average one is slow and unable to do anything like the proportionate work of a lighter horse. Of late years sufficiently large animals have been bred for heavy city teaming from stock imported into the Middle and Western States. They lack somewhat the flesh of the English horse, but are able, speedier, and more enduring. For lighter and quicker draught work, such as is especially called for by our express companies, probably there exists no better animal than the Eastern horse or than many of the horses now bred for such purposes in the West, not infrequently a cross of the imported Percheron with native stock. For a certain class of heavy work there is no such horse in the world as the Percheron. The omnibuses of Paris and the diligences all over France are drawn by these powerful animals, and at a good, if not rapid, gait. Within their limits they are not equalled. We have nothing nearer the Percheron than the Eastern express teamster.

Perhaps the most useful of creatures in a country of smaller means than ours is the pony. Until very lately no attempt has been made to domesticate him here. Shelties are now being raised in Iowa, but principally for children's use. For the multifarious smaller duties of town and country alike, where light loads only are to be hauled, it is odd that their utility has not yet been recognized. Pound for pound the pony can vie in endurance with the ass, and has speed besides.

The ass has never been domesticated in America. Except for breeding mules, or as an occasional pet, he is unknown. He belongs to the day of small things, which we, still over-rich in raw material, have not reached. And yet he is an extraordinary little fellow. In Spain or Italy, not to instance Africa or the East, the donkey, gauging his value by the work he does and the food he eats, is worth at least a dozen of the average population. He can give any horse odds of two to one, and distance him in every day's work.

His progeny, the mule, is, however, one of our most valued institutions. In the South he is indispensable. We are wont to prize the very big mule, and many stand seventeen and eighteen hands, can pull extraordinary weight, and thrive on exposure which would literally kill a horse. But abroad, where economy in feed is more closely studied, the smaller mule is found to do proportionately greater work, to live longer, and to be more generally useful. During the Civil War the Quartermaster's Department found mules, on the whole, decidedly preferable to horses for economy, efficiency, health, and durability, though it took six mules to do the work of a four-horse team. The question of relative inducement to profanity in their

The capacity of the country to respond to an extraordinary demand for horses was well shown during the war. "With reference to animals alone, the Quartermaster's Department supplied six hundred and fifty thousand horses and four hundred and fifty thousand mules. In the third year the armies in the field required for the cavalry, artillery, and trains one-half as as many animals as there were soldiers."—(General Vincent).

THE EASTERN WAR, AND AFTER:
A MILITARY STUDY.

THE EASTERN WAR, AND AFTER:
A MILITARY STUDY.*

"Don't never prophesy onless you know."

THE Mongols cover a larger part of the area of the globe than any other race; they make up nearly half its population. It is well for Europe that the predominant trait of the Turanian is inertia; if the Chinese had the colonizing instinct which many centuries ago drove the Aryans outward from their Asian plateau, there would to-day be nothing left of our civilization, even had they afforded our ancestors the leisure to create one. The "backbone of the earth," as the range on the west of their habitat has well been called, could scarcely have arrested their migration. But they are, as a rule, a stolid set of men, fatalists by religion,

* Published in The Forum, October, 1894.

satisfied with their little present, or, if not satisfied, making no effort to improve it. There is perhaps nothing which shows the inertness of the Mongol more than the fact that the sampan population of Canton, with its two millions of people, numbers over two hundred thousand souls. A sampan is a "slipper" boat plying for hire, owned by and housing a family whose members pass their entire lives therein, no more thinking of leaving their floating home than a serf tied to the soil dreams of quitting his lord's land. If you hire a sampan, you get aboard with the whole family, and while you cross the harbor may be actual witness to a birth, a marriage, or a death. How long would a European Aryan thus live?

One of the surprises encountered by the traveller when he is first cast among Mongolians is their physical development. Americans are wont to judge their bodily structure by the specimens in the laundry-shops of Sam Lee or Wi Ping; and the loose clothing of the Chinaman conceals his brawny arms and legs when he has them. Seeing Thibetans in the Himalayas—stocky chunks of men with an abnormal muscular development—had not brushed away my idea that the China-man was rather a slim, unmuscular Oriental, something like the willowy Hindu; but when I landed in Singapore and first saw numbers of coolies stripped to their work, I was thunderstruck at their massive proportions. The Chinese are commonly said to be a diseased race, a people permeated with blood-poisons: but one does not see it in the average specimen, and one does see at every street corner men with limbs and torsos like a Sandow, who would be marked down for football-players in any American college. Not but what disease is always an accompaniment of so crowded a population; not that its manifestations fail to impress you: but the Chinaman, far from being a taper-fingered mortal, is a tough, sturdy, fine fellow, with thews and sinews like an athlete, and plenty of ambition and courage—within his racial lines. Nor have I found any exception to the rule. The Mongol, from the borders of India, where, going east, you first strike his homely coarseness, to the confines of Japan, where you say good-bye to his lovely cherry-blossoms and his smiling bows, is everywhere, in physique, the same strong, enduring man. The Chinaman is filthy in mind, body, and estate; the Japanese is equally clean; but in mere physical quality they are very much alike. That the Mongol's nervous structure is less fine than the Aryan's is evidenced by the fact that the average Chinaman will endure unblenched the pain of a surgical operation which would seriously compromise the reactionary power of most white men; and this, if anything, adds to his value as a mere human animal.

But there be Mongols and Mongols; and perhaps no two European Aryan nations are quite so dissimilar in their traits and tendencies as are the inhabitants of the mainland of eastern Asia and those of the adjacent islands of Japan. The lapse of generations since the continental dwellers put over to the islands is one reason for the difference. It does not take many generations to work a climatic change in races,—look at the spare, quick, nervous Yankee, who in eight generations has been transformed from the beefy, easy-going Briton,—and all isle-dwellers are apt to develope a peculiar type. Religion is another reason; and while Shinto is not Christianity, it has produced a people with more qualities approaching those which are undoctrinally taught by the New Testament than can be found within what we are wont to entitle Christian lands. If honest helpfulness, unending amiability, loyalty to the powers that be, filial piety in its highest expression, law-abiding steadiness, and a keen sense of honor be not fair equivalents of the Christian virtues, where shall we find them?

The history of the Japanese testifies to abundant courage; their internal wars have been long and bloody. It is hard to reconcile this quality, which is the usual comrade of the grosser virtues, with their hyper-artistic sense. That the Japanese, as a people, lead the world in their feeling for the beautiful, seems now to be an accepted fact; and it must be confessed that there springs from this temperament that lack of practical directness which always characterizes the true æsthete. The business instinct is quite apart from the artistic; and the Japanese, when he promises you a thing for to-morrow, fully meaning at the moment to deliver it as agreed, may actually put you in possession of your property at some time between now and Christmas, or he may not. Now the Chinaman will do as he agrees; not that he has half the good intention or kindly feeling toward an outer barbarian which the other possesses; but he has found that honesty is practically the best policy, and he always pays his note when due. So well recognized is this difference that the cashier of every large commercial house in the treaty ports of Japan wears a pigtail. Business is business with the Chinaman—always; with the Japanese it is not so—if the chrysanthemums be in bloom.

One cannot expect all the cardinal virtues in one man; nor do you get them in the Japanese. He is far behind his distant cousin of China in all which makes for orderliness; but the latter can in no sense be compared to him in those qualities which make life worth living. The "Jap" has the "*mañana*" of the Spaniard, or the "*pacienza*" of the Brazilian, always on his lips; time is as nothing to him, and he will arrest the chariot of state to pen (or rather paint) a poem on a piece of rice-paper and hang it on a flowering plum-tree.

This long initial digression is not wasted if it conveys to those who do not know them the idea of the divergent characters, aims, and habits of the two nations who are now fighting in the Corea: the idea of the fatalistic but utilitarian Chinaman; the idea of the æsthetic, unmethodical Japanese. And the wonder of it all is that the latter, despite his tendency to carelessness, has adopted and is fast assimilating our practical Western civilization, while the former, with all his sharp-cut tendencies, still adheres to his Eastern ignorance; the one has got arms of precision and an able navy, while the latter, barring a small modern equipment, is still in the era of junks and stink-pots.

Now it is rather odd that the Chinese have not further adopted European inventions. To be sure, they have (or had) a few iron-clads; but they are by no means as well equipped as the Japanese with a tenth of their population. They have (or had) a few brigades of troops drilled according to the modern method; but only a fraction of the aggregate of their little enemy. Whether it be their bureaucratic structure of government which makes changes hard to introduce, or those peculiar racial characteristics the sum of which is utter passiveness, it is hard to say. One might guess that a nation where a man condemned to be beheaded can buy a substitute for a few pieces of silver, and thus satisfy an easy criminal code and his own convenience, had scarcely arrived at the perceptivity of electric search-lights and melinite shells. But this does not satisfy the inquiry; and one is at a loss to explain to himself the true inwardness of what one might call Chinese astigmatism in viewing the value of our modern devices. The larger the body, the more slowly, proportionately, will it move. The greyhound is more active than the bullock. Is it the volume of China, the impossibility of penetrating the whole mass with any one idea except conservatism, which keeps her so backward? It is only on the coast that there are any European ideas to-day; and what all China possesses of our modern machines and methods would scarcely equip a nation of ten million souls.

With Japan it is just the reverse; and while islanders are more get-at-able than continentals, it is little short of a miracle what she has accomplished since Perry rapped at her front door only so far back as 1854. It is hard to state the utter dissemblance between the Japanese and ourselves. Some one has truly observed that when you speak French or German you are only speaking by using a new set of words. "How many people are there in the hotel?" would be almost word for word the same in any of our Aryan tongues. But when you have to say, "Honorable guests under roof how many as to?" it argues a new form of thought, not language. And from what is to us an abnormal form of thought as well as life, the Japanese had to start in order to adopt our modern civilization. They have swallowed our inventions with wholesale gluttony; but their digestion is good, and they have assimilated them.   Every centre in Europe and America is full of Japanese students of our arts and manufactures. Among the best customers of our trading-marts are the merchants of their treaty ports.   All who were familiar with what Japan has been doing knew how it would be; but she has fairly startled the world by the speed and splendor of her mobilization and the sharp and effective directness of the offensive movement to, in, and about Corea.   How is it that a nation confessedly unbusinesslike, which adjourns from work at regular short intervals to play under the flowering trees, which twists a wistaria into a valid excuse for a popular holiday, has been able to make strides in civilization involving such exceptional stewardship, such unswerving directness, and such unremitting labor? The answer to this lies in the fact that Japan possesses its share of able men, and, above all, a dutiful people.

At the head of old Japan were the daimios, or nobles; beneath them the samurai, or gentry; and to the wants and wealth of these the heimin, or peasants,— nine-tenths of the population,—contributed all their toil and gain save only a bare subsistence.   Though Japan now possesses that portfolio of civilization, a written constitution, the demarcation between the two upper classes, which have much intermingled, and the lower class still remains.

The Japanese have no decalogue; their commandments are but two: Obey the Mikado; Love and obey your parents,—having done which they may follow their own sweet wills within the pale of the law, for nothing is wrong which does not inflict hardship on others. Simple as is this rule of life, it has, in Japan at least, shown its ability to produce a people happy and happy-making; a fair proof that too many laws tend to confusion. The second commandment, inculcating filial piety, is carried out in its broadest sense; the first is observed blindly; but in old Japan the orders of the Mikado trickled down to the commoner through several mouths, and they were wont to reach him as construed by his immediate lord. While to the European who only sees the railroad-opened cities, old Japan is a thing of the past, it suffices to go a day's 'ricksha journey from the tourist track to discover that modern Japan is confined mostly to the governing class of the capital and to their immediate surroundings. Where the Japanese has cut his hair à la brosse, and wears a derby and a "boiled rag," he is, or is trying

to be, Europeanized; when you get to regions where
the paint-brush queue points at you from the top of
his poll, and he wears a kimono and walks home from
his bath *in puris naturalibus*, there is old Japan still
resident. And the time-honored motto of old Japan is
unquestioning obedience.

Japan is a bigger country than we imagine. In area
and in population it equals Great Britain and Ireland;
and its strength lies in the absolute subservience of the
people to one man's will, or to that of one small set of
men,—the Mikado and his ministers. However much
we may hear of the efforts of Japan to make a representative government, or however pertinently she may
show, as in this war, that she has adopted European
methods, the people will for many generations remain
the patient, law-abiding, duteous folk of yore. And
so long as this exists, and the peasant retains his hardy
courage and exceptional power of endurance, Japan
will be able to deal a blow out of all proportion to her
weight.

The Japanese is brought up to work, to bear bur-
dens, to be patient under exhausting toil, to live on
little, and to keep his temper. This latter has been so
long inculcated, that babies never cry. If a child

tumbles and hurts itself, every one laughs, and it is surprised into laughing too. The six-year-old boy carries his six-months-old sister; the ten-year-old girl works with her two-year-old brother strapped to her back, to keep him out of mischief. Add to this the fact that the peasant is healthy and sound, and what can better produce an infantry able to march to the end of the world? He is plain, your Japanese, but the stuff is there.

The tone of the Japanese people is artistic, but the man of action in Japan possesses strength, intellectual and moral. A land where strong men too much abound may be torn by faction; this has not happened in new Japan, though in olden days the history was made up of the quarrels of rival shoguns. Since 1854 her course has been moulded by few men, but able ones.

Japan proudly dates her autonomy back beyond the Christian era. Tenshi-Sama, God of Heaven, whom we call Mikado, is the fountain of all authority, but centuries ago he was compelled to delegate this to a "ring" of his powerful subjects, known as shoguns. The last family of shoguns, the Tokugawas, reigned two hundred and fifty years, and up to 1868 the Mikado was a sort of Pope, infallible, but confined to a species of Vatican. In 1868 the Satsuma and Choshu clans rose against the Tokugawas and wrested their power from them; since when the "Sat-Chos" have been absolute rulers; and it is they who have built up the new Japan. Count Ito, who represents the progressive idea, but who does not wish the power to pass from the Sat-Cho ring; Count Itagaki, the head of the radicals; Count Okuma, leader of the Liberal party, which would make the government responsible to Parliament; and many others,—are truly able men; and they will lay aside their political disputes to work success out of their present complications.

A twofold ambition inspires Japan: to make herself a first-rate Power in the eyes of Europe, as by her native wealth, her territorial extent, and her population she may properly aspire to become if she adopts our ways; and as a sequence, by placing herself in the sisterhood of nations, to demand the revision of her treaties, especially that part which claims ex-territoriality, or the right of Europeans to be tried by Europeans for acts committed on Japanese soil. Her war in Corea is inspired perhaps as much by a Jingo desire to make a mark, and thereby show her claim to equality in the European economy, as by any feeling of having been imposed upon by China. She intends to be ranked no longer as an effete Mongol, and is fast proving her case. It may be seriously questioned whether Japan has taken a wise step in entering upon this Corean war; but, being in it, what are her chances of eventual success?

About China I know little. Who does know much? There is no new China; the proverbial hills are no older nor more inert. Though she has an immense territory, a dense, immeasurable population, and a species of negative force, the events of the past generation show that, despite the adoption of a few European methods, she has so slowly assimilated what she has taken, that she has been forced to yield to the successive demands of several of the Powers, though backed up by a naval and military display no less than grotesque when viewed from the light of armaments destined for the European theatre of war. The true cause of this supineness I cannot pretend to give; China is like a mammoth pachyderm; the blow from an elephant-hook which would kill a horse, merely makes the monster flap his ears; and it seems as if the body of China was not homogeneously sentient,—as if the nervous system of the mass was so subdivided that a lesion to one part did not reach the nervous centre of the whole structure. Nothing that China has done of late years demonstrates her capacity to act as one body. Her crew does not pull together, however bulky each oarsman. Granted the strength, the prowess of the Chinaman. That he can face death with stolid indifference is true. But that is not the desideratum of modern war, and, once demoralized, the Chinaman decamps. In no age has immobility won against activity. The Persian hosts could not resist the handful of Macedonian sarissas, or the passionate charges of Alexander's few Companions. Tilly's dense Spanish battalions were broken by the three-deep Swedes of Gustavus. Heavily manned works have been easiest taken by thin and active lines of skirmishers pushed on in quick succession. Assuming China to rise in her might and to deliver a blow at Japan with a directness in any sense comparable to her weight, the result could not be doubtful. But she has never done this; can she do it now? I see nothing to make me believe that she can or will. Her European equipment is no greater than Japan's, and it has been, in the initial engagements on land and water, smashed by the intelligent violence of the Japanese. To be sure, Corea is an easy battle-ground for Japan; but her landings have been admirably made, and while her division of forces at Ping Yang was not quite defensible, it succeeded,—and that is better. And at the Yalu fight, despite Admiral Ting's bravery, and the fact that he had two battle-ships and almost as great tonnage and average speed of vessel, he was bested by Admiral Ito by initiative and skilful energy.

The Corean war, so far, is rather interesting than great. In the absence of grave contests elsewhere, it looms up into undue prominence. Much talk was devoted to Big Bethel, when some of the battles around Petersburg—a score of times more deadly— were barely noticed. By no means to underrate Count Yamagata and his gallant divisions, the Ping Yang battle was no huge affair, except in its results. How it can be compared to Sadowa, as I have seen done, it is hard to say; for though battles are not properly measurable by numbers or losses, these have a certain bearing on the subject which may not be overlooked. Many a brigade has fought to a standstill with a loss out of all proportion; but you would not liken its struggle to the Moskwa or Gettysburg. The Yalu battle was greater as being typical of a new naval method. I see that the experts are drawing conclusions from the latter, to the effect that to attack is the policy of the future. But this is no discovery; to attack has been the policy of all great soldiers from Cyrus down. No vast result has ever been accomplished by defensive strategy or tactics. The trend of events sometimes dictates a defensive policy. Circumstances may bring results to a man who waits, but it is not he who has won them. The Yalu fight has no more shown the desirability of attack than a hundred battles on land and sea for the past five-and-twenty centuries. It is of more interest to know how the attack was made, whether "all along the line," or on some one spot in the Chinese front; what was the percentage of hits; and what the actual effect of the fire was on each and all the ships. Perhaps its lesson is that many small and swift are better than few heavy and slower vessels,—shall we say cruiser instead of battle-ship?

There are two dangers to Japan. One lies in her overreaching herself in too keen eagerness for success. This is the graver. To learn when you have won enough is the hardest lesson of all. The other danger lies in foreign intervention. Who shall have Corea is a question which interests all the Powers,—England

and Russia most. Like the Balkan peninsula, England feels that Russia must not have it; but Russia wants it none the less. May Japan play the part of Turkey and hold it so that neither the lion nor the bear shall prowl therein? These be questions of international policy which it behooves me not to answer—even if I could.

Another question is as to how far the Corean war may stimulate China to arm à l'Européenne, and how much danger such an act might threaten to Oriental, and, as a next step, to European peace? There lurks no danger in Japan. She has but forty million souls, and even if aggressive could do no harm. But China, the vast, the incalculable? This matter has already been partially answered by the above. Races are either migratory or they are not. Some races have been spasmodically migratory, as when led by some viking, thirsting for war and plunder; others have been consistently migratory, tempted by the colonizing instinct. China has never been either. The influx of Chinese on our Pacific slope has brought us scarcely a bubble of the froth on the surface of the population of that vast nation. And had the immigration of these dirty folk not been checked, while their advent might have produced a prejudicial effect on California, it would scarce have deluged America. Their migration hitherto has been individual, not national. Unless the Celestial changes the character he has possessed for generations untold, I should have no fear of his becoming inflated with the idea of conquest. His rôle is defence: "What we want is to be let alone!" China has able men, but they are not at the helm of state to-day. Their work does not dovetail, even when of the best. Li Hung Chang has not succeeded, because his hands were tied; nor is he the first able man to fail; and in any case the ability of the Chinese does not run on the lines of modern practice. Again China is not rich in the sense that she can spend millions on such armaments. Her recent expense-account, despite treasures said to be hoarded in Pekin and Moukden, had to be footed by robbery of the people; while Japan raised her loan three-fold. There seems to be neither centralization, energy, nor antagonism in China sufficient to lead her to create a dangerously great army or navy. More-over, these things mean years of preparation and out-lay.

At the outbreak of hostilities Japan had on foot and ready for duty in the outland five divisions, what we should call army corps, or a total of one hundred thousand men; and at their head a general staff composed of officers mostly trained in Germany. The reserve and landwehr could not be included in the tale of forces to be sent on a rapid foreign expedition, but were more than equal to home defence. This hundred thousand men, thoroughly organized and equipped in modern style, and with an *esprit de corps* bred of thorough discipline, was well ahead of any army China could throw into Corea. At sea, Japan likewise felt stronger than the enemy, and, though this was more doubtful, has since proven herself to be so in personnel, manœuvring, and marksmanship. Moltke's motto, "March in separate columns; unite for battle," was evidently the Japanese scheme for operations in Corea; their divisions worked on several lines; and against the Chinese the plan culminated in success. Yet, in front of an active enemy, unless you know just where he is and are convinced that he cannot fall on you in detail, this motto may not be construed too broadly. From Ping Yang, for quite a period, an able captain might have seriously disturbed the Japanese concentric manœuvres. The latter relied on their speed; they were right; and it is a truism that an operation

crowned by success shall not be criticised.   Ping Yang
was a Sedan on a rather small scale in all but results,

This ancient city is an important strategic point.
At this very place, some three hundred years ago,
China won from Japan the control of Corea.   From
here leads a road northward, substantially following
the coast, which it strikes at Sin-Chin, and thence continues on to the Yalu river, a hundred and twenty
miles from Ping Yang.   From the farther bank of the
Yalu, a better road runs a hundred and seventy-five
miles onward to Moukden, a capital of Manchuria,
parent of the present Chinese dynasty, and the Mecca
of the Chinese pilgrim.   But these roads are poor at
any season; in many places two carts cannot pass each
other; the many rivers are bridgeless; and through
the rice-growing districts they are at times so deep as
to be impassable.   Other Corean roads there are practically none.   The rainy season in northern Corea is
over in September, leaving a number of weeks for
campaigning before the winter snows set in.   The
Japanese are stubborn marchers, and the distance to
Moukden, apart from military or other obstacles or
delays, might be made in little over three weeks.   The
invaders must, however, consider not only the advance,

but the feeding of an army in Moukden; and this is a practicable thing by water, if the Japanese take Niu-Chwang and keep control of the sea.

Manchuria, though its home of origin, is not without rebellious feelings toward the Chinese Imperial family, which, in its turn, has done little to conciliate the province. It was only so late as 1891 that the Manchurian rebels, who were projecting no less than a march on Pekin, were luckily stopped at Kin-chu-fu by the Chinese army. This antagonism is all in favor of the Japanese, and if they can take Moukden they will have struck a sufficient blow at China to warrant their claim to Corea.

Not only are soldiers gratified with the Japanese strategy, but the thoroughly civilized manner in which these Europeanized Asiatics have gone to work stands out in marked contrast to the mediæval methods of the Chinese, whose wrath at being beaten seems to have threatened the security of all foreigners within her borders. The effect of the moderation of Japan has been to commend her cause to the entire world.

It is quite within the possibilities that there may be intervention between China and Japan on the part of the Powers, jealous lest any change in the strength or aim of either contestant may disturb the balance of power in the Orient, or, what is more to the point, the current of trade. Proposals to this effect are already afoot. Should intervention take such form that Japan must accept it, it would so far alter the conditions that the merely military situation would count for no more than a make-weight in the final forced settlement. Should the contestants be left alone, the probabilities run strongly in favor of the islanders. They will scarcely face the rugged and difficult territory between Ping Yang and Moukden with its severe winter climate. But Moukden is readily turned by a descent on Niu-Chwang, and the configuration of the theatre of war affords excellent means of coöperation by the Japanese army and navy; they will probably command all the waters west of Corea, as well as their communications with home ports; they can now readily move their troops by sea; Corea seems to be fairly won; they have the initiative; they have more modern troops, arms and vessels than the continentals. And though it is true that there is matter in nature which continues to compress before a blow or a missile, so that this can penetrate its substance only so far; while China may have a density of population and a stolidity

of racial traits which would make it impossible for any
army to march through the length and breadth of her
land without coming to grief; yet, in view of the near-
ness to the coast of Tientsin and Pekin, in view of the
historical certainty that well-led, well-armed troops
may safely defy mere numbers; in view of the fact
that the Chinese fleet will not be able for at least some
months to hold head to the Japanese vessels convoying
transports; in view of the personal equation, the strongest force in war, and which in this instance is markedly with the islanders; in view of the momentum
acquired by the attacking party and of the good cheer
as against loss of morale following the initial battles;
in view of the almost certainty that China will not put
out any efforts commensurate with her bulk,—it is
equally within the possibilities that Japan may dictate
peace at the capital of Manchuria or of China.   I am
inclined to think, however, that the Japanese would be
wiser to aim for Moukden than for Pekin.   Their
claim would be urged with equal force at either place,
and with far less danger at Moukden.   In fact all they
have started out to get they may rightfully claim when
their occupation of Corea is made secure.   For this
brilliant consummation there is yet one thing wanting—

a leader. At least three-quarters of the value of an army or a navy resides in the mental and moral equipment of one man. This suggestion of the possibilities must be Celtically answered by a query:

Has Japan a Von Moltke? We shall see. *Finis coronat opus.*

THE DEATH OF THE CZAR
AND THE PEACE OF EUROPE.

THE DEATH OF THE CZAR AND THE PEACE OF EUROPE.*

THE norm of peace in Europe has been stated at a maximum of twenty years. This is not borne out by the facts. Taking the last three hundred years, and counting only such tremendous conflicts as the Thirty Years' War, the Franco-Spanish War, the Wars in the Netherlands, the War of the Spanish Succession, those of the Austrian Succession, the Seven Years' War, the wars of the French Revolution and the Napoleonic Wars, the Crimean War, the Franco-Sardinian-Austrian War, the Prusso-Austrian-Italian War, the Franco-German War, the Turko-Russian War, there appear to have been more than one hundred years when the business of the world was killing. Should we count such minor conflicts as the wars

* Published in The Forum, December, 1894.

of Grecian Independence and Italian Unification, the
wars of the partition of Poland, the many wars of
Russia and Austria with the Turks, those of the Scan-
dinavian nations, and the numerous civil wars and rev-
olutions everywhere, there would be a record of more
than two hundred years of actual fighting in three
centuries. The periods between great wars vary from
one year to forty. Apart from the Malthusian theory,
the most solid comfort to be derived from the rehearsal
of all this slaughter lies in the fact that wars tend to
grow farther apart, as they grow more potentially terrible. We may not be on the eve of a general disarmament, nor indeed, despite the example of the English-
speaking nations, quite near an era of international
arbitration; but it may be confidently claimed that the
periods of war will be vastly fewer, and the intervals
between wars markedly longer than heretofore. This
means less waste of human life and less infliction of
human suffering; for what exterminates armies is long
and arduous campaigning, not general engagements,
whatever their list of casualties.

In a certain sense, armies are provocative of peace,
not war. It is the statesman or the journalist-politi-
cian who brings on war; it is the soldier who is com-

pelled to conquer peace. The latter is the passive element, the former the active, however inverted these rôles may appear. If any one dreads war, it is the soldier of modern times; not because he lacks stomach, for every young knight longs to win his spurs, but because he knows, if he has ever seen it, what war means. The mercenary swashbuckler who lived on war is, happily, a creature of the past, unless his mantle has fallen on the over-excitable members of the press. The citizen to-day protects his own fireside; and no one prays for peace more ardently than he upon whom the terrors of its rupture are first and most heavily to fall.

At no period of history has the world been so well equipped for war as to-day; at no period has every one more honestly desired peace. It is always among the possibilities that a spark may set the structure aflame; but, though it would burn with a fiercer heat and a shorter, it is not so quickly kindled as of yore. There is a disposition on every side to be less thin-skinned, which clearly makes for peace; and if the Socialist movement will occupy the attention of European statesmen at home so that they may have less leisure to brood over foreign encroachments or diplomatic provocations, then Socialism is *pro tanto* a blessing.

There is, in passing, a disposition to rob Socialism of the credit of such good as it is actually doing, by dwelling too much on the harm which its so-called off-shoot, Anarchism, occasionally does; but the fact remains that Socialism, despite its rather disputatious congresses, is only the natural protest of the many to the arrogant rule of the few, and that it is, on the whole, gradually accomplishing the good which our Republic set out to do—to help the peoples govern themselves. In the good old *ante-bellum* days, when eighty per cent of all the property in the United States was owned by poor men, say those worth from five hundred to five thousand dollars each, Socialism, let alone Anarchism, could find small footing with us. Now that the Republic has become a plutocracy, and that eighty per cent of its property is owned by a small group, whose numbers are about as one to two thousand of the population, there is a better breeding-ground for both lawful and lawless creeds. What the event will be at home, where our decentralization can barely put down riots, it is hard to say.

But this is wandering. In view of the death of the Czar, what are the prospects of the interruption of a peace which has enabled all the Governments to prepare so stupendously for war? Every nation has its internal troubles, financial and social; but, after all, the question put is the only international one, and on its answer depends the happiness of nearly every household in Europe.

Alexander III. of Russia will go down to future generations as a broad-minded man whose every instinct was firmly set for peace. In the thirteen years that he reigned, he earned the growing respect of the whole civilized world, and it is sad, indeed, that his life should have been cut short of even fifty years. For us Americans it is hard to appreciate the inner economics of Russia; but few of us know what the ignorant, heterogeneous population of the vast Empire is; and fewer can judge the difficulties incident to raising such a mass to a level with other nations. Whatever may be said of the home institutions, perhaps the Russian Empire may be gauged by the fact that more knees bent in earnest prayer for the Great White Father than there could possibly be for any other man upon whom Death might set his mark. Despite Nihilism, Alexander the man and monarch was beloved; and, so far as his influence on foreign affairs was con-

cerned, there is but one voice. He will be remembered
as a ruler of exceptional common-sense, of quiet firm-
ness, and of strong statesmanlike views. An autocrat
ruling over more than one hundred millions of souls,
what he has said and done has had unusual weight.

In personal character and bearing he was strongly a
Slav, and very devoted to Russia. Slavic methods of
thought are not ours, and with equal intelligence and
honesty it is not easy for a Slav and a Western European Aryan to understand each other in other than
mere society problems. Keenly jealous of his prestige,
it was largely the exclusion of Russia from what became the Triple Alliance that made him show the
rapprochement for France which has been so eagerly
coveted and so much exaggerated in Paris; but, for all
this, there is no Germanophobia to be detected in his
attitude. In his simple home-life, in his earnest habits
of work, in his education, he was more like a German
than a Gaul. He desired so to place himself as to
have his voice in European leadership, which the
Triple Alliance threatened to monopolize.

In frame the Czar was, in his youth, big, sound and
athletic. He was fond of exhibiting his strength. He
could, it is said, tear a full pack of cards in two, bend

a ruble-piece, break a horse-shoe, or force in any locked door. Simple of habit, he had done no more of court ceremony than he must; and he keenly enjoyed plain fare and real toil. Like Gladstone, he used an axe; he would mow the grass on his lawn; his ministers have often found him hanging pictures or doing joiner-work. He was sincerity itself. Attentive to business, he rarely used a secretary, but jotted down his obser-vations on state papers in his own hand. Though he received little and went out still less, he kept abreast with all that was going on in his own court and the world at large; and he dearly loved to hear the gossip of the day.

He was not a *gourmet*, but rather a hearty eater, preferring the plain Russian dishes, such as cabbage-soup. He was unapt to pay heed to his medical ad-visers. In his family-circle amiable and affectionate, kindly to inferiors and domestics, he was sober and somewhat stiff outside. While full of warm feeling, he found it difficult to utter words of praise; but he was able to give vent to his displeasure in very forc-ible Russian. For years he lived a life of worry:—the nation's financial straits, fear of attempts on his life, a natural habit of brooding over wrongs, care for the

Czarina, who has been something of a nervous invalid. No one but his physician knew of the fatal disease under which he labored, and there was no little complaint in the court and army-circles that the Czar had given up the saddle, so that he no longer took part in military reviews, and that he gave each year less and less heed to palace-ceremonial.

The new Czar, Nicholas II., was born in 1868. By those who have known him informally, in his travels and elsewhere, he is said, while lacking the Romanoff physique, to be as strong as he is earnest and truthful, given to a fondness for scientific study, and interested in all that pertains to the good of Russia. More modern than his father, he is none the less pacific in habit of thought so far as the outside world is concerned; but, above all, he has the amelioration of Russia at heart, especially in what relates to the welfare of the middle classes and peasantry.

It is a tremendous responsibility which rests on the shoulders of the twenty-six-year-old successor to the throne of all the Russias; and, however sturdy may be his mental and moral equipment, he has not had the training which only years bring—years of trial, of danger, of yearning to do, and of failure in seeking to do, the right thing. We have had in the neighboring Empire a sample of what exhuberant youth can be guilty of in unnecessary excess of inexperienced zeal; and we know that there is oftener wisdom in leaving undone than there is in doing. The one is the silver of speech, the other the gold of silence. Whether Nicholas II. will err in sins of commission or omission, and how he will fill the throne of Alexander III., cannot yet be said.

The multiplicity of serious questions for him to face is appalling; and each of them is laden with the potentiality of peace or war. Just what his personal sympathies are the public does not know. How he will adjust himself to the Triple Alliance and to its complement, the *entente cordiale* of Russia and France, with neutral England and her huge new appropriation for the navy as an enigmatical background, is yet to appear. How he looks upon the traditional Russian aspirations to the Balkan peninsula; how deeply he is imbued with Panslavism; how he views the Russian possibilities in the Corean war; how far he may desire to push forward Russian influence in the States abutting on India—all these are questions no one can answer for a while. Nicholas himself can scarcely be clear in the matter. It would seem that the internal economics of his vast Empire are complicated enough to keep his mind for some years from international entanglements. It is said that his father devoted much time to training the young Czar into his own method of thinking. He was scrupulous in selecting his governor, an old-fashioned, rigid, pious man. He watched over his associates. He strove to make him worthy of the crown. When a Nihilist bomb placed Alexander III. on the throne, the same dark anticipations were indulged in which confront us now. It was thought that the new Czar might be urged on by the young nobles' war-party to do some act which would interfere with general peace; but the strong, even current of his bearing was through his whole career one of the guarantees of quiet. May it be so with Nicholas!

There has been some recent prophesying of war, or, rather, strong hinting of its possibility. Some of this talk is idle, some of it vicious. To gag a few of the journalists would indeed be a public blessing. Such phrases as the "contagious influence of war," "the lust for slaying," "the intoxication which the sight of successful campaigns has on nations," and "the human

tiger has tasted blood once more and the appetite grows
with eating"—are surely noxious, even if flippant.
If war is contagious, and European nations must rush
to arms on account of the Corean struggle, why did
our Civil War, which every week ate up more men
than the entire campaign will cost Japan and China,
not breed a conflict in Europe? Though wars are
largely sentimental, nations do not plunge into them
without a cause, real or imagined. Luckily the level-
headed journalists do not indulge in such flourishes.
I do not look for war out of any conditions now existing. There is no reason why the old Bulgarian sore
should be prodded into activity so as to poison the
political blood of Europe. Madagascar ought not to
do so. The most proximate set of factors which might
so eventuate lie hidden in the Corean struggle and concern Russia and England.

Our British cousins very naturally look askance at
everything Russia may do; that she is their prime
opponent makes her course appear crooked, if not ignoble, in every instance; and the fact that Lord Rosebery paid a handsome personal tribute to the Czar in
his Sheffield speech does not conflict with this popular
mistrust of the Muscovite. But Russia has as much

right to extend the borders of her garments as Great Britain has; and John Bull is not habitually slow to run up his flag on any available spot he may safely grab. Russia does no more.

Despite society imitation of her ways, there seems, at the moment, to be a curious antagonism to England manifested by all the powers, save Italy. It is hard to trace this feeling to its source; but such *gauche* incidents as Lord Rosebery's recent reference to Agincourt do not tend to decrease it in France, any more than the irritating delays in the Madagascar business, or the continued occupation of Egypt. While there does not exist fuel enough to fan into a war-blaze even with France, Great Britain stands alone. Germany, in the event of war, would scarce lift a finger to aid her, and has lately been coquetting with Gallic susceptibilities; in fact, many people in France have begun to look on the loss of Alsace and Lorraine as ancient history. Thus Great Britain cannot boast an ally, and has the three strongest powers in a certain sense against her, a fact of which the recent refusal to listen to her suggestion for intervention between China and Japan was but a sign; and it is not improbable that, should Russia wish to seize a big strip of Manchuria, so as to straighten

her Siberian railroad, she would be aided not only by
Manchurian hostility to China, but also by the silence
of Germany and Austria, who are not unwilling to see
her Christianizing influence grow in those benighted
lands, and by the consent of France, which might want
Russia to wink at an increase of her own holding in
Tonquin.

All this, added to the fact that Great Britain, while
she can out-weigh Russia by her Pacific squadron, cannot compete with her on land, seems to place the settlement of the Corean question rather in St. Petersburg
than in London. That Japan shall not occupy Corea
in permanency herself will surely be the insistence of
both Russia and England; but if Russia saw fit to
claim the right to guide the destinies of that peninsula,
it might be hard for Japan alone to prevent it; and
Japan and England will scarcely join hands. Russian
diplomacy is keen; and it is altogether probable that
in dealing with the question so vital to her, Russia
would know how to satisfy Japan by consenting to her
taking her reward out of another part of China.
Should this be so, England is scarcely in a position to
do more than protest; and in case she demanded her
slice, some territorial compensation near Hong-Kong

The position of Great Britain was pointed out in *The Forum* for October by Dr. Geffcken. We Anglo-Saxons are wont to overrate ourselves. Inasmuch as our self-esteem has for centuries been coupled with the true colonizing fervor and with the habit of putting in big licks, the quality has been helpful, not only to us but to the world at large; but when we use this quality as an international yardstick, we are not always happy in our figuring. We are impatient at being judged by a "foreigner." M. Paul Bourget, despite his generous keenness, makes many of us writhe. So with the English in matters international. They jeer at the estimates by foreigners of their position in the world's economy; and yet, to arrive at the truth of the military situation—and all politics is to a degree measured by the length and quality of the sword-blade—you may not overlook the conservative utterances of the leading continental authorities. We are all too provincial "to see oursel's as ithers see us."

Here I wish to maintain that the best American is he who has been fortunate enough to see the world and to be able to gauge both his country's faults and virtues by the measure of many other nations. Such a man returns home with a higher appreciation of and love for America, just because he sees her shortcomings. I do not believe in the expatriated American; but I do believe in him who intelligently views the world, and judges his country by the greater standard. An American yard is not six feet long, as we are fain to urge; but it is a good thirty-six inches—which is more than every other nation can boast.

No one disputes the greatness of England. It is only necessary to travel with her citizens to the climes where they civilize and broaden the world all round its vast circumference, to feel that were you not an American you would wish to be a Briton. She is indeed a mighty element in the welfare of the earth. But other nations have learned her ways while she has not learned theirs. Anglomania is not all imitation; it teaches many a lesson; and it is a serious question whether England can continue to be as relatively great as she has been. Continental nations have grown to be colonizers, and are gradually acquiring the knack of it. A yet more trenchant idea is Dr. Geffcken's "key of the situation: namely, that the British Empire as it stands is *safe* only so long as it has supremacy at sea." This word cuts the knot of the problem. It is not only the preëminence of England, but perhaps her safety,

which might be at stake should she drift into a war.
The battleground of England is the Mediterranean.
She must hold this or forfeit her high-road to India,
her control of the Suez Canal, her immense and easy
superiority in commerce. Russia has managed to slip
some vessels through the Bosphorus; should this continue, she might yet gain a slight say-so in the Mediterranean; and with France as ally, and Italy neutral,
England might be put to it to do herself justice. Still
Russia knows that she can best hamper England in the
Orient; and she will not be lightly persuaded to try
conclusions elsewhere.

John Bull is wise. He stands alone, but he gets
rated at a premium, and he knows how far he may go;
and in the Oriental question he will not insist too
much. Were it possible for Great Britain and Japan
to join hands, the union would outweigh Russia in the
pending questions. But as she did in 1861, England,
prompted by commerce, has now chosen the losing side,
and such a union is scarcely on the cards; it is vastly
more probable that Russia will be able to play into the
hands of Japan, enough to avert her suspicions and
satisfy her demands, without losing her own hold on
what she aims to get: a better climatic harbor than

Vladivostok. Russia can bide her time; and when her trans-Siberian railroad shall have got finished, she will be the power of the Pacific Orient. It is, moreover, true that Russia makes friends of the peoples she subdues, a thing in which Great Britain often fails. Though it is probable that the result of the Corean war will extensively modify commercial relations with the East, and will rub off some of the cuticle if not lop off some of the limbs of monstrous China, there is no reason why there need be any immediate change in the world's political centre of gravity. Japan has rightfully become a member of the sisterhood of nations; but she will play for a generation a modest part, except in the far Orient.

We Americans can but hope that Great Britain will retain her present position: it is a healthful one for the world's peace; but other nations are making gigantic strides in British specialties. So long as her navy can hold head to any two others—a matter of present doubt—and is not too much scattered, she will maintain herself; but she must beware of any complications which shall call for what other nations would deem a respectable land force. She has none. And what is more, when a few hours' fighting can entirely disable a fleet, as we have just seen done in the Yellow Sea, who shall predict the outcome of any naval encounter? It is no longer the old day of gunpowder and gin, of boarding-cutlass and human brawn: accident is king; and one lucky shot may disable a battleship full of mettle enough to win a kingdom.

Between France and England there always has been and always will be a series of little miffs; or, to use the French phrase, a succession of *moues;* and it needs more than this to breed serious trouble. Neither has anything to gain by war; the Gaul seeks it no more than the Briton; and, though the press on both sides of the Channel is full of little irritating thrusts, each will go a long way to avoid it. Could France be certain of active Russian support, a small incentive might suffice to make her cast her glove at Great Britain; but the Double Alliance is not of the strongest; and nothing but a clash on other ground between lion and bear would induce Russia to join in a French attack on her island neighbor. Bar France and Russia, Great Britain has no immediate prospect of drifting into war.

The mercurial German Emperor is again dealing in surprises. Since Bismarck's retirement, nothing so pic-

torial has happened as the dismissal of Caprivi and
Eulenberg. If William II. could have his way, he
would be a Barbarossa, with all the accompanying
mediævalisms. But this is his habit, and some months
since he surprised us by again "sidling up" to France.
Alsace-Lorraine is claimed to have become Germanized
—indeed, part of the population is so; and though, at
the outset of this Emperor's career, folks feared an outbreak of the bellicose Hohenzollern blood, or an error
leading to equally grave results, he has now sobered
down into a peaceful monarch. Socialism to-day is
a factor in the peace problem in Germany. There
exists no danger from her. The Emperor will be kept
busy with his new team of ministers—behind whom he
may himself hold the reins—for more months than he
calculates. Poor old Bismark now has a companion on
the shelf. One can imagine his grim smile. Will he
see a third one added to the row?

France will not attack Germany. Hatred used to
be a good reason for wars; and a *casus belli* can be
found hanging on even the smallest political disagreement. For twenty years "*Revanche*" has been thought
to be such a reason; but the oncoming generations cry
"*Revanche!*" less lustily than their sires. Hatred of

the bilious Briton, or revenge for a beating a quarter-century old, will not suffice to breed the feeling which generates war, even in Gallic breasts. Germany and Russia have no cause of quarrel, proximate or indeed within several removes; and it may be said that Austria-Hungary and Italy are not in a position to take the initiative in any question. They are mere lieutenants of the ponderous German captain. Italy would scarcely jeopardize her standing in the Triple Alliance by adding her fleet to England's.

There is no safety in predicting any turn in a game in which a youthful monarch holds a strong hand; but, though many rumors have been running around about the new Czar, Nicholas II., there seems no probability of his undertaking any inflammable rôle. Russia has so much more to gain by peace than war. Barely a third of her army has the new small-bore rifle, and it will be two years before the other regiments are so equipped. Her revenues are none too great. Russia needs her money for the trans-Siberian railway; and she ought not to blow it out of the mouths of big guns. No doubt there is tension in many of the international relations; but that is always present; and diplomats are growing more reasonable. It is probable that what has been said of the character of Nicholas is in the main true; and this should lead him to follow in the footsteps of his illustrious father and make Russia still the dictator of peace.

No man will be rash enough to say that war may not come. Every one of the continents has spots where an accidental outbreak, the blunder of an over-zealous servant, may work such a hardship, actual or ideal, to some great power as shall call for an excited demand for reparation. It is then that cool heads, if not thick skins, are in demand; and it is then that the effervescence of journalists in search of circulation or notoriety does most harm. The human animal, according to his kind, is the silliest of all animals, if we measure him rightly: I know of no other that is capable of such irrational freaks; and it is on these that peace or war hangs by a hair. But, to resume, I do not believe, despite all the talk, that there is in the present status of the world a set of conditions which will lead to early war. The sentiment of the leading rulers, statesmen and journalists does not trend that way.

BISMARCK:
THE STRONGEST PERSONALITY
IN EUROPE SINCE NAPOLEON.

BISMARCK: THE STRONGEST PERSONALITY IN EUROPE SINCE NAPOLEON.[*]

THE Thirty Years' War left Germany a desert, its people half-savage. The land had lost all save religion. The peasantry had much ado for a generation to feed itself; there was no time to think of education or liberty, for the tillers of the soil were in every practical sense serfs. The city-dwellers were less crushed; but the rulers had gone into the struggle as autocrats, and autocrats they remained. About the same period there had arisen in our New England several small colonies of men hardy enough to thrive in a fierce climate and on sterile soil; courageous enough to give up all they held dear and to face the savage and starvation for what they deemed their liberties; intelligent enough to found a university within ten

* Published in The Forum, May, 1895.

years of their landing. It is scarcely to be wondered at that for eight generations the American has possessed political and personal liberty which the German has not yet won; nor, indeed, is it at all strange that it is so hard for us to take his point of view.

The Hohenzollern who was the petty ruler of Brandenburg and of the Polish fief of Prussia during the fearful war in which Gustavus Adolphus laid the corner-stone of the equality of creeds in the economy of nations, was not a fair representative of the race. But his grandson, the Great Elector, was a man and ruler worthy of the crown which Frederick I. placed on his own head in 1701, and an ancestor from whose loins such a hero as Frederick the Only might rightfully descend. If Frederick II. was the Last of the Kings, truly Bismarck has been his prophet. That Prussia belonged to him by divine right to make or to mar as he saw fit was the *motif* of all that great monarch's acts; but despite the drain of his terrible wars, Frederick did not mar, he made Prussia; and what he did in the eighteenth, Bismarck has carried forward in the nineteenth century; and has put the keystone in the splendid arch by creating a Germany one and indivisible.

Otto Edouard Leopold von Bismarck was born April 1, 1815, just before the battle of Waterloo, at Schönhausen in the Alte Mark, of a family of country nobility which had always numbered plenty of soldiers, many of whom, indeed, had died on the field of battle. His education was got at one of the gymnasia in Berlin and at the University of Göttingen; but though we hear little of his devotion to his studies and much of his wild ways, his naturally alert mind managed by infiltration to grasp the foundation of a very thorough knowledge. He was a furious fellow, big and burly, good-natured and reckless, quick in speech and ready to follow up a word by a challenge. A mighty man with the *Schläger*, he had some thirty duels to his score, in each of which he came off the victor. Having, like all the other German college men, served his year, he undertook the management of his father's Pomeranian estate. Extremely fond of a country life, he went into his work with zeal, but he coupled his economic activity with so much of what we should call "horseplay," that he earned the soubriquet *der tolle Bismarck*, and frightened out of all propriety the good folk of the region, and especially their sisters and their cousins and their aunts. He could drink almost any one under the table; he galloped about the country on the wildest hunts and larks, and was generally surrounded by a company of boon companions of the kind who played practical jokes. But for all this exuberance of spirits he neglected not his work; and finally, having with difficulty won the hand of Johanna von Puttkammer, the daughter of a pious house, he married in 1847 and settled down. Up to her death, in 1894, his wife, a rare helpmeet of the true Teutonic sort, and a lady of culture and executive ability, made a home for Bismarck to which he never failed to return with a glad heart. The tone of the Prussian nobility forty years ago was pious almost to Puritanism, though they possessed not the "tyranny of the Puritan Sabbath." Bismarck had indulged in free-thinking, but after his marriage he joined the church, and though by no means a consistent attendant, was wont to go to communion twice a year; and he was a thorough stickler for religion among the people and in the state.

A deo rex, a rege lex was the motto of the Hohenzollerns, only modified in our day. To us Americans this is a doctrine absurd enough, but once accept it and the Hohenzollern scheme was well carried out. With all his tyranny, no monarch ever slaved for his people

more earnestly than grim old Frederick; and it would
not be far from true that a kindly despotism is the
best government—if one could but insure the adjective.
The writer lived in Berlin in the 'fifties, and became
familiar with what Prussia was before she grew to her
present bulk; and he has never seen any class in any
community more earnest, more high-toned, more patriotic, more self-sacrificing, than the Prussian nobility.
"For God, King and Fatherland!" was a cry which
came not from perfunctory lips, but from the heart of
hearts of the upper classes; and, not to underrate the
middle classes of to-day in Prussia, up to the nineteenth century the brain and brawn of the land was in
its titled land-owners. The peasant was in the bonds
of a feudalism extinct by law, but alive by custom.

The successors of Frederick the Great were incapable,
his glorious structure rusted out, and at Jena, Prussia
bit the dust. But in 1813 her people threw off the Napoleonic yoke, and at one stroke freed their country and
themselves; gaining however no semblance of represen-
tation until, in 1847, Frederick William IV. created a
species of skeleton parliament. Representing his dis-
trict in this body, Bismarck was, from the start,
strongly against permitting the King's concessions to

go too far. "I am no enemy of the constitutional system," said he later; "on the contrary I deem it to be
the only possible form of government; but had I believed that a dictatorship — absolutism — in Prussia
would have speeded the unification of Germany, I
should assuredly have advised absolutism." The spirit
of the Prussian nation is essentially monarchial; the
king not only reigns but governs, and Bismarck held
that the constitution must be construed to leave to the
monarch all power of which he had not specifically
divested himself; nor would he ever allow that a majority vote in parliament—which was but a majority
of a majority—represented the people. Bismarck was
plus royaliste que le roi; but curiously it was on the
ancient republican soil of Venice, where both happened
to be in 1847, that he first attracted the personal notice
of the king, who rejoiced to find a man who still held
intact the old-fashioned ideas of the Hohenzollerns.
There is no need to recapitulate the revolution of 1848,
with its barricades and Commune furies in Berlin; but
the end of it all was that the king granted a constitution to his people, and the first parliament was summoned for February, 1849. The king now put to use
Bismarck's rugged fealty and stanchness, and he earned,

even so early as this time, the ill-will of the progressists. No man was ever more cut out to invite antipathy. "I have been hated by each party in turn," quoth Bismarck. But the love of united Germany was an ample compensation.

The aspirations for unity in Germany dated back to the revolution of 1830, but it was not until 1848 that the first National Assembly met at Frankfort-on-the-Main, where it devised a constitution and offered the King of Prussia the crown of a German empire. This was refused on the score that the offer emanated only from the people and not the princes; but the German sentiment was aroused, and Saxony, Hanover, and Prussia soon joined in an effort to secure a lasting alliance. In 1850 another attempt was made at Erfurt by the princes, but this too lapsed; the governing and the governed could not amalgamate. The only residuum of both assemblies was to show that Austria and Prussia were striving for the leadership of a to-be-united Germany; and this outwardly amiable but inwardly burning strife ended at Olmütz in November, 1850, by the complete triumph of Austria and the humiliation of Prussia. As a part of all this Bismarck had earned a reputation for unswerving loyalty to the

crown. One of his strong points—not often coupled
to so much obstinacy of purpose—was his willingness
to bow to the expedient; and bitter a dose as Olmütz
was, Bismarck approved it, for the time was not yet
come to measure strength with Austria.

Bismarck's next duty was as a representative of
Prussia in the Diet of Frankfort, which met in 1851
as the mouthpiece of the forty-odd states of the Ger-
manic Confederation; and it was here that he first
became intimate with the Crown Prince, the later King
and Emperor William.   His reports to the home offices
from the diet are photographic in their characterization
of the men with whom he was concerned.   His duties
were to make Prussia prominent in the diet; but this
was no easy task, for Austria had nearly all the minor
powers under her thumb.   The sole point on which
Prussia and Austria agreed was in the cautiousness of
their recognition of Louis Napoleon's *coup d'état* of
December, 1851.   Only in the matter of the Zollverein
was Prussia able to hold head to Austria; and in Prussia's dispute with Switzerland in 1856 Austria dictated
the settlement.   Indeed Prussia had a tortuous path to
tread between Russia on one side, Austria on the other,
and France across the Rhine; and Prussia in those

days was not the Prussia of the late 'sixties. The so-
called great powers could not gauge her reserve power;
though she so far stooped as to beg for a seat in the
peace congress succeeding the Crimean War, it was
barely accorded her; and many were the ill-turns she
pocketed from Austria while piling up wrath against
the day of wrath. "Who is Herr von Bismarck, this
Landwehr lieutenant?" was asked at the diet. But
he soon made his mark, and there is no better instance
of the trenchant, if scarcely diplomatic, way Bismarck
had of cutting the knot of a difficulty than his conversation with Baron Prokesch, the Austrian plenipoten-
tiary and president of the diet, in the early days at
Frankfort. The Austrians were much in the habit of
bullying, and of assuming as a basis of negotiation
things which were not facts. One evening, when at a
large social gathering, Bismarck and Prokesch, surrounded by a brilliant group of diplomats, were discussing a protocol based on certain equivocations,
Prokesch said, looking straight at Bismarck: "If that
were not true, then I, in the name of my Imperial
master, should have been guilty of lying!" Returning
his gaze without a symptom of faltering, "Precisely so,
Your Excellency!" slowly said Bismarck. The group,

thunderstruck and embarrassed, scarcely knew which way to turn. Prokesch moved away; but later, at the supper-table, he came over to Bismarck with a glass of champagne and "Well, let us make peace!" "Assuredly," said Bismarck, "but the protocol must be altered." And it was.

In the Crimean war the policy of Prussia was dictated by a desire to keep on good terms with the czar, and meanwhile not to truckle to Austria. This was no simple work, but it was expedient if labyrinthic. "*Cette politique là va vous conduire à Jena,*" said the French ambassador at Berlin to Bismarck in 1855. "*Pourquoi pas à Leipzig ou à Waterloo?*" proudly replied Bismarck—and it did, to Sadowa and Sedan.

From Frankfort Bismarck went as ambassador to St. Petersburg in 1859, when the later King William was prince regent; and here he remained three years. It was at this time that occurred the Franco-Austrian war in Italy, and that Napoleon's aspirations to the left bank of the Rhine came to the surface. The French Emperor's "*L'Empire c'est la paix!*" was well twisted into "*L'Empire c'est l'épée!*" for his wars never ceased. In October, 1860, the rulers of Russia, Prussia, and Austria met in Warsaw to discuss the

European situation. Bismarck was present and forcibly impressed himself by his clean-cut knowledge and purpose upon both his sovereign and the prime minister, Prince Anthony. His help was sought, and thereafter he was the chief counsellor of William I., who succeeded to the throne in January, 1861. In the ten succeeding years Bismarck made his master the most powerful sovereign of Europe.

William was a true soldier. The Prussian army, defensively mobilized in the Franco-Austrian War, had revealed grave defects, notwithstanding Napoleon declared to his army that its threatening attitude arrested his victorious march. To correct these shortcomings, William and his military advisers at once applied themselves, with what effect was shown at Sadowa. In 1862 Bismarck was recalled from St. Petersburg and sent to Paris, to spy out the nakedness of the land. His grasp of mind had already compassed the inevitable conflict with France for ownership of the Rhine, as it had already prophesied the struggle with Austria for supremacy in Germany. Though his residence in Paris had been useful, he was summoned back within a few months. The chamber had refused to vote the military budget; and to the surprise of everybody the king appointed Bismarck president of his ministry. William was one of those men with a genius for selecting servants. The conflict between parliament and king grew to be constant. Bismarck's schemes, already ripened and only awaiting time and place, could not succeed if proclaimed from the housetops; the country would not vote supplies for an army for which it could see no necessity. The foreign complications could be but partially enlarged on, nor the future policy of Prussia openly indicated, and Bismarck was heartily sick of the much parliamentary talking and loss of time. "Eloquent people remind one of women with pretty feet, who wear boots too tight for them and thrust them out to be admired." "Debate should only serve to orient people." "The wildness of the declamation makes me think of the Neapolitan command which used to follow the Charge Bayonet!—*Faccia feroce!* (Make a ferocious face)—Forward! March!" "Not by speeches and majority votes can the great questions of the day be settled," said he, "this was the error of '48 and '49—but by iron and blood!" For four years this conflict went on; and what the government could not get by votes, it took. The trio of men who made the German empire—Bismarck, Moltke, and Roon—

well understood each other; their master reposed full confidence in them, and so matters went on.

In the Polish insurrection Prussia stood by the czar, and the purpose of England, France and Austria to intervene proved impotent. Europe learned that Bismarck had nothing akin to fear in his foreign policy. With Russia as a friend, he could now speak out more plainly to Austria; the time for truckling had passed; Vienna was given to understand that she could no longer lead in Germany. In 1863 came up the interminable Schleswig-Holstein question, the details of which are as complicated as, and far less useful than, Bradshaw. The Danes, in short, on the accession of Christian IX., had attempted to incorporate with their kingdom the duchies of Holstein and Lauenburg, a thing they were bound by treaty not to do; the German diet protested, and Austria and Prussia joined to enforce the protest. Again the Prussian parliament refused to grant a *groschen* for war; and again William and his ministers took what they needed. "If we find it necessary to go to war, we shall do so with your approval or without!" boldly said Bismarck. The man stood alone; no one could see the true policy of Prussia. So well-hated a premier has not calmly pur-

sued his way during the century. He complained that
the bitterest insults were heaped on him under the protection of so-called debate. "I found on the average
that the same insults to the prime minister which
would condemn a master-mechanic to a heavy fine and
perhaps imprisonment if spoken of his fellow, were
expurged, if uttered in parliament, by a fine of ten
thaler." "For ten pitiful thaler, any one had a right
to heap insults on me."

Go to war Prussia did. She mobilized, and swept
the Danes out of Schleswig. Despite storms of protest
from within and without, to which Bismarck turned
an adder's ear, Prussia, backed by Austria, forced the
fighting. England tried cajolery, then menaces; but
Bismarck knew the temper of Russia and of France,
and cared not a straw. At Düppel the backbone of
the war was broken; Denmark succumbed and Schleswig, Holstein and Lauenburg were turned over to
Austria and Prussia to deal with "as they should
agree." In this simple phrase lay a fruitful source of
future complication. Finally, at Gastein, it was agreed
that Austria should retain Holstein; Prussia Schleswig;
and William bought the emperor's half of Lauenburg.

This modest war—a pigmy in hard fighting com-

pared to Grant's coincident Wilderness campaign—
was just what Prussia needed to complete her already
perfect army organization; and William, aided by Roon
and Moltke, was not slow to repair every gap which
the mobilization, the manœuvring, and the fighting of
the Prussian divisions had shown to exist. But the
honorable issue of the war by no means placated the
parliament or the people, and the hatred of Bismarck
was practically exemplified by the attempt to assassinate him in 1866.

The tension with Austria continued to increase, and
the latter's antagonism in Holstein finally brought an
intimation from Bismarck that "Prussia would resume
her liberty of action and consult only her own interests;" to which unequivocal hint Austria responded
by assembling troops on the frontier. This meant
blood and iron. Prussia was ready, for Russia was
friendly, and Italy, anti-Austrian to the core, was aiming to grab Venetia. In April, 1866, the fruit of
Bismarck's consummate policy, a treaty offensive and
defensive was signed between Italy and Prussia.
Napoleon suggested a European congress; Bismarck
made signs of agreement, knowing that Austria—as
she did—would reject the proposal. All was ready,

but King William was loath to draw the sword: Bismarck was put to it to invent a *casus belli* which he would act on, when Austria herself furnished it. She pretended to submit the Holstein question to the German diet, but meanwhile convoked the estates of Holstein to decide upon what it desired. This latter act ruptured the treaty of Gastein, and Austria's procedure consequently trenched on Prussia's condominate rights in Holstein. General Manteuffel was at once dispatched into that province and drove out the Austrians helter-skelter. War was in full swing.

It was now a question as to how the German princes would side; and on Hanover, Saxony, and Hesse-Cassel returning evasive answers to Bismarck's demand for prompt declaration of their attitude, Prussia marched troops into their capitals within two days and summarily choked them off. This act, quite in the slashing style of old Frederick, was prompted by Bismarck. Italy and Prussia declared war at the same moment, and Bismarck, the premier, could now sit down to watch Moltke, the marshal, manœuvre his army-corps. This work, the most brilliant done since the early part of the century, culminated in Sadowa.

Napoleon now threw himself into the scale for a cessation of hostilities; but Prussia would listen to no truce until Austria succumbed. Napoleon was playing for the Rhine frontier of 1814, and his minister, Benedetti, offered to let Prussia have her own way with Austria, as against this concession to France. Bismarck dawdled with Benedetti until terms were forced on Austria, under which Prussia took Schleswig, Holstein, Hanover, Hesse-Cassel, and Frankfort, and then threw him over. He could afford to do this, for, after the crushing defeat of Austria, the south German states signed the long-discussed secret treaties by which they agreed to serve under the lead of Prussia in case of a national struggle: German unification had been begun, and it was with the whole race that France must reckon. Benedetti stormed, even threatened war, but Bismarck was immovable. This incident was a master-stroke.

Sadowa not only made Prussia the centre of German influence, but better still, it reconciled king and people, and new elections brought in a parliament with which Bismarck could work in unison. Never was a more splendid triumph than the day when William, preceded by Bismarck, Moltke, and Roon, moved down the *Unter den Linden* between rows of over two hundred cap-

In February, 1867, the North German Parliament opened in Berlin, with some three hundred members representing twenty-two states north of the Main, and in April a constitution was agreed on, and Bismarck was made Chancellor of the Confederation. The threatening attitude of France had speeded on the new work. Balked in his claim for the Rhine frontier, Napoleon now suggested that Prussia should wink at his seizing Belgium and Luxemburg. But he got neither—Bismarck's political acumen was more than equal to Napoleon's greediness. He did, however, finally agree to a conference of European powers on the subject, and this eventuated in preventing the grab-game of France.

The three years preceding 1870 were spent by Bismarck in consolidating the union of north and south Germany; by France in thwarting Bismarck. Unaware how close the bond already was, Napoleon pretended to more influence with the south German states than the chancellor, and how well Bismarck succeeded in his unification structure, in despite of Napoleon the Little, was proved in a very few days of 1870. In closing the fourth session of the Reichstag in May of that year, King William congratulated the country on having become substantially one. Bismarck was not the only man to forsee war with France: but the premier was waiting for north and south to shake hands in real earnest. It needed some cataclysm to bring this about; and midsummer of 1870 furnished the shock. Napoleon's worm-eaten dynasty was tottering; nothing but stirring events which should appeal to the Gallic love of glory could shore it up. A resort to war was the only means, and Prussia was the only opponent. How the military authorities of France could have believed her army to be fit it is hard to see; but France is the land of surprises, and while, under his many splendid leaders, from Vercingetorix to Napoleon, the Gaul has always been unsurpassed as a soldier, in adversity or led by mediocre men he cannot rival the steadiness of the Teuton.

The absurd pretext that a Hohenzollern must not accept the throne of Spain was a weak enough *casus belli;* but to demand that the head of the Hohenzollerns should give pledges for the future—and especially Benedetti's insolence to King William at Ems—well showed that the Boulevardists of Paris had predetermined war. It is not uncommonly claimed that Bismarck led France into this step by insidious diplo-

matic practices. Were this so, as war was certain,
wherein would Bismarck have been at fault in hurry-
ing its advent? The fact is that Napoleon was bound
to have war; Prussia was waiting and ready. So soon
as a mobilization was ordered, Bismarck's labors were
for the moment finished. The last war had crushed
the arrogance of Austria; would this one crush the
insane war fury of the Gaul? The answer came in a
battle song: from Alps to Baltic feuds were forgot,
every German flew to arms, and the "*Wacht am Rhein*"
was chanted by millions of throats along the banks of
that ever blood-stained river. Under Bismarck's leading, German hands and hearts were knit; the outcome
of the war was assured.

No need to recapitulate the avalanche which swept
over France during August, 1870. Bismarck followed
his master; he had little to do but watch the stupendous drama, until on September 1, at Sedan, Napoleon
surrendered his sword. Was ever such a triumph?

First to meet the crestfallen emperor was Bismarck;
and of this meeting, which took place in a small room
in a mean house in Donchéry, Bismarck afterward said
that he felt as he used when, as a youth, he had invited
some young lady to be his partner in the cotillon, had

absolutely nothing to converse about, and no one would come up and take her out for a turn.

At a banquet next day the king drank to the health of his army: "You, General von Roon, have whetted Prussia's sword; you, General von Moltke, have wielded it; and you, Count von Bismarck, have made Prussia great by wisely directing her policy!" Almost greater than the military result was the triumph of Bismarck's long struggle for German unity. At last north and south saw the truth of United we Stand, Divided we Fall! and there arose an immediate and universal demand for union. The south came of her own free will and claimed that political kinship with the north which had been so long a dream. The harvest of Bismarck's prescient sowing had ripened. Though there still had to be some give and take in the settlements of detail, it was with the hearty consent of all that William became the first emperor of the new Germany. The King of Prussia was placed on the imperial throne by people and princes together.

Meanwhile the French republic succeeded the empire; and both Favre and Thiers unsuccessfully essayed to win a truce while German siege guns were being mounted around Paris. The siege went on, and finally came negotiations for peace. To these both Favre and Thiers were parties. The former Bismarck by no means gauged high; he esteemed Thiers at his true worth. But Bismarck was a hard man to deal with, and France could not readily acknowledge how low she had fallen. When negotiating with Thiers in Versailles—they talked in French, of which Bismarck is a master—at one of Bismarck's demands, Thiers sprang up with "*Mais, c'est une spoliation véritable, c'est une vileté!*" Bismark showed no annoyance, but at once began talking German. "*Mais, Monsieur le Comte,*" said Thiers, after a moment, "*vous savez bien que je ne sais point l'allemand.*" Bismarck again resumed in French: "When you spoke of *vileté,* I saw that I did not know enough French, and I preferred to speak German, in which I appreciate the value of the words I utter and hear." Thiers gave way and agreed to the clause in question. Finally terms were made: France ceded what she had vowed she never would part with, and paid the sum she had vowed she never could raise; the German army, on March 1, 1871, entered Paris, and the Franco-German war was over.

For handsomely standing by Prussia during 1870 Russia had earned her reward. This she now took by repudiating the treaty of 1856, under the *ægis* of Germany. Austria made up her mind to forget 1866; Beust yielded to the logic of events; and at a meeting in August, 1871, at Salzburg, William and Francis Joseph exchanged a Teutonic embrace. A year later the three emperors met in Berlin, and Bismarck thus began to see mature his plans for isolating France— for cutting short her fury for revenge. As the fruits of the two wars that he had foreseen to be necessary had proved all-sufficient, Bismarck was now a "fanatic for peace." Return visits were made to St. Petersburg and Vienna, and Victor Emmanuel came to Berlin. All central Europe, with Russia in the background— the *Drei-Kaiser-Bund*—stood arrayed against France, demanding peace.

The attitude of Germany in the Russo-Turkish war had much to do with preventing a general European struggle, and when in the summer of 1879 the powers met in Berlin to deliberate upon the treaty of San Stephano, Bismarck was presiding officer. A wonderful change was this from 1856 when Prussia was barely admitted to a minor seat at Paris; and during the stormy sessions Bismarck, with all his patience and persuasiveness, had much ado to keep Russia or Eng-

land from leaving the conference in anger. Gortchakoff could not have his way; Bismarck did have his,
and the two were finally quits for more than one act
of arrogance by the Russian diplomat in bygone days.
Owing to this disappointment, the court of St. Petersburg, feeling that Bismarck had been somewhat less
than friendly, fell away from the court of Berlin—and
there arose danger of a Muscovite flirtation with
France. Alarmed at this attitude, Bismarck hurried
to Vienna. Austria was grateful for German support
in her Eastern policy, and signed a defensive treaty
against Russia in October, 1879, which was but reluc-
tantly approved by the Russophile Emperor William.
Thus again was created a guaranty of peace; and
when, in 1885, Alexander III. succeeded his assassin-
ated father, the war-maniacs of Russia were permanently shelved. Three years previous to this, Bismarck's dealings with Italy had borne fruit in the
accession of that kingdom to the Triple Alliance; and
this put it still further out of the power of France to
think of war. One more power—Spain—remained to
be placated in order to isolate France, and this neatly
came about in the silly ebullition of Gallic jealousy
when King Alphonso was made a Prussian colonel;

in his being insulted in Paris as the '*Roi Uhlan*'; and in a visit of the Crown Prince of Prussia to Madrid. Again the Triple Alliance, the friendly attitude of Spain, and—despite an occasional misunderstanding—the kindly relations with the czar's government made Germany secure from a war of revenge; and all this was the work of the Iron Chancellor's skilful hand. It was he who had preserved the peace of Europe.

It must not be supposed that Bismarck's astonishing success in the Franco-German war relieved him from difficulties at home. The new imperial constitution was far from a perfect instrument. The Reichstag was a mere body for discussion. Initiative and veto remained with the Bundesrath, which represented the rulers, and the Bundesrath was overawed by Prussia—in other words by Bismarck. This meant eternal vigilance. Germans are not only factious but are never-ending debaters—"Show me two Germans and I will show you two opinions"—and such was the Reichstag. But this was not all. The antagonism between church and state grew apace. Alsace-Lorraine—the glacis of the Empire—was not easy to govern, until in 1880 these provinces were given a sort of autonomy, and conciliation became the maxim of the government.

Considering their sudden acquisition, the five milliards received from France were spent with fair judiciousness, in rewarding the leading heroes, in creating a war-chest, and in building fortresses, strategic railways, and a fleet; but their disposition created many a heart-burn. And a never-ceasing source of worry was the triennial army bill. Moltke had truly said that what Germany had won in half a year she would have to defend for half a century; but the interminable squabbles over the army were a load to weigh down any man, until the parliament finally agreed to surrender the military budget to the emperor for seven years; and this has since been repeated. The never-ceasing opposition of the clericals, the Kultur-Kampf, the railway imbroglio, the location of the federal supreme court at Leipzig, the attempts of Hödel and Nobiling to assassinate the emperor, and the difficulty in passing a repressive law, sadly pressed on the aging chancellor. In 1877, wearied by the eternal struggle, by ill health and vexation of spirit, Bismarck sent to the Emperor his petition for leave to resign. All Germany rose in protest to this act; and William returned the petition with *"Niemals!"* written on the margin. Bismarck might have unrestricted leave, but chancellor he must remain. Had Bismarck not discovered in this universal reliance on his ability and strength a means of forcing compliance to his will, he would have been more than human, and thereafter the threat to resign was at intervals covertly utilized—indeed, so often that it finally lost its potency.

It was in consequence of the wounding of the Emperor by Nobiling that the laws against the Socialists were finally passed, and these were remorselessly administered. To us Anglo-Saxons it is hard to say which was worse, anarchism or the tyranny employed in seeking to uproot it. The police resorted to the methods of mediævalism to suppress the Socialists. This gave trouble enough; but by far the gravest struggle Bismarck had to wage was the Kultur-Kampf—the war between church and state. In 1870, simultaneously with the declaration of war by France, was announced the papal dogma of Infallibility, and that, with the French leanings of the Holy See, there was some connection between these two events has always been thought probable. The dogma the German Catholic bishops, as in duty bound, accepted and sought to force upon their flocks, demanding, for instance, of the theological professors of Bonn, its acceptance under pain of suspension. On the appeal of the professors, Bismarck assured them they could not be touched. A lay Catholic teacher in East Prussia was excommunicated for refusing to teach the dogma, and upheld in his place by the government. The Jesuits plotted in Alsace-Lorraine, and bred so much mischief everywhere, that even the Old Catholic party sided against them, and many demanded their expulsion from the land. Laws were passed against them. They were excluded from all priestly and scholastic functions, and most of them left Germany. Contumacious prelates were fined or mulcted of their pay; and Bismarck was now as roundly abused by the pope and the Catholics as he had ever been by the French. The clericals held doctrines highly dangerous to the government, and "Pope or Kaiser?" was the question of the day. Guelph and Ghibelline again strode through the land. Should a man be a German or a Catholic first?

In May, 1873, the Falk repressive laws were passed: the Catholics disregarded them; and their acts— christenings, marriages, funerals—were declared null and void; their records were seized; the archbishop of Posen was even imprisoned; and a later law deprived refractory priests of their civic rights and subjected them to banishment. Civil marriage was made obligatory. So heavy was the hand of the government that Bismarck, from being the best-hated man in Germany, became the best-hated man in Europe; and a further attempt to assassinate him occurred in July, 1874. The laws were pitilessly enforced, and the imperial mission was withdrawn from the Vatican. The Pope stormed; Bismarck acted: he would show who was ruler in Prussia. The incomes of recalcitrant prelates were impounded; all but Samaritan religious orders were expelled from Prussia; Catholic church property was vested in the congregations, subject to the control of the state; and the Old Catholics, heretics in the eyes of the Jesuits, were given usufruct of their churches and church funds. These were the "Bread Basket and Cloister Laws." So long as Pius IX. lived, there was no peace in Germany for any Catholic who did not obey the law—"*Pio Nono, Cui Bono?*"

When Leo XIII. became pope in 1878, a policy of conciliation was fostered by both sides, and in 1882 a Prussian minister was again accredited to the Vatican. Despite a certain ,measure of success Bismarck had found that the Church of Rome was a mighty opponent, with whom to live in peace was easier than to be at war. From this time on the state, under the pressure of the clericals, gave way more and more, and the Holy See and the German government became reconciled—so much so indeed that the pope threw the entire weight of his influence in favor of the Septennate Bill. Bismarck who, with his policy of iron and blood, had defeated Danes, Austrians, French, had overridden law and gospel, had made Prussia a mighty nation, and had created the German Empire, found Rome a power quite beyond his strength. Thiers was wise enough to foresee this, and in reference to it once narrated to Count Arnim an anecdote of Waterloo. Near the end of that struggle of giants, some one appoached Napoleon with "Sire, the English have lost a terrible number of men." "Yes," replied the great soldier, "but I have lost the battle." Two things Bismarck could not cope with: the deep-rooted persistence of all-pervading Rome, and the nameless secrecy of leprous anarchism.

In March, 1888, splendid old William was gathered to his fathers. That Bismarck was still the executive was well shown in his preventing, by a threat to resign, the marriage of the Princess Victoria to Alexander of Battenburg, ex-prince of Bulgaria, which union he deemed dangerous to the interests of Germany. The imperious habit had grown on the chancellor, but it worked with moribund Frederick. When in the same year William II. came to the throne, Bismarck was still at the height of his influence; and that the young monarch leaned heavily on the man of blood and iron, and had the utmost affection for him, is abundantly testified. Then came the unfortunate incident of the publication of the Crown Prince Frederick's Diary— which was twisted into an arraignment of Bismarck; the trial of Dr. Geffcken and the accusations against Sir Robert Morier and the English court, with its unfortunate implications. In all this imbroglio William stood at his chancellor's side. But Bismarck, now really Mayor of the Palace, weighed on the high-strung potentate's sense of Hohenzollern ownership. In March, 1889, there came another "chancellor crisis," now a common means resorted to by Bismarck to force his will on emperor or parliament, and this time William determined to take him at his word. The threat had been used once too often. The real reason lay in the purpose of the young emperor-king to have ministers responsible to himself directly and not through any chief, were he even a Bismarck. The chancellor had become *imperium in imperio*—an anachronism. The manner of his release from his duties was in the highest degree honorable, but to Bismarck it was after all but "a first-class funeral." He left Berlin in a species of triumph, sad as it was, and with the sympathy, respect, and admiration of universal Europe. But, after all said, the master was right; Bismarck was no longer a servant of the state. He dominated it.

There are many important things which for lack of space we must pass over in silence—such as the German colonial policy; the accident, sickness, old age and indigence assurance laws; the malodorous Arnim quarrel, which was the protest of a jealous small man against the power of a level-headed great man; and many interesting occurrences in Bismarck's public life. They were incident to his office, rather than part of his life's work. His restless retirement, his initial difficulty in grasping a true *otium cum dignitate*, his final reconcilement to the Emperor, and the ripening quiet of octogenarianism every one knows.

One of the common slurs against Bismarck in Prussia is that he is a *Junker*—that is, belongs to the class of country nobles who, after the old feudal fashion, faiu would ride roughshod over the rights of the mid-

dle and lower classes. In so far as Bismarck is a lifelong believer in the divine right of the king his master,
he is a *Junker*, and he comes of honest *Junker* blood;
but his course throughout life evidences scrupulous
regard for the rights he believes the people to possess;
and that he is essentially a friend of the poor is shown
in his ultra-socialistic efforts to create by law a fund to
assure the laboring man against the distresses of old
age. He is rather a disciple of militarism than a
Junker. Accused of anti-Semitic tendencies, he dis-
claimed being a foe of the Jews, but acknowledged a
belief that they should not hold high office in a Christian country.

Bismarck is too broad-minded to be always consistent. "I am not one of those who say they have
nothing more to learn. If any one says to me that
twenty years ago I was of his opinion, which he has
not since changed, and that now I am no longer so, I
reply to him: 'Yes, as wise as you are to-day I was
twenty years ago; to-day I am wiser; I have learned
in the twenty years.'" His idea of government is:
"There are times when one should rule liberally, times
when one should rule as dictator. Everything changes.
Here is no eternity." On Thiers urging him to raise

money in a fashion not warranted by Prussian law, Bismarck said: "*La patrie veut être servie, pas dominée;*" but he added, on Thiers speaking of a majority vote, "*La majorité n'est pas la patrie.*" "I have never belonged to a party since I became minister, neither liberal nor conservative. The king is my only associate, and my only effort is to defend the king's power and to strengthen the German Reich." This was indeed his one life's work, and his proudest title to fame is that he has increased the fatherland. But his precept and practice alike must be confessed to be dangerously akin to absolutism. As a despot his natural feeling for justice would have made him mild; still the *motif* of his character was undeniably autocratic. One of the best histories of Bismarck's career and growth in the affections of the German people is to be found in the pages of "Kladderadatsch," the Berlin comic weekly. From 1862 on, the drawings and poems reflect the man as seen from the familiar standpoint. Beginning with censure, the tone gradually changes to admiration after 1866, and unbounded enthusiasm after 1870. He is the one of all the Germans, not excepting the monarchs, who monopolized the weekly pages of this journal.

As a statesman, Bismarck has been essentially wise and far-seeing. His knowledge suited to diplomacy is vast and varied. He is an adept in French, he speaks English and Italian well, he understands Polish, and has acquired a good knowledge of Russian—which one day he exhibited, much to the astonishment of the czar. His wisdom in active measures is rarely at fault. To accomplish a greater end here he can give way there. To bring the south German states to a point where he could depend on them to act with Prussia, so as to head off Napoleon from acquiring a frontier on the Rhine, he made easy terms with them; but how much more was gained than lost. He has never swerved from his ultimate objective, however much he might vary his course thither to suit the changing conditions. He gracefully recognized the moment to yield; he instantly seized the moment to strike; he has been apt at misleading his opponent and always ready to accept the responsibility of a decision; he has essentially a cool head and a warm heart. Busch calls him "Achilles and Ulysses in one." An arch enemy of all sham, of shuffling, of mere speechifying or posing, a man of deeds, unusually open and above-board, but able to conceal what was solely his own business, his horizon is extended, he takes the larger view of everything, and subordinates details to the main object. He has been a tremendous worker, never sparing himself when the state or the king needed his services. "There is so much *I must* in my life that I rarely reach *I will.*" Able in conference beyond most men, of a rugged force and grandeur and a will which imposed on all, he is yet not a fluent or powerful speaker, except that he deals in great ideas—some of his utterances are like the unfinished blocks of Michelangelo; but he is a capital *raconteur*.

Bismarck is fond of nature; no life would have suited him better than that of the plain country-baron. He likes and knows a good horse, he has been a never-tiring rider, and has always had about him some splendid specimens of dogs—such as Great Danes—and he was an exceptional shot and a lucky hunter. There is a story of a bear hunt in Russia, in which he and six other gentlemen joined. Three bears were shot, all, as it happened, by Bismarck, after each had been missed by several of the others. Of powerful frame, he has been expert in all athletics, and a stanch swimmer. His first decoration was given him by the king for saving the life of a drowning man under peculiarly

Lacking time, he has not been a great reader; but his prime favorites are Shakespeare and Göthe. His wife was an able musician, and Bismarck is fond of music; but he is not a performer. He rarely visits the theatre or opera, Teuton to the backbone though he is; his amusements have rather led him out of doors. He has been a hearty eater, loves good wine, and smoked continually until he suffered from its effects. In later years he has undergone much pain. Very slightly near-sighted, he yet can read and work without the aid of glasses. His hearing is extremely keen.

It is said that Bismarck is rather superstitious in a mild way. He put off the completion of the Bazaine negotiations one day because he would not sign them on the 14th of October, the anniversary of Hochkirch and Jena. He believes in the influence of the moon on the growth of vegetation. He is stated not to like thirteen at table, nor to undertake important things on Fridays—though he himself denies this. And he really believes that he has once seen a supernatural vision.

Bismarck is said to resemble in person his great-grandfather, Augustus Frederick von Bismarck, who, as a colonel of dragoons, fell in the Seven Years' War.

. .

The ancestral estate in the Alte Mark, Schönhausen, contains two thousand eight hundred *Morgen*. In 1867 Bismarck purchased, with the gratuity of four hundred thousand marks voted him by Parliament, the estate of Varzin in Hinter Pommern, which contains thirty thousand *Morgen*. In 1870 the emperor presented him with Friedrichsruh, near Hamburg, an estate of twenty-eight thousand *Morgen*. All this made Bismarck a wealthy man according to the simple German notion; his estate is not large by the reckoning of our plethoric plutocracy.

Prince Bismarck is one of the monumental figures of the nineteenth century. It is scarcely too much to say that, in Europe, only Napoleon played a greater part, in the world's economy only Abraham Lincoln. Except Frederick, he is the most noble individuality in the history of Prussia. Going back to 1861, when he first became the counsellor of the King, compare his accomplishment in Prussia with that of the other peoples of Europe. Russia has increased only in Asia; Austria has fallen from her high estate; Italy, though united, has come to the very verge of bankruptcy; Spain remains of no political value; France is rich and powerful, but has been shorn of territory and honor; England

barely holds her own by her insular position, her
wealth, her fleet and her colonies. Of all the countries,
Germany is the only one which has markedly gained.
Prussia, in 1861, was a power of questionable strength
even within Teutonic territory; to-day she holds the
hegemony of all Germany, far and away the most
puissant of the powers of the earth; and it is mainly
to the strength, wisdom, patience, sagacity, and courage
of Otto von Bismarck that this is due. Generations to
come will point to him as the *Mehrer des Reichs*.

NAPOLEON AND WELLINGTON.

NAPOLEON AND WELLINGTON.*

[*The Decline and Fall of Napoleon.* By Field-
Marshal Viscount Wolseley, K. P. (Boston:
Roberts Brothers. 1895. Pp. viii, 208.) *The Rise
of Wellington.* By General Lord Roberts, V. C.
(Boston: Roberts Brothers. 1895. Pp. x, 196.)]

THESE admirable monographs, by the new Commander-in-Chief of the Forces, and by the special
pet and hero of to-day's British soldier, giving in a
crisp *resumé* the last half of the career of Napoleon,
and the entire career of Wellington, form an initial
part of the Pall Mall Magazine Library, and contain
information, not indeed new, but so concentrated that
the reader, whom sparse time forbids Jomini or Napier,
may refresh his knowledge of the era which the restless Corsican made immortal.   Limited by space, there

* Published in the American Historical Review, October, 1895.

is yet a well-digested mass within these covers, clearly collated and tersely expressed. To the British public they must be highly acceptable; their chief interest to us lies in their thoroughly British point of view. To the average Briton, the Titanic wars from 1796 to 1815 seem to have been mainly waged by England; Napoleon's downfall to have been due to her men and money; the gigantic continental armies and equal expenditure to have counted for less. "It must be generally admitted," says Lord Wolseley, "that it was the war maintained by England against France, in Spain by land, and all over the world by sea, together with . . . her lavish subsidies, that eventually destroyed him." This view is traceable to that Anglo-Saxon singleness of aim which has conquered the world, the inheritance of which indeed has built up our own great country. Were one of us to write from the "Greater Britain" standpoint, he might reach the same wrong estimate. From a national standpoint the sense of international proportion is lost, and too much stress is laid upon the work done by one's own people. Should these volumes fall into the hands of a man unfamiliar with those stupendous twenty years, he must conclude that England, with her three-score thousand British soldiers in the Peninsula, was the main instrument in forcing Napoleon's first abdication; and that Wellington, with his 25,000 British soldiers at Waterloo, was the absolute cause of his ruin. The millions of men raised by the continental nations, their death-roll greater many fold than all the men England put into the field, seem to vanish from the stage; and "Marschall Vorwärts," without whom Waterloo would have a French triumph, is quite forgotten. In the same manner, Eugene is never mentioned in connection with Marlborough: Blenheim becomes a British victory. This is inseparable from any strictly biographical sketch; only scrutiny of the subject from a point of view not national will gauge the relative values. The facts are that England's supremacy at sea was a considerable factor in the problem; that her subsidies were important; that her military aid on land was trivial. Were it possible for an unprejudiced statistician to reduce to percentages her value in the entire struggle, it would surprise one to see for how much less she counted than these volumes indicate.

Not but that the eminent writers aim to be fair. Lord Wolsely characterizes Napoleon as a Colossus among men, the greatest of all captains; he does

abundant credit to his supreme military genius.
Napoleon's decline, traced to a mysterious malady,
Lord Wolseley begins in 1812; but it is clear that in
1809 there was distinct failure of his early decisive-
ness; mental and nervous strain were reacting on his
physique. The sketch is able and forcible, and the
volume, except for the modernized punctuation, which
distinctively hampers instead of helps, is very pleasant
reading.

In his busy life, as his articles show, Lord Wolseley
has studied our civil war quite superficially. The continental critics have gone into them more *au fond*, and
have discovered their good as well as their weak
points. Lord Wolseley insists much on the value of
regulars, forgetful that (as Lord Roberts points out)
the best of all schools is the school of practice, and
speaks of our 1865 troops as "undisciplined and un-
trained." The fact is, that in 1865 (eliminating all
foreign-born) there were on both sides a million Anglo-
Saxons, the residuum of over three million enlistments,
who were the veterans of four years of war and 200
pitched battles, a body in which over a hundred regiments lost in killed in some one action a percentage
higher than that of the heroic Balaclava charge,—

many almost twice as much; a body in which from
1861 to 1865 the killed and wounded in battle averaged over 400 men a day; a body hardened by marching and fighting unsurpassed in any age; a body as
good as and far more numerous than any army England ever boasted. Though they might not have
saluted as stiffly, or pipe-clayed their belts as white
as Tommy Atkins, they had learned their duty
in a struggle against equal opponents. England stands
alone in not having, for many generations, had a war
which jeopardized her very life; her campaigns for
eighty years have been much like our Indian struggles;
since the Crimea she has not faced a civilized opponent; war according to the larger standard is unknown
to the British soldier. To Lord Wolseley the trivial
Tel-el-Kebir campaign naturally appears to exhibit
greater skill and fortitude than the Wilderness, where
in thirty days some 70,000 English-speaking men bit
the dust; but the soldiers who have most studied and
who have seen serious war, will not felicitate him on
depreciating the American volunteer. As a raw recruit
he did, in truth,—after an all day's battle against an
equal Anglo-Saxon foe, in which he had suffered losses
unknown to Englishmen of this generation—stampede

at Bull Run, for which act it would not be hard to find many precedents, even among British regulars; but he later learned to stand decimation unequalled since the battles of Napoleon. Dating from 1862 he was as good a soldier (whether regular or not) as has stood in arms since the disbandment of the Old Guard. Lord Wolseley never commanded—has never known—his equal.

Lord Roberts places Napoleon less high than Lord Wolseley does—possibly second to Wellington. He underrates him, charging him, for instance, with many mistakes in the Waterloo campaign, while Wellington made none,—an opinion quite untenable. Such estimates, however, to those who know this era, lend the book additional color.

Great Britain has always rewarded her heroes with royal munificence, and her sons serve her the better for their blind belief. In addition to many earlier gifts, Wellington was voted in 1814 £400,000, the equivalent to-day of five millions of dollars. What would Grant or Sherman, over whose paltry $15,000 a year for life Congress fought so stingily, have said to this? England's coffers have been always full, and if money is the sinews of war, then she truly bore her share in the Napoleonic struggle, for her subventions to her men-rich, coin-poor continental allies, in 1815, rose to £11,000,000 a month.

In Lord Roberts' sketch of Wellington's character, he conceals no weakness nor (except in the comparative values) exaggerates his strength. The Peninsula campaign is lucidly summarized, the story of Waterloo happily told. Wellington had many of the qualities of the great captain,—a marked fondness for the offensive, judgement rarely at fault, tenacity of purpose, industry, push, patience and self-control under reverses, exceptional discrimination, and the ability to control though not to win the love of his men. Curiously, his despatches give small credit to the quality of his armies; and yet they marched and fought, as the Briton always does, superbly. The one quality Wellington lacked was that imagination without which no general reaches the highest rank. That he, with Blücher's aid, won at Waterloo, no more places him beside Napoleon than Zama raises Scipio to the level of Hannibal. Wellington may be fairly classed with Turenne, Eugene, and Marlborough. He can be ranked higher only from a British point of view.

The matter of these volumes never loses its interest.

The manner of its presentation is what one might expect from the brilliant initial volumes of the biographer of Marlborough, and from so able and straightforward a soldier as the man who marched from Kabul to Kandahar.   They are a welcome addition to any library.

PHILIP HENRY SHERIDAN.

PHILIP HENRY SHERIDAN.*

HIS PLACE AMONG THE GREAT CAPTAINS.

———

IT is perhaps unusual, so soon after the death of a
great soldier, at a time when eulogy alone is the
common tendency, to endeavor to place a hero in that
niche among the leaders of men which he may properly fill. But it is not an ungracious task. Truth,
simple and unvarnished, is praise enough for the brave
heart which has at such short warning ceased to beat.
Sheridan was a typical soldier; the very ideal of a *beau
sabreur*—though indeed the greater part of his service
was in command of infantry or bodies comprising the
three arms; and one is often apt to feel that when he
rode at the head of his splendid corps of 10,000 horse
in the fall of 1864 he was in his truest element. But

* Published in The Boston Herald, August, 1888.

Sheridan was more than a general of cavalry; he had the stuff of a great commander. Just how great among soldiers was he?

The captains of the world who stand distinctly above all others are quickly numbered—three before the Christian era, Alexander, Hannibal, Cæsar; and after the lapse of sixteen centuries, three others, Gustavus Adolphus, Frederick, Napoleon. These are the men from whose campaigns and battles we have gathered the art of war; who are great, not alone because they had the genius to plan and the courage to do the great deeds which remain our pattern, but because their lot was so cast that their genius and their courage could bear its richest fruit. Opportunity is ever the co-efficient of genius, and it is rare indeed that the first, and human, element is handmaiden to the second,, the divine. To this order no other soldier can by any means claim to aspire. Following the six great captains is a class which numbers many illustrious names —Miltiades, Xenophon, Epaminondas, the Consul Nero, Scipio,—as exemplars of the ancients; Wallenstein, Turenne, Prince Eugene, Marlborough, Wellington, not to come down to a later date, as examples from modern times. Besides these latter, equal often in ability, differing from them only in that they were not in supreme command, but worked out the plans of others, is the class which contains such famous names as Seydlitz, Prince Henry, Masséna, Murat, Ney. In such a classification, which the history of the military art appears to make distinct, what may the place of Sheridan be honestly gauged to be?

In what he accomplished he cannot properly take rank with the great army commanders; in what he was, in character and qualities, he certainly may. All great soldiers are cousins-german in equipment of heart and head. No man ever was, no man can by any possibility blunder into being a great soldier, without the most generous virtues of the soul, and the most distinguished powers of the intellect. The former are independence, self-reliance, ambition within proper bounds, that sort of physical courage which not merely does not know fear, but which is not even conscious that there is such a thing as courage; that greater moral quality which can hold the lives of tens of thousands of men and the destinies of a great country patiently, intelligently and unflinchingly in his grasp; powers of endurance which cannot be over-taxed; the unconscious habit of ruling men and commanding their love and admiration, coupled with the ability to stir their enthusiasm to the yielding of their last ounce of effort. The latter comprise business capacity of the very highest order, essential to the care of his troops, keen perceptions, which even in extraordinary circumstances or sudden emergencies are not to be led astray; the ability to think as quickly and accurately in the turmoil of battle as in the quiet of the bureau; the power to foresee to its ultimate conclusion the result of a strategic or tactical manœuvre; the capacity to gauge the efforts of men and of masses of men; the many-sidedness which can respond to the demands of every detail of the battle-field while never losing sight of the one object aimed at; the mental strength which weakens not under the tax of hours and days of unequalled strain. For, indeed, there is no position in which man can be placed which asks so much of his intellect in so short a space as that of the commander, the failure or success, the decimation or security of whose army hangs on his instant thought and unequivocal instruction under the furious and kaleidoscopic ordeal of the field. To these qualities of heart and head add one factor more — opportunity, and you have the great soldier.

Those who are familiar with Sheridan's character and military career well know that he possessed all the qualities thus enumerated in abundant measure. Perhaps no general of the North or South had the native qualities of the soldier in more marked a degree. But, like Stonewall Jackson, Sheridan lacked opportunity to rise beyond the position of lieutenant. When he had made his way by crisp merit to the command of a corps, circumstances had already selected Grant and Sherman as the two men who should guide our armies, east and west, to the outcome of the war. No more changes in supreme command were to be made. The confidence of the people had been given to Grant and it was never recalled. There was but one great rôle beside that assumed by Grant, and this was undertaken and grandly played by Sherman. There was no leading part left to which Sheridan could aspire.

Sheridan's Valley campaign cannot fairly measure the whole man. He commanded overwhelming forces, and, if capable, must win. But incidents in that campaign do directly illustrate the qualities of the soldier, and show how truly he possessed them. Rarely does the divine spark break forth from any man's soul as it did from Sheridan's at Cedar Creek. From Dinwiddie through Five Forks to Appomattox, Sheridan showed the true capacity for command, and in his remorseless pursuit of Lee exhibited what is perhaps more rarely shown than any other quality, the ability to follow a retreating enemy to the bitter end.

That Sheridan was the making of a captain of no common order seems unquestionable. That his youth and the fortunes of war kept him a lieutenant to even so great a man as Grant in no wise militates against his powers. It merely limited their scope. He was potentially a commander of a high class. He was actually one of the best lieutenants that any modern war has developed.

MOSBY'S RANGERS.

MOSBY'S RANGERS.*

[*Mosby's Rangers: A Record of the Operations of
the Forty-third Battalion Virginia Cavalry*, from
its Organization to the Surrender, from the
Diary of a Private, supplemented and veri-
fied with Official Reports, etc. By JAMES J.
WILLIAMSON, of Company A. (New York:
Ralph B. Kenyon. 1896. Pp. xii, 510.)]

NONE of the brave men who fought through our
civil war is qualified to write its final history;
yet whoever is able should deem it a duty to jot down
the facts which alone can lend local color to the work
of the future historian. With characteristic national
patience, the German general-staff has compiled an
unprejudiced narrative of the War of 1870; but in
America we are not so fortunate. Though there is no
lack of even-handed treatment of the subject, the

* Published in the American Historical Review, December, 1896.

majority of our war-books lean markedly to one or the other side; and despite the glamour environing Mosby, the volume before us is somewhat marred by its unconscious bias. War on the large scale is a universally engrossing topic; the operations of small war must be narrated with exceptional dash to ensure an audience beyond the immediate personal circle; and this book will be chiefly read by those who served on the outskirts of the Virginian armies.

John Singleton Mosby was a born partisan. In 1861 he was twenty-eight years old, a college-bred lawyer, a man of quiet character, gentle though firm, cool and daring, and an unusual judge of men. Our author describes him as "a rather slender, but wiry-looking young man of medium height, with keen eyes and pleasant expression." During the first two years of the war he played but a modest part, awhile in the Old Capitol prison; nor until June, 1863, does he appear in a masterful rôle on the Virginia theatre of operations. His habitat, "Mosby's Confederacy," was a quadrangle between the Blue Ridge and Bull Run Mountains, whose debouches lay at the four corners—Manassas, Thoroughfare, Snicker's and Aldie Gaps. His troops were farmers, many of whom had suffered at the hands

of the United States troops; they were called together
for a raid by couriers; they dispersed after the event;
any Virginian would shelter and feed them.   Though
they were regularly mustered in the Confederate army,
and though Mosby reported directly to J. E. B. Stuart
and later to Gen. Lee, we Federals persisted in calling
them guerillas, bushwhackers, freebooters, and sought
to deny them the rights of the soldier who served in
the ranks.   Yet it is doubtful if war was ever conducted by an invaded population without recourse to
to irregulars—*Freischützen, francs-tireurs, Cossacks*—
doubtful if conflict was ever freer from vandalism.

From his "Confederacy" Col. Mosby sallied forth at
intervals of a few days or weeks, and by his intimate
knowledge of the *terrain*, the aid of the country people,
his exceptional speed, and his power of getting work
out of his men and horses, he created for himself an
importance quite beyond his actual power.   He cut
out army trains, burned bridges, pounced on sleeping
camps, waylaid scouting parties, wrecked trains and
captured paymasters with funds, rode into towns and
took general officers prisoners in their beds, attacked
cavalry columns with a mere handful of men, and generally played havoc with the minor operations of our

armies. No wonder that his boldness and skill made him a Southern hero and Northern plague. Yet it savors of extravagance to herald him as the dread of Grant and Sheridan, as a factor in their problem overriding Lee and Early. As Hannibal's Numidians pestered the Roman legions; as the Austrian Pandours more than once upset old Frederick's best laid plans; so Mosby's brilliant success was won because the conditions had bred for us no body of men which could play his game. This was all: Æsop's gad-fly all but drove the lion crazy. Excellent chronicle as is Mr. Williamson's book, in this it lacks perspective: that it has just a trifle too much of the "we did it all" spirit. And yet the author is fair according to his light, admits occasional defeat gracefully, is not offensive in his accusations of "barbarities" committed by the Union troops, and verifies his statements by copious foot-note extracts from the *War Records*. Still, when one finds that it is "nothing contrary to the usage of War" for Mosby to wreck a train and "kill and wound a large number" of our people, but that it is "brutal conduct" deserving retaliation for us to arrest some Confederate citizens, and make them ride on future trains as a deterrent, one is tempted to smile at the honest obliquity of the

If Mosby was an irregular *beau sabreur* of pure water, so were his men brave, devoted, skilful and enterprising. They covered the country from Gordonsville to Gettysburg, from the Shenandoah to the lower Potomac, and left their impress wherever they went, in distinctly inverse ratio to their numbers. They were naturally horsemen as our men were not; they left sabre and carbine behind and rode at the enemy with their six-shooters; and their heavy percentage of loss testifies to their fighting capacity. In line of battle, however, they would not have counted for much—until they learned their trade. They did precisely what New England farmers did a hundred years ago, and would do again—no more, no less.

The two hundred portraits, both Union and Confederate, are interesting as giving occasion to compare the Northern and Southern soldier's looks and attire, as well as to gauge the difference between the outward man of to-day and him of a generation past. The inward man varies only as he gains (or loses) by civilization.

THE CAMPAIGN OF MARENGO.

THE CAMPAIGN OF MARENGO.*

[*The Campaign of Marengo*, with Comments. By
HERBERT H. SARGENT, First Lieutenant and
Quartermaster, Second Cavalry, United States
Army. (Chicago: A. C. McClurg and Co. 1897.
Pp. 240.)]

————

IN 1800 Napoleon was thirty, within two years as
old as Alexander at his death. He had won his
rank as a strategist and tactician in 1796; he had
deservedly made himself First Consul. Mainly by his
efforts civil war had been suppressed; France had been
saved from financial ruin; the morale of the nation and
the army had been restored. Napoleon had deserved
well in that he had not despaired of the republic.

Peace was desired; but events were set for war.
England commanded the sea, but remained inactive.

* Published in the American Historical Review, July, 1898.

Austria held all northern Italy with 120,000 men under brave but aged Melas, confronted in the Genoa region by tenacious Masséna with one-third the force; while on either side of the Rhine stood Kray and Moreau, each with an army of about 125,000 men.

Napoleon, in supreme command, was secretly raising an Army of Reserve. Assembled near Geneva, it could succor either Masséna or Moreau. Austria was attacking on two lines separated by the Alps, while France might debouch from central Switzerland against either of her armies. The best Austrian soldier, the Archduke Charles, had been shelved, and the Aulic Council assiduously kept both Kray and Melas misinformed. The Army of Reserve was assembled without their knowledge. Kray and Melas believed that every French soldier stood in their front. From Paris Napoleon watched each move, understood the meaning of every situation. No man has comprehended the great game of war in the same broad and yet detailed sense. Lesser lights have since jeered at Napoleon's pincushion maps, and at Jomini's diagrams; but the man who, for his own instruction or another's, can so give a clear object lesson, proves that he has mastered his subject. The captain must think clearly before he can act

Masséna's duty in the general scheme was to occupy the attention of Melas; and he was abreast of the task. Though literally starved out of Genoa, he contained his thrice greater opponent until Napoleon could descend upon his rear. Though able, Moreau lacked his chief's audacity, and rejected Napoleon's bold manœuvre, by which he might turn Kray out of his position and compromise his army. But rank and file confided in Moreau; Napoleon needed the man, and he was permitted to play his own game. This he did respectably, not brilliantly. He might have destroyed Kray; he did actually defeat him.

Meanwhile Napoleon assembled his Army of Reserve, 55,000 strong, and crossed the Alps. This march he and his adulators have been fond of likening to Hannibal's daring feat. It was in no sense comparable to that wonderful performance, nor indeed to the march of Alexander across the Hindu Kush. But it was splendid in execution as in conception, utterly unexpected by the enemy, and successful. By the 25th of May, despite the almost fatal check at Bard, his five corps had descended into the valley of the Po. He was within reach of the communications of Melas; his own were secure.

The pass of Stradella, where the Appenines meet the Po, has always played its part, as all great topographical features must, in the campaigns of northern Italy. Hannibal calculated on it; Prince Eugene won Turin because of it; Napoleon saw that it was the gate through which Melas must retreat. Hastening to Milan, after a diversion leading Melas to believe he was aiming at Turin, Napoleon was compelled to await his reïnforcements; but he reached Stradella and camped there on the 6th of June, astride the line of retreat of Melas, who had just awakened to the meaning of the problem. Melas had not drawn diagrams, mentally or otherwise.

The strategy of the campaign of Marengo was magnificent; that leading up to the battle and the tactics of the battle itself were full of audacity, but lacking in discretion. Purposing a battle near Stradella, Napoleon failed to concentrate all his forces there, lest Melas should escape by the north of the Po; he advanced ·to Marengo without sufficiently reconnoitring, detached Dessaix, and was outnumbered and surprised on the battle-field. Had not Melas's personal exhaustion prevented continuance of the handsome effort which defeated the French in the

forenoon; had not Dessaix marched back to the sound
of the guns; had not Napoleon been fortunate in his
lieutenants—had he indeed not been Napoleon—
Marengo would have been a lost battle. His manœuvre was perfect up to Stradella; he then gambled
on the chances; and any one but Napoleon would
have miscarried.

All this is told by Lieutenant Sargent in an interesting and especially perspicuous manner. What may be
called the modern military criticism, i. e., that which
the reader may compare to modern examples, often
within his own experience, dates only from the present generation. Jomini, though we all go back to him
with a keener sense of enlightenment, appeals rather
to the soldier than to the civilian; but out of the
modern critic's book any intelligent reader may, without effort, grasp the salient points of a military situation. Turgid criticism preceding Lloyd arose from
turgid ideas. Lloyd was the first to see and tell why
Frederick accomplished his astounding results. Jomini's
diagrams first enunciated what Napoleon had evolved
from the deeds of his predecessors—the modern art
of war. Since Jomini, military criticism has grown
to appeal more directly to the civilian. Just as now-

adays a layman may better understand the law applicable to his own peculiar case than in the days of Coke, so may he better comprehend the underlying motives of this or that manœuvre on a strategic or tactical field, than a century ago.

Lieutenant Sargent is one of the most interesting of our modern military critics; and, recognizing that no single chapter can do a campaign justice, he is happy in choosing to devote each of his volumes to a single campaign.

Marengo has been so fully discussed heretofore that it is no detraction from this work to say that there is perhaps small room for novel ideas upon the subject; but the author's presentation of the events which led up to the battle and of the battle itself shows a good sense of proportion, keen appreciation of the value of facts, and an agreeable, easy style. Future volumes will be warmly welcomed.

CRITICAL ESTIMATES

OF

COLONEL DODGE'S BOOKS

From the Instantaneous Photograph of Patroclus and Owner.

BY
THEODORE AYRAULT DODGE,

BREVET LIEUTENANT-COLONEL UNITED STATES ARMY (RETIRED LIST), AUTHOR OF "THE CAMPAIGN OF CHANCELLORSVILLE," "A BIRD'S-EYE VIEW OF THE CIVIL WAR," ETC., ETC.

PATROCLUS AND PENELOPE:
A CHAT IN THE SADDLE.

Since—as it has been our fortune to be long engaged about horses—we consider that we have acquired some knowledge of horsemanship; we desire also to intimate to the younger part of our friends how we think that they may bestow their attention on horses to the best advantage.
— XENOPHON on Horsemanship.

This book is written from an experience extending over thirty years, — in the English hunting field, the Prussian army, the plains of the West, active service during the Civil War, and daily riding everywhere. The author has studied equestrianism as an art, and, though believing in the Haute École of Baucher, enjoys with equal zest a ride to hounds or a galop on the Western prairies.

The experienced equestrian will be delighted by the author's breezy talk and thorough knowledge of his subject. The young horseman who may have purchased a colt just broken to harness can by the use of its hints make him as clever as Patroclus. Even the man who rides but a dozen times a year will be interested in the book, while the every-day reader will be charmed by its simplicity, geniality, and heartiness.

AMERICAN NOTICES.

Col. Dodge has given the beginner in the art of horsemanship the best possible introduction to his pleasurable task. The author has had a much wider store of practical experience in horsemanship than his predecessors in this field of instruction. — *New York Evening Post.*

The practical horseman cannot fail to admire the firm, easy seat which the beginner will do well to copy: "Patroclus" is ably described, and, if up to what is said of him, must be a gem of the first water. — *New York Times.*

It is written in a frank, refined, and genial style that is peculiarly ingratiating; while underlying this is a thorough knowledge of the subject treated. — *Dial* (Chicago).

Col. Dodge's book is liberalizing. It may be both warmly and safely commended to all lovers of horses and to all who ride. — *Atlantic Monthly.*

Col. Dodge is an expert in all the *finesse* and paraphernalia of horses and horseback-riding. . . . The advice is sound and simple, and very direct. — *The Critic* (New York).

It abounds in excellent suggestions, the fruit of sound experience, accurate observations, and good common-sense. It is an excellent book for the amateur. Withal it is told in a pleasant, easy way, as if it had been written in the saddle instead of at the desk. — *Christian Register* (Boston).

The chapters on the training of horse and rider are full of sound information, clearly stated, and practical to the last degree. — *Journal of Military Service Institution* (New York).

A lover of horses will find in this volume a book which will give him unlimited pleasure. — *The Book-Buyer* (New York).

This book will be given an enthusiastic welcome by all lovers of equestrianism. — *Chicago Journal*.

The hearty animal spirits which galop through its pages are catching. — *New York Mail and Express*.

Col. Dodge is a charming teacher. — *Boston Herald.*

ENGLISH NOTICES.

Col. Dodge has a right to offer himself as an authority on horsemanship. . . . We recommend Col. Dodge's work as one of the most important and valuable treatises upon the art of riding that we have in our language. — *Saturday Review* (London).

Amongst experts Col. Dodge enjoys the reputation of being one of the very first horsemen. . . . The book is not one to be read through and put aside, but to be kept on a convenient shelf for reference. — *Illustrated Sporting and Dramatic News* (London).

Col. Dodge has handled his subject with an ability beyond the average, and is also very amusing in his lectures. — *Pall Mall Gazette.*

A very learned and charming book. We may very well recommend it as a delightful one to all who care for horses. — *London Graphic.*

The spirit of a sportsman pervades it throughout. There is very much that is worth reading and thinking over. — *The Field* (London).

Published in two styles. Illustrated with fourteen phototypes of the horse in motion, one volume, octavo, gilt top, half roan, $3.00. Illustrated with fourteen drawings by Gray Parker from the instantaneous photographs, 12mo, half roan, $1.25.

HOUGHTON, MIFFLIN, & COMPANY, PUBLISHERS.

ALEXANDER.

A History of the Origin and Growth of the Art of War, from the Earliest Times to the Battle of Ipsus, B. C. 301 ; with a detailed account of the Campaigns of the Great Macedonian. With 237 Charts, Maps, Plans of Battles and Tactical Manœuvres, Cuts of Armor, Uniforms, Siege Devices, and Portraits. 8vo, two volumes in one, pp. xxiv, 692, $5.00.

By THEODORE AYRAULT DODGE,

Brevet Lieutenant-Colonel United States Army.

Colonel Dodge has made it clear in this well-written book that there was room for at least one more study of the great Macedonian, and that new light could be thrown upon his achievements by examining them from a military point of view. The observations of Colonel Dodge on many points of military science are pregnant and weighty. — *N. Y. Tribune.*

Colonel Dodge points out with great skill what Alexander was as a great captain, and what he did for the art of war. This book is of the deepest interest to those who wish to fully comprehend how Alexander conquered the world. — *Boston Herald.*

We cannot name an author who can describe a battle so clearly and simply, make the object of manœuvres so plain, the reason of defeat or victory so clearly understood. — *Boston Advertiser.*

He has certainly made the story more intelligible than did his less military predecessors, not only by his admirable and abundant maps and plans, but by the clear and careful narration of the military transactions. — *Philadelphia American.*

Colonel Dodge follows Alexander with critical analysis, and in a style specially suited to the needs of the modern reader. — *Dial* (Chicago).

A book of much interest to the ordinary reader from the freshness of its matter . . . which invites perusal from the outset. — *Christian Union* (New York).

It is the first work which has treated the subject in such perfect detail and with such a profusion of aids to the reader in the way of maps and illustrations. — *Boston Transcript.*

American scholarship has reason to be proud of this successful inauguration of Colonel Dodge's great undertaking. — *Chicago Evening Journal.*

The author's work, modest, clear, entertaining, and full of information, deserves cordial recognition from scholars and warm praise from critics. — *Hartford Courant.*

Creditable to the unfaltering industry as well as to the sagacity of its accomplished author. — *Boston Beacon.*

The style, which is clear and interesting, flows on with a certain vividness which carries one along with it to the very last page without weariness or disappointment. — *N. Y. Critic.*

Nothing apparently has escaped his research in ancient records or modern travel. — *Christian Register.*

Colonel Dodge writes out of so fresh an interest in his subject that he is sure to find interested readers. — *Atlantic Monthly.*

Colonel Dodge has the excellent faculty of making things clear in no mean degree. — *London Saturday Review.*

A work of immense research and labor and prepared with unusual intelligence and ability. — *Brooklyn Standard-Union.*

The book represents an amount of research and labor really enormous. — *Boston Courier.*

The author's accounts of Alexander's campaigns are vivid, picturesque, and entertaining. — *Book Buyer.*

In every respect creditable to the industry and scholarship of the author. — *Magazine of American History.*

A conspicuous feature of the book is the historian's perfect fairness. — *Public Opinion.*

It is plain, clear history, with frequent pithy criticisms. — *Inter-Ocean.*

A remarkably interesting as well as valuable book. — *Providence Journal.*

A well-digested and admirably classified work. — *Philadelphia Ledger.*

The clearest tale of military history we have ever read. — *American Grocer.*

The book is interesting on every page. — *Journal of Mil. Service Inst.*

Vivid, picturesque, and entertaining. — *Minneapolis Tribune.*

HANNIBAL.

A History of the Art of War among the Carthaginians and Romans, down to the Battle of Pydna, 168 B. C. ; with a detailed account of the Second Punic War. With 227 Charts, Maps, Plans of Battles and Tactical Manœuvres, Cuts of Armor, Weapons, and Uniforms. 8vo, two volumes in one, pp. xviii, 684, $5.00.

By THEODORE AYRAULT DODGE,

Brevet Lieutenant-Colonel United States Army.

Especial praise is due to the chapter on crossing the Alps . . . and to the general summing up of Hannibal's character and career. . . . They commend themselves to the critic from the first word to the last. — *London Athenæum.*

Having once begun, the reader does not wish to lay down the volume until he closes the cover on the last page. — *Journal of Mil. Service Inst.*

The result of exhaustive research and enthusiastic interest in the subject. — *N. Y. Critic.*

Colonel Dodge marshals the evidence . . . and fills out the story with whatever authentic material has survived, and thus gives local color and increased interest to the whole. — *N. Y. Nation.*

Colonel Dodge has brought to his task a very thorough preparation and equipment. . . . The accounts of Hannibal's battles and sieges and marches are clear and spirited. — *N. Y. Tribune.*

The book is an example of how life can be infused into apparently exhausted classical themes by fresh study and vigorous presentation. — *Providence Journal.*

Colonel Dodge's views are carefully considered and his opinions are presented with clearness and force. — *N. Y. Journal.*

Although a careful historian, the author is also a graceful and forcible writer, with the true soldier's faculty of expressing himself concisely. — *N. Y. Herald.*

CÆSAR.

A History of the Art of War among the Romans, from the Second Punic War down to the Fall of the Roman Empire; with a detailed account of the Gallic and Civil Wars. With 275 Charts, Maps, Plans of Battles and Tactical Manœuvres, and other Cuts. 8vo, two volumes in one, pp. xix, 792, $5.00.

By THEODORE AYRAULT DODGE,

Brevet Lieutenant-Colonel United States Army.

The distinguishing characteristic of this excellent series is the extraordinary care the author has taken to make each volume approximately, as nearly as is permitted to fallible humanity, the standard of absolute accuracy. — *Public Opinion.*

One charm of Colonel Dodge's Great Captains Series is the absolute frankness with which he makes known his estimates of the campaigns and the character of his heroes. — *N. Y. Times.*

The portrait of Cæsar has often been drawn, but Colonel Dodge has reproduced it in singularly lifelike lines and colors. — *N. Y. Sun.*

The work will add to Colonel Dodge's reputation as a clear and on the whole unprejudiced writer concerning topics which appear to possess peculiar difficulties. — *N. Y. Independent.*

The work is a monument of patient labor, and so clear in style and free from technicalities as to make it a popular work. — *American Grocer.*

Colonel Dodge's Great Captains, when complete, will be an enduring monument of conscientious study and industry. — *Magazine of American History.*

Again we have to praise the author's unwearied perseverance in tramping over sites of battles. — *London Athenæum.*

Richness of resource, vividness of portraiture, and candid impartiality lend to this work a fascination which holds a sustained interest. — *Minn. Tribune.*

The author has added to his reputation as a military historian in the present work. — *Brooklyn Eagle.*

It is as if we were with Cæsar himself and looked on as a disinterested observer. — *Boston Herald.*

Colonel Dodge's series . . . has already taken established rank among English histories of ancient wars. — *N. Y. Nation.*

Colonel Dodge has given facts in which the ordinary scholar and reader will find unusual pleasure. — *N. Y. Herald.*

A model of clear description and critical military analysis. — *Boston Transcript.*

A wonderful amount of careful, painstaking research. — *Boston Advertiser.*

We commend the whole series, judging the volumes to come by those we have, to all students. — *Dial* (Chicago).

Colonel Dodge convinces us that he understands the business of war. — *London Saturday Review.*

The military student owes a debt of gratitude to Colonel Dodge. — *Military Service Inst. Journal.*

All students of the subject will want to possess the volume. — *Hartford Courant.*

No little point escapes the Argus eyes of the historian. — *Philadelphia Ledger.*

Colonel Dodge is well fitted to give freshness to the old story. — *N. Y. Evening Post.*

A vivid picture of the great game of war. — *Providence Journal.*

Colonel Dodge has certainly fulfilled all expectations. — *N. Y. Herald.*

A historian of broad views and logical opinions. — *Boston Beacon.*

Singular clearness and accuracy. — *Boston Courier.*

One of the most profoundly interesting of books. — *Philadelphia Press.*

His criticisms are most valuable. — *Boston Traveler.*

RIDERS OF MANY LANDS.

Profusely illustrated by Remington, and from photographs of Oriental
subjects. 8vo, pp. 486, $4.00.

By THEODORE AYRAULT DODGE,

Brevet Lieutenant-Colonel United States Army.

A book that will gladden the heart of every lover of horses. — *Boston
Herald.*

A volume of rare and exceptional interest, full of information, modestly
and diffidently conveyed, written by a man who is not only a past master
of his subject, but who shows in every line that he is possessed of that fine
feeling — that sacred fire — which alone can create perfect sympathy between a high-bred gentleman and his equine counterpart. — *N. Y. Tribune.*

The reader who has a grain of humor in him no bigger than a pinch of
snuff will find endless entertainment in it. — *N. Y. Evening Post.*

His style is picturesque and breezy; he has opinions and he does not
hesitate to express them. — *Boston Advertiser.*

Every style of riding which deserves to be called a style is sympathet-
ically estimated. — *Boston Traveler.*

It is intensely readable, and it contains a variety of information with
regard to horsemanship and the horse which could not possibly be found
elsewhere. — *Boston Beacon.*

Colonel Dodge is more than an enthusiastic lover of dogs and horses; he
is a most genial and clever writer. — *Portland Press.*

It is fortunate that so fair-minded and cosmopolitan a critic of equitation
has arisen as Colouel Dodge. — *Springfield Republican.*

To an unlimited knowledge of the horse and the art of horsemanship the
author adds vast experience as a traveler. — *New Haven Register.*

What Colonel Dodge does not know about horses and how to ride them
could be put in very few words. — *Providence Journal.*

It is one of those delightful books in a conventional world which comes
upon us not once in a decade. — *N. Y. Nation.*

It is a book which all who love horses or the fields and the open air will
take up with delight. — *N. Y. Independent.*

The writer passes in review the riders, horses, and the methods and equip-
ments of about every people under the sun, chatting with the charm of an
accomplished raconteur. — *Commercial Advertiser.*

Riders are discussed with the science of one who knows everything about
a horse that is worth knowing. — *Philadelphia Item.*

Colonel Dodge has studied riders from the saddle, and has observed
things, women. customs, and costumes. — *Detroit Free Press.*

Colonel Dodge's claim to know something about horses is amply and
pleasantly maintained in nearly fourscore delightfully written chapters. —
New Orleans Times-Democrat.

Readers will insist on finding out for themselves the good things in this
excellent work. — *Boston Herald.*

A charming volume it is with its lively text, full of interest and anecdote.
— *Army and Navy Journal.*

Colonel Dodge's latest work is of distinct military value. — *Journal Military Service Inst.*

A series of charmingly written chapters, in a breezy, unconventional style. — *Boston Transcript.*

A delightful feature of Colonel Dodge's book is its sympathetic tone. — *Boston Courier.*

A book every one interested in equitation will desire to possess. — *Boston Gazette.*

His observations on horses and men in many lands are sensible, intelligent, and bright. — *Portland Argus.*

He writes with an energy that carries his readers with him. — *N. Y. Mail and Express.*

Marked in every paragraph with the knowledge of the specialist. — *Outlook.*

A book that will gladden the heart of every lover of horses. — *Brooklyn Times.*

Colonel Dodge is an adept whose knowledge of horseflesh is both wide and deep. — *Philadelphia North American.*

It will appeal strongly and favorably to every lover of a manly spirit. — *Philadelphia Press.*

Opinions that are heartily outspoken; a breezy, broad-chested way of saying things. — *Philadelphia Record.*

A charm of sprightliness which holds the reader's attention throughout. — *Philadelphia Bulletin.*

Every horse lover will delight in Colonel Dodge's intelligent and sympathetic demonstration of his subject. — *Philadelphia Telegraph.*

If ever a man was qualified to write of horses and riders it is Colonel Dodge. — *Washington Star.*

Nothing bearing on the equestrianism of the various peoples has escaped his notice. — *Rochester Herald.*

What the colonel does not know about the horse and his gaits is not worth knowing. — *Buffalo Commercial.*

The discourse is easy and free from cant or technicality. — *Christian Advocate.*

Vivid glances of life with opinions that are heartily outspoken. — *Louisville Courier-Journal.*

The most magnificent tribute ever paid to the combined horse. — GEN. CASTLEMAN, *President Society of Saddle-Horse Breeders.*

Combines to an unusual degree interest, use, and beauty. — *Chicago Times.*

Sound horse lore is dispensed all through the book. — *Boston Commonwealth.*

He writes of a subject of which he is easily master. — *Boston Commercial Bulletin.*

Marked by the enthusiasm of a genuine horseman. — *Boston Journal.*

Will delight those who love a good anecdote or a good horse. — *Zion's Herald.*

Contains a vast amount of curious information. — *Portland Advertiser.*

Both instructive and extremely entertaining. — *Hartford Courant.*

The collection is one of rare value and most entertaining quality. — *Book Buyer.*

An exceptionally attractive book. — *N. Y. Critic.*

A delightful and most instructive book. — *N. Y. Press.*

Bright, chatty, sparkling, and abounding in sage observations. — *Christian Intelligencer.*

A volume of surpassing interest. — *N. Y. Rider and Driver.*

Colonel Dodge writes *ex cathedra.* — *Episcopal Recorder.*

Colonel Dodge is a judge of horseflesh. A breezy and outspoken book.— *Philadelphia Ledger.*

Lots of entertainment. — *Philadelphia Times.*

A breezy, off-hand way quite refreshing. — *Presbyterian.*

Colonel Dodge has studied the horse and horseman everywhere. — *Albany Journal.*

One of the choicest holiday books of the year. — *Buffalo Courier.*

Full of interest. — *Toledo Blade.*

Colonel Dodge's style is easy and vivid. — *Cincinnati Commercial Gazette.*

Colonel Dodge is thoroughly qualified to speak from experience. — *Cleveland Plain Dealer.*

One of the most entertaining books of the day. — *Louisville Post.*

Abounding in anecdote and comment. — *Chicago Journal.*

Will not only entertain but instruct equestrians. — *Inter-Ocean.*

Colonel Dodge is master of his theme. — *Dial.*

A feast of reason and a flow of soul. — *Chicago Interior.*

His style is animated, his pen graphic, and his knowledge of the subject infinite. — *Chicago Saturday Evening Herald.*

From Russia to Africa, from Japan to Westchester County. — *New Orleans Picayune.*

An authority which it is safe to follow. — *San Francisco Bulletin.*

An expert judge of horseflesh. — *San Francisco Post.*

Leaves no part of the world untouched. — *San Francisco News Dealer.*

Colonel Dodge clearly speaks as one having authority on horses, saddles, months, and manners. — *Breeders' Gazette.*

ENGLISH NOTICES.

Colonel Dodge writes with wide knowledge, keen sympathy, and trained judgment. — *London Times.*

One of the best books on horses and their riders with which we have met. — *London Athenæum.*

Colonel Dodge is an exceedingly agreeable companion. — *London Saturday Review.*

I am inclined to think no living man is a more profound authority. — *Sporting and Dramatic News.*

The book displays a knowledge of the ever-fascinating subject which is nothing less than bewildering. — *London Sketch.*

Very well done. — *London World.*